The Human Tradition around the World

Series Editors

WILLIAM H. BEEZLEY, Professor of History, University of Arizona
COLIN M. MACLACHLAN, John Christy Barr Distinguished
    Professor of History, Tulane University

Each volume in this series is devoted to providing minibiographies of "real people" who, with their idiosyncratic behavior, personalize the collective experience of grand themes, national myths, ethnic stereotypes, and gender relationships. In some cases, their stories reveal the irrelevance of national events, global processes, and cultural encounters for men and women engaged in everyday life. The personal dimension gives perspective to history, which of necessity is a sketch of past experience.

The authors of each volume in this historical series are determined to make the past literal. They dismiss the post-modern concerns about true descriptions and instead write accounts that identify the essential character of everyday lives of individuals. In doing so, these historians allow us to share the human traditions that find expression in these lives.

Volumes in The Human Tradition around the World Series

William B. Husband, ed. *The Human Tradition in Modern Russia* (2000). Cloth ISBN 0-8420-2856-0   Paper ISBN 0-8420-2857-9

K. Steven Vincent and Alison Klairmont-Lingo, eds. *The Human Tradition in Modern France* (2000). Cloth ISBN 0-8420-2804-8 Paper ISBN 0-8420-2805-6

THE HUMAN TRADITION IN

MODERN RUSSIA

THE HUMAN TRADITION IN
MODERN RUSSIA

EDITED BY

WILLIAM B. HUSBAND

NUMBER 1

A Scholarly Resources Inc. Imprint
Wilmington, Delaware

© 2000 by Scholarly Resources Inc.
All rights reserved
First published 2000
Printed and bound in the United States of America

Scholarly Resources Inc.
104 Greenhill Avenue
Wilmington, DE 19805-1897
www.scholarly.com

Library of Congress Cataloging-in-Publication Data

The human tradition in modern Russia / edited by William B. Husband.
    p. cm. — (The human tradition around the world ; no. 1)
  Includes bibliographical references and index.
  ISBN 0-8420-2856-0 (alk. paper) — ISBN 0-8420-2857-9 (pbk. :
alk. paper)
    1. Russia—Social conditions. 2. Soviet Union—Social conditions.
3. Russia—Civilization. 4. Soviet Union—Civilization. I. Husband,
William. II. Series.

HN523.H86 2000
306'.0947—dc21   00-028518

To Jeffrie

About the Editor

WILLIAM B. HUSBAND is the author of *"Godless Communists": Atheism and Society in Soviet Russia, 1917–1932* (2000) and *Revolution in the Factory: The Birth of the Soviet Textile Industry, 1917–1920* (1990). He has published numerous articles on religion, politics, education, foreign policy, and society in the former Soviet Union, and he is currently working on a social and cultural history of nature and wilderness in modern Russia. He received his Ph.D. from Princeton University and teaches in the Department of History at Oregon State University.

I believe in aristocracy, though—if that is the right word, and if a democrat may use it. Not an aristocracy of power, based upon rank and influence, but an aristocracy of the sensitive, the considerate and the plucky. Its members are to be found in all nations and classes, and all through the ages, and there is a secret understanding between them when they meet. They represent the true human tradition, the one permanent victory of our queer race over cruelty and chaos. Thousands of them perish in obscurity, a few are great names. They are sensitive for others as well as for themselves, they are considerate without being fussy, their pluck is not swankiness but the power to endure, and they can take a joke.

—E. M. Forster, *Two Cheers for Democracy* (1951)

Acknowledgments

This project has been enjoyable from beginning to end. I especially thank Bill Beezley for offering me the opportunity to edit a volume of essays on the human dimension of the Russian past, something I have wanted to do for many years. At Scholarly Resources, Richard Hopper was highly supportive, and I thank him particularly for his openness and flexibility throughout the early stages of our work together on this publication. Carolyn Travers and Michelle Slavin have been models of patience and professionalism. And I thank Sandy Eldridge.

Individually and collectively the contributors owe a variety of debts. We thank the International Research and Exchanges Board (IREX) for its ongoing support of the study of Eastern Europe and Eurasia. Although no IREX grant specifically backed the present enterprise, many of the essays derive from larger research projects in part supported by IREX. All eligible contributors have received IREX support in the past, several on more than one occasion, and all have benefited from the multiple ways in which IREX has enriched our field. We also thank the Summer Research Laboratory of the University of Illinois at Urbana-Champaign for its unstinting support of Russian studies in North America.

This volume employs the Library of Congress system of transliteration, with certain exceptions. Diacritical marks have been eliminated except where doing so would appear artificial (hence, Tver, not Tver' and Shulman instead of Shul'man, but Gorbachëv, not Gorbachev). The transliteration of well-known proper names in the text employs their most common Western spelling (for example, Mayakovsky, not Mayakovskii). Abbreviations used in archival citations follow common scholarly practice: *opis* (op.), archival inventory; *fond* (f.), archival collection; *delo* (d.), *dela* (dd.), file(s); *list* (l.), *listy* (ll.), page(s); *oborot* (ob.), reverse side of page.

Contents

Introduction: The Persistence of Memory in Modern Russia

William B. Husband

With his proposed reforms being sabotaged by entrenched bureaucratic interests and inertia, and lacking energetic support among the population at large, in January 1987 Soviet leader Mikhail S. Gorbachëv shifted the emphasis of his rhetoric from political and economic considerations to human issues. In orchestrated public statements he took aim at the systematic falsification of Soviet history familiar to every Soviet schoolchild, and he announced that in the future "history must be seen as it is" and that "blank spaces" would be removed from the record. The practices that had shaped history in the USSR—the manipulation and destruction of documentation, the sacrificing of accuracy to ideology, and the removal of politically inconvenient personages from accounts of the past—were to give way to a frank and truthful engagement of evidence, no matter how unpleasant the findings. Moreover, the schematic offerings that had dominated scholarship for more than a half century must now yield to work that integrated the "human tradition."[1] Gorbachëv's remarks a few days earlier at a meeting of the Central Committee of the Communist Party had made an even broader point. The transparent falsification of historical truth and failure to admit mistakes in the past had led, he said, to a "social corrosion" that adversely affected public consciousness and, by extension, ultimately undermined achievement in every sphere of national endeavor. The pursuit of truth in history would be one way to provide a corrective.[2]

Gorbachëv's motives are not difficult to discern. As the first Soviet leader to have matured professionally solely in the post-Stalin period, he was keenly aware of the part that systematic deceit by the regime had played in the demoralization of society. His announcement at the beginning of 1987 therefore had less to do with the pursuit of historical truth as an intellectual or academic goal than as a calculated political strategy. Attacking falsifications and speaking in terms that corresponded more accurately with society's collective memory were to become instruments to regain public confidence and in due course help relegitimize socialism in Soviet society. And integrating the human tradition into the new history would be a key element in that quest.

It is unlikely that Gorbachëv understood at the time all the intellectual implications of his position. In the full context of his remarks the human tradition appeared largely as an addendum to the political and economic record rather than a fundamental rethinking of the meaning and philosophy of history. In his presentation, a truthful approach to political history would be enriched by a fuller explication of the human dimension of the past, but there was no indication that he believed this would necessarily alter our definition of history writ large. To be fair, Gorbachëv presented the human factor as more than simply something "nice to know," but he stopped far short of reconsidering the question with which E. H. Carr has challenged more than one generation of students: What is history?[3] But forcing a reevaluation of received wisdom is exactly what the study of the human tradition does best. It redefines our criteria for identifying legitimate subjects for investigation and the methodologies that can best illuminate them;[4] it challenges conceptions of truth and objectivity and, by extension, existing understandings of knowledge, nationhood, and self;[5] and it even subjects the basic mechanics of the historian's craft—correlating supporting evidence with historical interpretations, for example—to scrutiny.[6] The act of reintegrating absent actors into the record therefore not only expands our base of information but also makes imperative a reexamination of received interpretations in light of new evidence. Once elements of the history of society receive full consideration (the history of women in Western historiography during the last quarter-century is a prime example), questions in political and other branches of history that were once considered resolved have to be reinvestigated from a different perspective. Consequently, to embark on the social history of modern Russia while simultaneously attempting to correct a falsified record of the nation's political history would be an undertaking far more complex than the Soviet leader's remarks of early 1987 indicated.

Given the legacy of the scholarship of the Cold War era in both the Soviet Union and the West, rethinking the Russian past proved difficult everywhere. A methodological consensus dominated Western scholarship on the USSR until the mid-1970s. Interpretations were far from homogeneous, but they were nevertheless informed by widely shared assumptions and united on key underlying points, notably their preoccupation with Soviet politics and institutions and their marginalization of the study of society. And while pursuing this research agenda, Western historians stridently denounced Soviet historiography. Conversely, Soviet scholars experienced their own internal differences,[7] but responded to their Western counterparts in kind. Amid this mutual incrimination, however, there arose an irony that is strikingly evident in retrospect: each tradition disagreed with the *conclusions and interpretations* of its rival, but in an operative sense historians in both camps tacitly agreed on *what constituted legitimate subjects of study*. Western and Soviet scholars alike produced a plethora of works on Russia's intellectual and revolutionary movements, statist and authoritarian traditions, the Revolution of 1917, Soviet political history, and the foreign policy of the USSR, to which must be added the general writings of the totalitarian school of political analysis. As revisionist historians began to challenge this research agenda in the West during the 1970s, they, too, began by co-opting yet another Soviet chestnut: the study of class, with a special emphasis on workers. And while this Western historiography first gave rise to an impressive and nuanced body of political analysis and subsequently began to turn productively toward the analysis of society,[8] before 1991 the social history of Russia was more a study of the social ramifications of institutional behavior than social history as historians of Europe and North America understood the term.

The disintegration of the Soviet Union and the opening of its formerly classified archives in 1991 dramatically altered the range of opportunities, but in a large sense scholarship on Russia during the past decade has everywhere found itself still working to overcome the influence of Cold War scholarship. The problems are deeply rooted. In the 1920s pluralism predominated in the study of history in Soviet Russia. M. N. Pokrovskii and his Society of Marxist Historians championed a view of history (much like the approach of Sergei Eisenstein in film) that centered on the proletariat as a class, not individual leaders, as the engine of history, but the general scholarly climate of the 1920s tolerated non-Marxist points of view as well. The rise of Joseph Stalin at the end of the decade, however, halted both pluralism in history as well as Pokrovskii's collectivist orientation. A new emphasis on the role of the leader in Bolshevik mythology became instrumental in the formation of Stalin's "cult of the personality," and the subsequent study of history in the USSR reflected this change in course. Stalin personally intervened in a key debate among historians with a pivotal letter to the journal *Protetarskaia revoliutsiia* (Proletarian revolution) in October 1931, which ended some historians' careers and—of greater long-term importance— intimidated survivors into professional timorousness, preemptive obedience, and self-censorship.

The link of ideology to history subsequently strengthened. In 1938, Stalin himself helped prepare the *History of the Communist Party of the Soviet Union (Bolsheviks): Short Course*, a textbook whose crude dogmas defined the only acceptable interpretation of party and national history. After 1938 the *Short Course* inverted the usual relationship between textbooks and academic scholarship: it put forward an official version from which professional interpretations could not deviate. During the post-World War II period, Soviet and Western scholarship therefore became mirror images. Despite temporary upheavals during the era of Nikita Khrushchev, Soviet historiography maintained a leftist course that employed Marxism in crude caricature. In the West, infusions of government support and the "know-your-enemy" mentality expanded the study of Russia and the Soviet Union exponentially. As noted above, however, the tendentious Western scholarship of the 1950s–1970s shared the foci of Soviet historiography, even as it reached diametrically opposed conclusions. And to this day neither side has fully resolved its internal disagreements that dominated those years.

The Human Tradition in Modern Russia enters this discourse by focusing on the role of individuals and groups previously underrepresented in scholarship. The study of change stands at the center of analysis. Beginning with Tsar Alexander II's attempt in the midnineteenth century to reinvigorate the autocracy through reform, and culminating with a discussion of individual life in contemporary Russia, this collection emphasizes the upheavals that individual Russians have faced in the most recent 150 years (which were dramatic even by the global historical standards of the tumultuous past century and a half). In the aftermath of Alexander II's reforms, the liberation of 90 percent of the population from serfdom, the social and economic dislocation that everywhere accompany the early phases of industrialization, and the world's first sustaining Marxist revolution all uprooted lives in ways unanticipated by everyday men and women. After 1917 the conscious attempt by Soviet power to alter how citizens viewed their material surroundings, the content of their belief systems, and even how they celebrated or spent their leisure time challenged existing customs on multiple fronts. Subsequently, the utilization of terror accompanied by widespread demoralization in late Soviet and post-Soviet Russia transformed mores in ways with which society will continue to grapple in future generations.

As important as it is to our story, change is only one part of the equation. No society is a *tabula rasa;* the interaction between individuals and their surroundings is deeply embedded in long-standing cultural constructions.[9] It is consequently unrealistic to think that the use of intimidation and repression—even by the authoritarian and determined Soviet regime—could alone be sufficient to change citizens' hearts and minds completely. The hold of the past is too strong, and—to complicate matters—"tradition" itself can be fluid. Elements in every society regularly attempt to use the past to legitimize their desires in the present, and, in so doing, they routinely reinterpret custom and tradition in light of current conditions. In other words, not only do certain ideas of what is traditional and therefore an entitlement correspond extensively to prevailing perceptions of immediate interest, but also customs and traditions can change, assume new functions in different contexts, or even be invented as required without weakening their ability to inspire loyalty. And when a given society is besieged, this propensity to reinvent the past frequently intensifies. "Customary" or "traditional" practices whose origins were actually historically recent have therefore often ignited tenacious adherence precisely because of their situational utility.[10] As more than one historian has noted, only partly in jest, "the past isn't what it used to be."

Consequently, in conditions in which serious transformations are taking place, continuity also requires an explanation. In the late prerevolutionary period the Russian Orthodox Church resisted pressures to liberalize the grounds for divorce, as one might expect, but it is noteworthy that church loyalists had joined outside reformers in bringing such pressure to bear in the first place. Among the religious traditionalists known as Old Believers, modernity was an evil to be resisted in its totality, while disenfranchised social elements such as women took refuge even in pre-Christian beliefs to express their anxiety at the onset of a new world. During the early years of Soviet rule, to which *The Human Tradition in Modern Russia* gives special emphasis, a long-standing infatuation with America and the West did not disappear but, in fact, deepened under the influence of foreign fashions and movies. Church officials and rank-and-file believers found multiple ways to resist Soviet antireligious campaigns, while Bolshevik reformism encountered insuperable obstacles as it attacked so-called bourgeois vices such as prostitution and alcohol abuse. And in spite of mounting evidence to the contrary, the educated elite continued to subscribe to beliefs about the peasants and their sexuality that did not conform to observed experience. From the time of Stalin to the present, repression remained a reality of Russian society, although under Stalinism it appeared in a modernized and even careerist mode. In the mature Soviet system, fields such as health care still fail to transcend the bureaucratism and corruption that had characterized the tsarist system. And post-Soviet society faces a pattern of dislocation not unlike what Russian citizens faced in the second half of the nineteenth century. All of these issues will be examined in this volume.

In sum, *The Human Tradition in Modern Russia* is not only a study of the old and the new in Russia but also an analysis of how the old has shaped the new. It brings together a group of senior and junior scholars united by a preoccupation with history "from below" and their extensive experience in working with state-of-the-art documentation, including but by no means limited to the formerly classified archives. This book makes no claim to comprehensiveness; no thirteen essays could accomplish that for a period so historically rich. Instead, this collection attempts to convey the spirit of the period since 1861 by allowing those who lived through it to speak, as far as is possible, for themselves. And while this may not conform exactly to what Mikhail Gorbachëv had in mind in January 1987, it is the authors' collective response to his challenge that "history be seen as it is" and "blank spaces" eliminated.

NOTES

1. "Ubezdennost—opora perestroiki: vstrecha v TsK KPSS," *Kommunist* 4 (1987): 4; *Pravda*, February 14, 1987. Gorbachëv used the expression *"chelovecheskii faktor,"* which translates literally as "human factor" but resonates more idiomatically in English as "human tradition."

2. *Materialy plenuma tsentralnogo komiteta KPSS: 27–28 ianvaria 1987 goda* (Moscow, 1987), 9, 11, 12, 15, 17, 35.

3. E. H. Carr, *What Is History?* (New York, 1961).

4. For a diverse overview see the essays in Lynn Hunt, ed., *The New Cultural History* (Berkeley, 1989). An analysis pertinent to modern Russia is Laura Engelstein, "Paradigms, Pathologies, and Other Clues to Russian Spiritual Culture: Some Post-Soviet Thoughts," *Slavic Review* 57 (Winter 1998): 864–77.

5. Joyce Appleby, Lynn Hunt, and Margaret Jacob, *Telling the Truth about History* (New York, 1994).

6. Anthony Grafton, *The Footnote: A Curious History* (Cambridge, MA, 1997).

7. Soviet historiography is discussed in Nancy Whittier Heer, *Politics and History in the Soviet Union* (Cambridge, MA, 1971); Donald J. Raleigh, "Translator's Introduction," in E. N. Burdzhalov, *Russia's Second Revolution: The February 1917 Uprising in Petrograd*, trans. and ed. Donald J. Raleigh (Bloomington, IN, 1987), ix–xvii; William B. Husband, "Secondary School History Texts in the USSR: Revising the Soviet Past, 1985–1989," *Russian Review* 50 (October 1991): 461–63.

8. In the late 1970s the work of Moshe Lewin and Sheila Fitzpatrick definitively established social history among historians of Russia in the West.

9. James C. Scott, *Seeing Like a State: How Certain Schemes to Improve the Human Condition Have Failed* (New Haven, 1998); Yi-fu Tuan, *Cosmos and Hearth: A Cosmopolite's Viewpoint* (Minneapolis, 1996).

10. David Lowenthal, *The Heritage Crusade and the Spoils of History* (Cambridge, Eng., 1998); E. P. Thompson, *Customs in Common* (New York, 1993), 1; Eric Hobsbawm, "Inventing Traditions" and "Mass-Producing Traditions: Europe, 1870–1914," in Eric Hobsbawm and Terence Ranger, eds., *The Invention of Tradition* (New York, 1983), 1–13, 263–67, 303–7; Keith Thomas, *Religion and the Decline of Magic* (New York, 1971), 422–29.

PART I

REFORM, MODERNIZATION, AND IMPERIAL SOCIETY

When Tsar Alexander II enacted the Great Reforms during the 1860s, his principal objective was not to alter Russia for humanitarian or idealistic reasons, but to find ways for his empire to maintain its central place in European politics and diplomacy. At the beginning of the nineteenth century, Russia had received significant credit for its role in the defeat of Napoleon. Consequently, the perception of Russian military prowess became one cornerstone of the Congress System—engineered by Prince Metternich of Austria—that existed in various permutations from 1815 until the Crimean War (1853–1856) as both the predominant diplomatic alliance in Europe and an international instrument to combat revolution. After 1825, Tsar Nicholas I particularly embraced Russia's role as the "gendarme of Europe" as well as a belief in the divine origin of his powers, convictions consistent with his opposition to instituting progressive changes in Russian society. A humiliating defeat in the Crimean War, however, graphically demonstrated the error of such policies. Although fighting on its own borders, the Imperial Government failed to supply its troops effectively; civil and military institutions lacked the flexibility to respond to initiatives even from reformers loyal to the regime; and the malnourished and illiterate Russian peasant could no longer be molded into a fighting man equal to his European counterpart. When Nicholas I died in 1855, Alexander II inherited this war that he could not win, and he took it upon himself to correct the situation once the fighting ended.

Alexander's motives were openly pragmatic. Determined, as he stated matters, to remake Russia "from above" before the peasants did so "from below," he set into motion reforms that emancipated 90 percent of the national population from serfdom; transferred key functions of social welfare—primary education, basic medical services, instruction in agronomy for the peasantry—to a newly created local institution called a *zemstvo*; fundamentally revamped the judicial system; eased censorship; granted greater autonomy to universities; and eliminated some of the more draconian elements of military service. Although much was rescinded or seriously modified after terrorists assassinated Alexander II in 1881, by the 1890s Russia undertook a major industrialization drive, much of it subsidized by the state, that created the world's fifth largest gross national product at the beginning of the twentieth century. Despite recurrent disastrous decisions—mishandling a major famine in 1891–92,

1

an ill-advised declaration of war on Japan in 1904 that precipitated a general strike and revolution at home the following year, a suspicious and heavy-handed approach toward labor unions and organizations of professionals—Russia entered World War I with much of the same confidence and jingoism witnessed among the other leading combatants. But if the Great Reforms and what followed were intended to enable the Imperial Government to modernize and survive, we can only judge them as failures. In February 1917 the strains of the war combined with domestic discontent to end the Romanov dynasty within a matter of days.

What went wrong? In the realm of politics and policy, reformism never became an effective force in Russia between 1861 and 1917. Progressives argued that the Great Reforms had not gone far enough, especially in redressing social ills. Consequently, when Alexander III and Nicholas II, the final two tsars, attempted to reassert centralized autocratic authority after 1881, they only worsened relations between reformers and the state. In practice, even philanthropic work had a radicalizing influence, since the experiences of civic-minded volunteers who attempted to help the regime deal with catastrophes increasingly led many to conclude that the tsarist system was itself the chief problem. Conservatives, on the other hand, argued that change fostered instability, and in the most extreme cases they blamed the spirit of the Great Reforms for the terrorism that claimed Alexander II's life. From the Imperial Palace to the national universities to the administration of local areas, the guardians of tradition therefore pursued the contradictory aims of trying to transform Russia into a modernized state in the first rank of European nations and to suppress public opinion and initiatives from society. In this environment, moderation failed to find a significant voice in national affairs, and Russian politics never fully adopted the concept of a loyal opposition. In fact, during its final decades the tsarist government feared even the reformers who worked in the state bureaucracy, and it was more suspicious still of the business community and professionals whose trust and cooperation it now needed. Among the lower classes, emancipation brought too few meaningful improvements into the lives of the peasants, while industrialization gave rise to increasingly visible problems among the growing body of factory workers. As the government thus alienated society both high and low, the revolutionary movement that eventually triumphed was able to take root.

The collapse of autocracy in Russia owed as much to social displacement as it did to politics in the narrow sense of the term. Between 1861 and 1917, Russia's national institutions, grounded in the needs and interests of an agricultural society, fell increasingly out of touch with emerging social reality. Most obviously, the emancipation of the peasantry deprived the landowning nobility of its permanent pool of free labor.

The loss of peasant labor dictated a change of the aristocratic life-style—nobles had to convert agricultural estates into viable economic enterprises or face bankruptcy—and challenged the value system of a class that looked down on aggressive entrepreneurship and commerce. Many, such as the befuddled characters of Anton Chekhov's *The Cherry Orchard*, succumbed, and those who survived either faced decades of economizing or had to adapt to different career and life patterns. As happened elsewhere, industrial modernization created new professions in business and service and expanded or modified existing ones, such as law and medicine, in turn giving rise to an unprecedented level of professional assertiveness in Russia. As a result, by the beginning of the twentieth century the landowning aristocracy had lost its near monopoly on the top echelons of state and military offices. Even among those educated Russians still generally sympathetic to the regime and decidedly opposed to revolution, professional identities and values increasingly came into conflict with the principles of obedience and centralized decision making that were the hallmarks of tsarism.

Among the lower classes, emancipation granted the peasants increased rights to leave their villages for seasonal employment, and the rise of factories gave them somewhere to go. As hundreds of thousands streamed first seasonally and then permanently into urban areas, the cities underwent significant alterations related to overcrowding, a rise in crime, and the beginnings of a mass commercial culture. New experiences transformed the labor migrants themselves, who returned to their villages with different clothes, language, ideas, and attitudes toward the patriarchy they had left behind. And in their absence the villages changed, with women often assuming more assertive roles and the patriarchal system coming under increasingly greater scrutiny. The village by no means submitted passively to these developments—there is ample evidence that the reverse was true—but challenges to traditional authority everywhere increased.

At the center of this assault stood the link between society and the Russian Orthodox Church. Subordinate to the government through its governing Holy Synod, the church exercised significant influence over spheres such as education and marriage, functions that were then becoming increasingly secularized in the industrialized states of Western Europe. But beyond being an institutional presence, Orthodoxy was also a belief system deeply embedded in Russian culture. It shaped the ordering of daily and seasonal routines, household organization, rituals of hospitality and celebration, and rites of passage. Orthodox belief lay at the root of much popular wisdom, rumor, proverbs, and folklore, and it provided a profound symbol of national identity. As modernization challenged tradition in Russia, it consequently encountered Orthodoxy at virtually every turn, whether in a redefinition of the prerogatives of marriage and divorce (Chapter 1), the rejection of modernity through a reaffirmation of ancient legend and belief (Chapter 2), or multifaceted encounters that captured the very essence of redefining gender, personal responsibility, professionalism, and observed experience (Chapter 3). Emerging revolutionary ideologies may therefore have shaped the final assault on tsarism, but it was the extreme, far-reaching social displacement of the postemancipation period that provided its chief momentum.

CHAPTER I

Krylov vs. Krylova

"Sexual Incapacity" and Divorce in Tsarist Russia

GREGORY L. FREEZE

To control marriage, divorce, and the prevailing definition of a family is to possess considerable leverage in any society. The power to decide who may marry, at what age, and under which circumstances—and the authority to determine the conditions, if any, that may be used to dissolve such unions—carries social influence so pervasive that it cannot be measured. Historically, however, rules governing marriage and divorce have seldom been completely static. Rather, as the socioeconomic and political environment evolves, individuals and groups continually attempt to renegotiate their prerogatives.

The Russian Orthodox Church fully understood the social and spiritual significance of marriage and made its regulation a high priority from the outset. Following Russia's conversion to Christianity in 988, the church worked to displace pagan nuptial festivals, the abduction of brides, polygamy, and the use of sympathetic magic at weddings. In the eleventh century, it made its influence felt on Russia's first written law codes, which defined penalties for the abandonment of wives, bigamy, adultery, and incest. These early laws specified the levels of kinship within which marriage was forbidden, and they listed the causes for which a man could divorce his wife. In the sixteenth century, the Domostroi, *written mostly, if not completely, by clergy, defined the ideal family in terms of Orthodoxy and patriarchy, and the ecclesiastical courts that usually adjudicated cases of rape took into account both the marital status of the victim and her moral reputation. Enforcing church ideals, however, could be no stronger than the institutions of the church itself, which in premodern Russia sometimes left key decisions to local parishes by default. In this regard, prior to the mideighteenth century, laity and parish clergy exploited the institutional weakness of the church to dissolve marital unions relatively freely. Canon law and the dictates of bishops and high church officials notwithstanding, parish priests responded to local agendas, personal whim, and convenience in granting divorces even when formal prerequisites had not been met. It was only between the mideighteenth and midnineteenth century that national religious institutions became strong enough to prevent such light treatment of matrimony, and by the time of the Great Reforms divorce requirements in Russia ranked among the most restrictive in Europe.*

The sanctity of marriage and ease of divorce consequently serve as a virtual metaphor for social modernization in Russia between 1861 and 1917. By the midnineteenth century, even as the church increased its strictures against divorce in Russia, state authority was displacing church prerogatives in this important sphere elsewhere in Europe. Inevitably, Russian society, especially its upper echelons, began to exert similar pressure to ease divorce restrictions. With adultery, abandonment (including Siberian exile), and sexual and mental incapacity the only existing grounds—and the church placing expensive and time-consuming procedures in the way— educated Russians in particular lobbied for more liberal means of ending unsuccessful and unhappy marriages. The church responded, but at a rate well below European norms and too slow to satisfy demand. Ironically, when the Bolshevik state wrested authority over marriage and divorce away from the church with a series of decrees in December 1917, it actually relieved Russian Orthodoxy of one of its most contentious points of internal disagreement.

In the following article, Gregory Freeze captures the complex of issues that came into play during virtually any divorce proceeding. The case of Krylov vs. Krylova *explains the grounds and administrative church procedures involved, but it is equally important for illuminating points of strain in society that we do not usually consider strictly religious. Thus, the issue of divorce brought the church into direct conflict with the rising class of professionals, in this case medical doctors, who directly challenged the church for hegemony over their sphere of expertise and expected to have their opinions accepted. The financial dimensions of divorce raised the issue of women's rights (in this case the wife had given up a career to marry). It attacked male abuses of power and, by extension, questioned the legitimacy of patriarchy. Divorce was inextricably entwined with concern over a perceived breakdown of the family, and ultimately it involved a challenge to the legitimacy of the church as a social actor. This examination of a single case, in short, provides social insight that extends far beyond the fate of the litigants.*

Gregory L. Freeze is professor of history at Brandeis University. He received his Ph.D. from Columbia University, and his publications include Parish Clergy in Eighteenth-Century Russia *(1977);* The Parish Clergy in Nineteenth-Century Russia: Crisis, Reform, Counter-Reform *(1983);* Russia: A History *(as editor and contributor, 1997); and the two-volume* Church, Religion, and Society in Modern Russia, 1740–1940 *(forthcoming).*

In late 1907 a middle-ranking state official, Gavriil Krylov, filed for divorce from his wife of nearly seven years, Olga Krylova.[1] In his petition to Russian Orthodox Church authorities to terminate the union, Gavriil cited as legal grounds her "incapacity for conjugal relations." Specifically, he complained that his wife suffered from a congenital deformity—the lack of a vagina—that made sexual intercourse impossible. Although surgeons had created an artificial orifice, Krylov pronounced it unsatisfactory and declared that "no artificial vagina can replace a real one." Because the church recognized "sexual incapacity" (though not infertility) as legitimate grounds for divorce, the plaintiff asked the church to dissolve his marriage and permit him to remarry. To all appearances, Krylov had an airtight case, and he plainly expected a prompt and positive response.

In fact, however, divorce, while increasingly common in late Imperial Russia, was fraught with enormous difficulties, delays, costs, and even perils for the plaintiff. Divorce files such as this one abound in Russian archives,[2] all attesting not only to a serious crisis in the traditional patriarchal family order but also to mounting problems in the church's attempt to control and limit this social revolution. As Krylov was to learn over the next seven years, sundering the bonds of holy matrimony, especially when the spouse resisted, could be exceedingly difficult.

Ever since the 1860s the Russian Orthodox Church had gradually allowed a sharp increase in divorces. Although still determined to sabotage proposals to secularize and liberalize divorce, the church did acquiesce—however reluctantly—in the rising popular demand for a more tolerant policy on the dissolution of marriages. As a result, the annual number of divorces dramatically increased, escalating from fewer than 100 in the 1850s to nearly 1,000 in 1900 and then quadrupling again to nearly 4,000 by the outbreak of World War I. That increase was due partly to rising demand (that is, higher rates of family breakdown) but also to changes in church law. The most important change, adopted in 1904, abolished the life-long ban on remarriage for spouses guilty of adultery; to combat an upsurge in illegal cohabitation (as former adulterers were forced to live out of wedlock), the church agreed to permit them to remarry after they had undergone several years of penance under the supervision of their parish priest. Although the divorce rate in Russia was still several times lower than in most other European countries, the gap had closed significantly.

Despite this remarkable increase in the divorce rate (or, indeed, because of it), the church made every effort not only to subvert liberal reform legislation but also to thwart the dissolution of individual marriages. Its first response to every divorce application was to order an obligatory "exhortation" by the local parish priest, urging the spouses to reconcile. Such exhortations, interestingly, sometimes had the desired effect. If not, the church proceeded with the case, but carefully examined each file in a transparent attempt to find some pretext to deny or at least delay the divorce. After all, from the church's point of view, marriage was a holy sacrament—something not to be undone lightly by mere mortals. In many cases, procrastination took its toll as plaintiffs disappeared, died, or simply grew weary of the delays and mounting costs. Even when the plaintiff stubbornly persisted, in the great majority of cases the church found cause for denial, usually citing a lack of proper grounds or conclusive evidence.

The stymying of a divorce was especially likely if the accused spouse and witnesses refused to cooperate. The defendant had ample weapons to delay or even torpedo the case by simply refusing to come to the diocesan consistory (the board of clergy who actually processed such cases) for the obligatory hearing. Although the consistory could eventually hold the trial in absentia, such evasion served at least to delay and sometimes stall the proceedings altogether. No less important was the plaintiff's duty to provide the requisite evidence, the nature of which varied according to the grounds cited for the divorce application. Specifically, the proof could include medical documentation in the cases of insanity and sexual incapacity, community and official records in cases of disappearance and Siberian exile, and two eyewitnesses in the case of adultery. Only after the plaintiff provided the requisite proof, paperwork, and fees did the consistory make a formal verdict. But that did not mean an end to the case: its decision required the approval first of the local bishop (who often overturned decisions or required further investigation) and then of the Holy Synod, the governing board of prelates in St. Petersburg, which was no less vigilant in its oversight. Only after the latter gave its approval did the consistory issue the final divorce papers, empowering the innocent party (the plaintiff) to remarry and prescribing penance for the guilty spouse. In short, divorce remained a difficult, costly, and protracted process, one more likely to end in denial than in dissolution.

Divorce *was* easy only if both partners desired it, for they could easily collude, manufacture the requisite evidence, and arrange a prompt dissolution of their union. The surest, simplest method was to file for divorce on grounds of adultery; whether real or contrived, the evidence for such infidelity left no room for church authorities to quibble or prevaricate. As a result, by 1914 adultery accounted for 90 percent of all divorces granted by the church—a statistic attesting not to rampant sexual license but to the greater ease of obtaining divorce on these grounds. While the proof in such cases sometimes involved cohabitation (confirmed by the birth of illegitimate children), and even love letters and photographs, ordinarily the plaintiff cited at least two eyewitnesses to the physical act of sexual intercourse. The latter, for credibility, often involved an accidental sighting at a brothel or some other public place. In one typical case from 1913, a state official accompanied a friend, the male defendant, to a bordello and inadvertently entered the room as the latter "lay on a girl and performed sexual intercourse." Colluding spouses could also invoke the assistance of lawyers to assemble the requisite documentation and, in some cases, even hire "eyewitnesses" and bribe consistory officials to expedite the case. Such lawyers brazenly advertised their services in respectable, conservative newspapers. For example, in its issue of February 19, 1913, the stalwart *Novoe vremia* (New time) carried several advertisements from lawyers, including one that promised: "Divorce cases: unbelievably quick and extremely cheap, with guaranteed results." As a consequence, colluding couples—if they had the private means—could ensure a certain and relatively speedy divorce, sometimes within less than a year.

Most cases were not so simple, either because one spouse opposed the divorce or because the case raised questions not easily resolved by traditional canon law. In contested divorces, the defendants not only denied their own guilt but sometimes also filed a countersuit, often muddying the waters so thoroughly that the consistory was at a loss to ascertain the truth. And defendants had good reason to resist the divorce. Not only were there emotional motives (such as love and jealousy) but also sheer material interest in the allocation of assets and financial responsibilities. Matters were not helped by the fact that the church had authority to grant divorce but absolutely no right to address "worldly" issues such as alimony or child custody and support. Particularly in the case of dependent women who lacked their own assets, divorce meant loss of home and material support, with dim prospects of obtaining favorable adjudication in a state court. So long as the marriage remained intact, however, the wife could petition state authorities to divert a portion of the husband's income for her support.

In cases not involving adultery, modern science was increasingly at odds not only with the faith but also the canons pertinent to divorce, especially when the latter involved "premarital insanity" and "premarital sexual incapacity." Timing was critical: both had to be premarital, thereby obviating a voluntary conscious marital union (in the case of insanity) or consummation of the union (in the case of sexual incapacity). Modern psychiatry and medicine put traditional rules to the test. Indeed, such matters were now under the jurisdiction of "professionals" in psychiatry and medicine—specialists who were generally ill disposed to sacrifice modern science in favor of the traditional assumptions of the church. In the case of insanity, for example, professionals were far more likely to question the church's refusal to grant divorce on the grounds that evidence of premarital disorders was lacking; psychiatrists, instead, assumed the existence of premarital mental disorders that had simply eluded detection by lay observers, even close family members. Nor was premarital sexual incapacity (denoting the physical inability to perform the sexual act) easily demonstrated. The church sent such people to state medical examiners, who ordinarily reported only whether the sexual organs appeared to be "normal," not whether they were actually capable of physical intercourse. Nor could the traditional canons have foreseen a case where corrective surgery enabled a spouse, though born with a congenital premarital defect, to have sexual relations. That problem was at the very heart of *Krylov vs. Krylova.*

When Gavriil Krylov sued for divorce from his wife, Olga, on grounds of sexual incapacity, he invoked a relatively uncommon ground for divorce (accounting for about 3 percent of all divorces on the eve of World War I). Although the church taught that marriage was fundamentally a "spiritual union" consecrated through a holy sacrament, it did recognize this worldly physical dimension. It bears noting again that it recognized only physical incapacity, not infertility, as legitimate grounds for marital dissolution. Such cases were usually contested, whether by men facing shameful denial of their masculinity or by women fearing loss of material support. The Krylov case raised the thorny question of whether postmarital surgery, if successful, offset any premarital congenital deficiency. It also would shed light on the church's devotion to formal law and its sense of social justice, especially in a case where the wife underwent a dangerous operation in a desperate effort to satisfy her husband's carnal desires.

As Gavriil Krylov explained in his deposition, the pair had married on January 31, 1901. Both parties came from the relatively privileged, educated strata of society. As his marriage certificate attested, Gavriil was a midlevel state official, holding the rank of court counselor (*nadvornyi sovetnik,* the seventh tier in the fifteen-tier Table of Ranks) and serving at the Vilna regional court; his marriage certificate also listed him as Orthodox, age forty-five, and widowed. His bride, Olga, was the daughter of a retired collegiate assessor (*kollezheskii asessor,* rank eight); at the time of the wedding, she was Orthodox, thirty-five years of age, and with no prior marriage. Until the wedding, she had belonged to the stratum of economically independent women: she had a position in the state postal and telegraph agency and earned a monthly salary of 30 rubles. By marrying Gavriil, ten years her senior, she relinquished her position not only to assume the role of spouse but also that of stepmother, charged with raising the five children borne by Gavriil's first wife.

The newlyweds, however, were unable to consummate the marriage: to his dismay, the groom discovered that Olga had an "organic physical shortcoming—the complete absence of a vagina." Although this deformity precluded normal conjugal relations and therefore constituted grounds for divorce, the couple turned to modern medicine for assistance. On June 6, 1901, four and one-half months after the wedding, a team of doctors at the Hospital for Women's Illnesses performed a complicated operation to create an artificial vagina. As Olga lay sedated by chloroform, the surgeons made an incision between the urethra and rectum to create a small canal 5 centimeters (approximately 2 inches) in length. Although Olga still lacked a uterus and ovaries, she was now capable of having sexual intercourse with her husband. As a result, for the next six and one-half years the couple lived together, their relations apparently being quite normal.

Then, on November 22, 1907, after nearly seven years of marriage, Gavriil filed for divorce. He described briefly Olga's premarital physical deformity, made his wife solely responsible for seeking the operation, and complained that, notwithstanding the surgery, "sexual intercourse with my wife does not satisfy me and even causes me harm." He declared that her condition was irremediable (since no additional operation can "eliminate this congenital deficiency") and insisted that "no artificial vagina can replace a real one." He therefore asserted that "existing law gives me the right to petition for a divorce." The plaintiff also submitted the mandatory documents, including a copy of the wedding certificate, and paid the fees required to initiate a divorce suit in ecclesiastical courts.

In accordance with church law, the consistory first attempted to reconcile the two spouses by directing their parish priest to "exhort" the couple. In a report filed about six weeks later, the priest reported that Gavriil categorically refused to withdraw the suit and that Olga had declared her willingness to acquiesce in the dissolution of their marriage. Significantly, however, the priest went beyond his customary legal duty (that is, to exhort the couple and report on the results) and volunteered an impassioned statement on the true state of affairs. At issue, he wrote, was the husband's callous disregard for his wife's financial plight in the event of divorce. The priest complained that Gavriil had rejected reconciliation with Olga "despite her very tragic condition," specifically citing "her lack of material support," and added that he "saw her tears and heard her pleas to delay this matter until she found some minor position for herself." It was, he concluded. "a horrible family scene!"

Olga's acquiescence was short-lived. A month later she formally retracted her earlier statement and categorically rejected divorce. She claimed that she had signed the nonreconciliation statement "under duress" and accused her husband of refusing to provide support. As a result, she complained, "I have been left without any means for existence." Although the court record is silent, it seems likely that Gavriil won her initial consent with promises of postdivorce support but later, savoring imminent victory, had unceremoniously reneged. Whatever the reason, Olga declared her firm intention to fight the divorce tooth and nail. And she had good reason for doing so: as long as the couple remained legally married, she could appeal to Gavriil's superiors for assistance or file suit in the regional court demanding an appropriate portion of his salary for her upkeep. Once divorced, particularly if pronounced the "guilty" party, she might forfeit any hopes for a maintenance allowance.

The cumbersome procedures of ecclesiastical justice, not just her resistance, served to complicate matters further: Gavriil, as husband and plaintiff, bore sole responsibility for providing the requisite evidence. In cases of sexual incapacity, that meant subjecting Olga to a physical examination by the local Medical Board, an agency of the Ministry of Interior. The church itself lacked the means to arrange such an examination; while it did use the state administration in some matters (for example, the delivery of summonses), it had neither its own police apparatus nor the right to direct state officials to act on its behalf. The consistory therefore instructed Krylov to deliver his wife to the Medical Board for the necessary examination. That directive was also consonant with traditional patriarchal order, which bestowed authority on the husband and therefore presupposed his ability to bring his spouse before the Board.

The days of untrammeled patriarchal authority were now past. As Krylov complained in repeated depositions, his wife simply refused to obey and he had no way to force her to comply. He therefore demanded that the diocesan consistory, as the responsible agency, should enforce its own order for a full examination and take the necessary steps to ensure her compliance. Well aware of its limited authority, however, the consistory steadfastly declined to take action and reminded Gavriil of his husbandly duty to deliver Olga to the Medical Board. After months of delay and evasion, the frustrated Krylov finally appealed to the Holy Synod in St. Petersburg to intercede on his behalf.

Olga, meanwhile, had launched her own campaign to quash the divorce. In a moving petition filed with the consistory in April 1908, she explained that when her physical deficiency became apparent, she had offered to accept a divorce and at one point even returned to live with her parents. She claimed, however, that Gavriil had persuaded her to return to him and gave every indication that she "completely satisfied him." For several years, she wrote, all their "physical relations were normal and he was satisfied." The real problem, she declared, was not her artificial vagina but his carnal desires for another woman: "I became inadequate only because he took it into his head to marry a third time, and he has instigated this entire divorce proceeding at the intrigue of the woman whom he plans to marry." Olga noted that she had taken care of his children, currently ages sixteen to twenty-eight, of whom only one was married and the rest still in need of parental care and guidance. Moreover, Gavriil, now over fifty years old, was hardly in a position to start a new family "at his age." She added that for the past seven years she had "devoted her energy and health" to him, and now, after having become part of that family, "he is throwing me overboard." So long as she had been needed as a housekeeper and mother who "looked after them, sewed their clothing, and provided them with maternal care," Gavriil had praised her as a "good woman." Now that the children were nearing the end of their formal schooling and would soon be grown up, "I have become useless as a wife and housekeeper."

Given these facts, Olga insisted that "he does not have the moral right to a divorce." She believed that her husband's demand that she go to the Medical Board for a physical examination was not only a "caprice" but also an act of vengeance against her father, who (so her husband claimed) had promised a large dowry but had then deceived him. Olga emphasized the fact that she had sacrificed her career as an official in the postal and telegraph agency; now that "he is throwing me out onto the street," she had little chance of finding a suitable job. She appealed to the consistory, comprised exclusively of male clergy, "to understand the position of a defenseless, unfortunate woman," to prevent her husband from subjecting her to humiliation and to deny this "immoral petition" for a divorce. The consistory, evidently moved by her letter, drafted a memorandum to the Holy Synod contesting her husband's claims that he failed to have "adequate" sexual relations with his wife.

The Synod, however, as in so many other cases, insisted upon adherence to the strict letter of the law and canon. It took this position in a formal resolution of September 1908, which reaffirmed Gavriil's demand that his wife undergo a medical examination and settle conclusively the question of her sexual incapacity. Her refusal to appear for the examination, it declared, was tantamount to a failure to repudiate her husband's claims. That decision derived largely from the Synod's waxing concern about the massive problem of similar delays and procrastination in the ecclesiastical courts. Although the church, not without cause, blamed such breakdowns on recalcitrant spouses, these delays provoked growing censure of the church along with demands that the whole process be transferred to the state judicial system. Because the Synod (like the consistory) lacked its own executive arm, it resorted to sheer threat: it directed the consistory to issue one more summons for Olga to appear and, should she fail to do so, the consistory was to use the older medical records supplied by her husband. The latter, comprising the original medical reports on her physical condition, confirmed her deformity and described the operation but did not attest to her capacity for sexual intercourse. In short, should she refuse a new physical examination, the consistory was to rely upon the initial documentation that essentially mandated dissolution of the marriage.

Unmoved by this decree, Olga still refused to appear for a medical examination: she ignored not one, but two, more summonses from the consistory. At that point, one year from the date that Krylov originally filed for divorce, the exasperated plaintiff sent yet another petition to the consistory, with an unveiled threat to file a new appeal to the Synod about the malfeasance of diocesan authorities. His petition had the desired effect. Clearly fearful of a reprimand from the Synod, the consistory not only made another attempt to summon Olga for the examination, as Krylov demanded, but also solicited an official opinion from the provincial Medical Board. In January 1909, fourteen months after the initial petition for divorce, the Board filed its response, which concluded that "the condition of Olga Krylova can be deemed as premarital [sexual] incapacity for marital relations."

Her position plainly becoming critical, Olga fought back. She first petitioned the consistory, with the claim that in August 1908 (that is, *after* filing for divorce) Gavriil had pretended to reconcile and had even had conjugal relations with her. Indeed, he did so at the very moment when he was filing his appeal with the Synod. Olga also decided to go over the heads of the consistory and made a personal, impassioned appeal to the local bishop, imploring him "to intercede for a defenseless woman" and to prevent "my humiliation."

Her petitions fell on deaf ears. The local consistory, intimidated by the Synod's earlier decree, adopted a verdict in her husband's favor. It approved the divorce "because of the congenital incapacity of the wife for conjugal relations," with the customary stipulation that the husband be allowed to remarry and that she remain forever celibate. It then summoned the two litigants to read the text, giving each one an opportunity to verify its factual accuracy and to record approval or "dissatisfaction" with the verdict. Whereas Gavriil was predictably "satisfied" with the consistory's decision, Olga formally protested and filed new evidence on her behalf. The latter consisted of a deposition, signed on February 19, 1909, by her original surgeons, who attested that "at the present time her vagina has a length of 4.7 to 5.0 centimeters," thereby making "conjugal relations possible." In strictly formal legal terms, Olga had now gained the upper hand against her husband, since the most recent documents superseded the original diagnosis and explicitly confirmed her physical capacity to have sexual intercourse. In addition, Olga also demanded that her husband be examined (!), plainly hinting at *his* physical shortcomings.

Notwithstanding her statement and evidence, however, the local bishop confirmed the consistory's provisional resolution in Gavriil's favor and sent the file to the Holy Synod for a final review and approval. The decisive factor was Olga's refusal to comply with the Synod's instruction. Since the latter required that the verdict be based on the original medical evidence, the diocesan authorities had no choice but to dissolve the union. Surprisingly, the Synod decided in favor of Olga. Taking note of the failure to obtain a medical examination by state authorities, the Synod sent the file to the Ministry of Interior for an official evaluation. The latter, whether because of the available data or the private medical report filed by Olga, ruled that the earlier documentation was insufficient and that only a thorough examination could allow a definitive judgment on the matter of her sexual capacity. While rejecting her demand for a physical examination of Gavriil (citing his five children as proof of his sexual capacity), the Synod reiterated its earlier demand that Olga undergo a medical examination without, however, specifying precisely how.

For the next few years Krylov tried, in vain, to comply with this directive. As the exasperated plaintiff later explained, he made every attempt to deliver his wife to the Medical Board, but with no success. At first, she had taken up residence with his parents but later moved to another province (Grodno), where she obtained a position in a secondary school for girls. Despite further complaints from Krylov, the diocesan consistory insisted that he bore the exclusive responsibility for bringing Olga for the medical examination. Krylov appealed once more to the Synod, but to no avail. Whatever its private motive (sympathy for the woman, or alarm over the exploding rate of divorce), the Synod reiterated that the plaintiff "must himself take measures to deliver his wife to the Medical Board." In 1914, as the country edged toward the cataclysm of World War I, Olga's procrastination and appeal for sympathetic clerical intercession had triumphed: the case breaks off without resolution, with the marriage left intact.

By the early twentieth century the Russian family was now in the throes of a profound crisis, a complex of powerful forces steadily eroding the traditional patriarchal order. Accelerated geographic mobility, opportunities for male and female employment outside the village, erosion of traditional values, heightened self-consciousness (including a refusal to tolerate spousal abuse, physical or psychological)—these and many other factors undermined patriarchy and family stability, even in remote rural areas. Conservative institutions such as the church felt driven to accommodate these powerful forces or risk losing altogether their influence. The result was a steady increase in the divorce rate. As a liberal church journal (*Tserkovnyi vestnik*) observed in September 1913, "The disintegration of the family—notwithstanding the extreme difficulty of the divorce procedure—is one of the most grievous social ills of the present time."

Nevertheless, that accommodation lagged considerably behind the expectations and demands of society, for many bishops (and bureaucrats) regarded family breakdown as an alarming symptom of a broader social crisis and something to be resisted at any cost. As the Krylov case demonstrates, local and eventually central church authorities were predisposed to tolerate spousal resistance and thus help avert divorce, which, by definition, they regarded as evil and undesirable. Hence, Olga Krylova, exploiting through noncompliance the power of passive resistance, effectively sabotaged her husband's suit. However well grounded and logical his legal claim might have seemed, for years she simply declined to appear for a medical examination and succeeded in preventing the divorce. Significantly, first diocesan and then central authorities implicitly came to her defense, tolerating such noncompliance and denying her husband any effective recourse.

That family crisis produced a further crisis in the church itself: it led to an inexorable breakdown in ecclesiastical administration, which gradually lost the ability to handle the escalating volume of marital and divorce cases. As a result, bishops across the empire began amassing an enormous backlog of unresolved divorce suits. Diocesan authorities, operating with a tiny staff, soon found themselves overwhelmed by the sheer volume of new and outstanding files. Unless both parties desired the divorce, it became increasingly easy to procrastinate and defy, subverting the judicial process and denying divorces even on grounds recognized by the church itself. The St. Petersburg consistory, for example, reported that its caseload had more than doubled, with an ever larger set of unfinished and unresolved cases besetting its staff. This process accelerated rapidly with the outbreak of World War I, as the chaos of war and social dislocation (including the conscription of spouses and witnesses) made the processing of divorce cases all but impossible. Matters steadily deteriorated by 1917, with the revolution at once unleashing radical new expectations about immediate divorce and further subverting the regular operation of church administration. By the time that the Bolsheviks finally secularized marriage and divorce in December 1917 (effectively making this sphere the exclusive concern of state authority), the church had virtually lost its capacity to process, let alone resolve, the tidal wave of divorce applications. The conjunction—a growing demand for prompt divorce, a declining ability of the church to process such cases—fueled widespread disenchantment and alienation, even among staunch believers. Little wonder that the bishop of Kaluga affirmed popular support for the Bolshevik decree on the family, which many in his diocese called "the most useful" by the new revolutionary regime.

NOTES

1. In Russian, adding the suffix "a" forms the feminine form of a husband's surname.

2. The records of the case described in this article are preserved in the Historical State Archive of Lithuania as fond 605, opis 9, d. 845.

SUGGESTED READINGS

Bisha, Robin. "The Promise of Patriarchy: Marriage in Eighteenth-Century Russia." Ph.D. diss., Indiana University, 1994.

Engel, Barbara Alpern. *Between the Fields and City: Women, Work and Family in Russia, 1861–1914.* Cambridge, Eng., 1994.

Freeze, Gregory L. "Bringing Order to the Russian Family: Marriage and Divorce in Imperial Russia, 1760–1860." *Journal of Modern History* 62 (December 1990): 709–48.

———. "L'Ortodossia russe e la crisi delle famiglie: Il divorzio in Russia tra la rivoluzione e la guerra (1917-1921)." In *L'Autunno della Santa Russia, 1917–1945: Atti del VI Convegno ecumenico internazionale di spiritualità russa, Bose 16–19 settembre 1998*, edited by Adalberto Mainardi. Magnano: Qiqajon, 1999.

Goldman, Wendy. *Women, the State, and Revolution: Soviet Family Policy and Social Life, 1917–1936.* Cambridge, Eng., 1993.

Pushkareva, L. N. *Women in Russian History: From the Tenth to the Twentieth Century.* Armonk, NY, 1997.

Wagner, William. *Marriage, Property and Law in Late Imperial Russia.* Oxford, 1994.

Worobec, Christine D. *Peasant Russia: Family and Community in the Post-Emancipation Period.* Princeton, 1991.

Yvert-Jalie, Hélène. "L'Histoire du divorce en Russie Soviétique." *Population* 36 (1981): 41–61.

CHAPTER 2

Old Believers in Imperial Russia

A Legend on the Appearance of Tobacco

Roy R. Robson

Not everyone who opposed modernity in late Imperial Russia was reactionary or self-serving. One did not have to be an ardent supporter of autocracy, a dispossessed landowner, a marginalized peasant, or some other victim of socioeconomic displacement to prefer the familiar to the unknown. In every society a significant proportion of the population has a commitment to the status quo that transcends any reflexive or even opportunistic rejection of change. Indeed, few citizens anywhere relinquish what they know best unless compelled by events beyond their control or when converted to something they regard as demonstrably better. But for a significant plurality—perhaps a majority—of ordinary Russians in the late Imperial period, no such transition was taking place. Indeed, for those who had embraced the status quo consciously and even endured sacrifices to maintain it, and for whom the familiar was not simply the path of least resistance, dislodging what people lived by proved especially difficult. Neither revolutionary ideology nor paeans to progress, modernization, and secularism stood much chance of converting those who viewed the familiar not as an intellectual or even personal choice but as a divinely consecrated order of heavenly and earthly affairs.

The Old Believer sect constituted one such group. Old Believers saw themselves as Russia's only true practitioners of the Orthodox faith and as the main repository of piety in the country. Alienated both from the state and the mainstream church and characterized by their foes as confusing symbol with belief, Old Believers determinedly clung to ancient practice in the face of what they regarded as a world of blasphemy, heresy, and temptation. Given the circumstances of their break with the church hierarchy, matters could hardly have been otherwise. When Nikon became Patriarch of Moscow in 1652, he brought Greek texts to Russia in order to correct the mistakes that had crept into Orthodox holy books during the past seven centuries, and a year later he expanded his scope to include the revision of church rituals. The sign of the cross was presently being made with two fingers rather than three; two, and not three, "alleluias" were sung; the name of Jesus had been misspelled. At the same time, he took steps to strengthen the control of the central church over the parishes, and priests who opposed him found themselves imprisoned and exiled. Ultimately, a church council in 1667 upheld Nikon's reforms and excommunicated his opponents, even though it also took action against the Patriarch himself.

The Nikonian reforms thus created a schism in Orthodoxy that continues to the present day. Rather than accept what they considered anathema, Old Believer communities fled to Russia's hinterland, began a global diaspora, practiced collective self-immolation, or endured persecution as a subculture within mainstream society. Not surprisingly, a response of such depth stemmed from much more than a petulant adherence to old rituals. By the time it ran its course, this seventeenth-century revolt came to encompass a protest against serfdom and centralized state control as well as a general rejection of foreign—especially Western—influences. Although by no means monolithic, Old Belief survived as a subculture and not uncommonly prospered during the eighteenth and nineteenth centuries. But as the twentieth century approached, symbols of modernity, from vodka to tea to the city, placed obstacles in the path of their vision of the true faith.

Roy Robson presents the only extant English translation of the legend of the introduction of one leading Old Believer nemesis: tobacco. In this treatment, the legend allows us to view not only important inner workings of the Old Believers' faith but also to assess their rejection of modernity in the late Imperial period. Modernization challenged no group more directly than the Old Believers, and, as Robson shows, it is unlikely that any other group had given as much thought to its advent. The legend of the introduction of tobacco thus illuminates the experience of an important subculture in Russian history, but in its unflinching confrontation with modernity the legend also undoubtedly articulates feelings that resonated far beyond the circle of Old Believers.

Roy R. Robson is assistant professor at the University of the Sciences in Philadelphia. He is the author of Old Believers in Modern Russia *(1995) and of numerous articles on Old Belief in Imperial Russia. Professor Robson received his doctorate from Boston College.*

There was a Greek king named Anepsii who ruled in those lands. One night as Anepsii was sleeping in his bed, he had a dream. In his dream, he saw a maiden clad in royal robes who sat on his own throne and had his crown upon her head. The girl had a beautiful face and an attractive countenance, and she appeared joyous as she sat on his throne. He noticed that many old people who were looking at her looked frightened and awe-stricken. They were so overwhelmed with fear that many of them died on the spot. Then young people wanted to see the girl, and they climbed upon the corpses, and saw her, and trembled with fear, and died too. And then young children wanted to see the girl, and they climbed upon the corpses, and saw her, and died. And the king could not see her anymore; he could see nothing but the multitude of corpses. He woke up, consumed by horror and trepidation. He was so stricken that he did not dare to tell about his dream to his queen, his councilors, or his courtiers. He could not eat nor drink, and he had an uncontrollable urge to flee, as if a terrible storm was approaching.

So begins the Old Believer legend entitled "A Tale Taken from the Book Called Pandae of the Secret and Filthy Weed Called Tobacco, Where It Came From and How It Spread in the World." The legend first began to circulate in the eighteenth century but was not published until 1860. By then it had spread by hand-copying and oral tradition across Russia's far-flung Old Believer communities. But who were these Old Believers, and why would they develop a legend about faraway kings and relate it to horrific visions to describe tobacco use? And why would they despise smoking some centuries before science discovered its ill effects?

The term "Old Believers" encompasses a great number of traditional Russian Orthodox who lived across all the empire. In the midseventeenth century, Patriarch Nikon, leader of the Russian church, began to change details of the liturgical ritual and the church books. On the face of it, many of his changes do not seem to make much difference to a modern Western person—how to hold your hand when making the sign of the cross, walking clockwise or counterclockwise in processions, and saying "alleluia" two times or three.

For the Russian Orthodox of the seventeenth century, however, these changes cut to the core of their belief. Unlike the Western Christian church, which increasingly emphasized the biblical word as the key to salvation, Orthodoxy accentuated the process of "divinization" or "theosis." In the theology of divinization, believers hoped to find salvation—in part—through the ritual actions of the liturgy, thus becoming "godlike." (One Orthodox saint wrote that "God became Man so that men could become God.") Changing ritual actions and words, therefore, was tantamount to altering the faith itself and diverting the path to salvation. To make matters worse, Nikon based his reforms on Greek practices, which Old Believers claimed had been sullied by Roman Catholic influences. Why, asked the traditionalists, should Russians accept foreign rituals, tinged by the papacy, instead of their own?

Finally, Patriarch Nikon enforced his changes in order to centralize control of the church and to increase his own ecclesiastical power. Relying on Tsar Alexis, the patriarch brutally persecuted those believers who did not want to accept reforms: some were beaten, others burned at the stake, and still others smoked "like bacon." For their part, Old Believers (as they became known) built their religious ideology on retaining traditions, emphasizing local control over religious affairs, and fleeing from persecution. In the worst cases, Old Believers burned themselves in great church funeral pyres rather than accept changes in ritual or bow to the strong arm of the Russian army.

The earliest Old Belief was not an organized movement; it probably sprang from people who cherished their traditional religious independence and already resented the centralized power of government and church in Moscow. Quickly, however, the Old Belief appeared across Russia, and Old Believers became known as industrious, pious, and serious Russians who mistrusted influences imported from the West. Tobacco was such a substance, brought to Russia in the late seventeenth century by Western Europeans after its discovery in America. To continue the legend:

[Anepsii] indeed abandoned his realm and fled, taking only a meager amount of food with him. He ran for three nights and three days without so much as stopping to eat or drink, and committed himself to fasting and labor. God saw his humility and sent His angel to him to interpret his dream. The angel, disguised as a eunuch, that is, an aristocrat [sic], was to reveal to him that in the last days of the world, humanity and the whole world would be corrupted by a secret poison. This was the meaning of his dream.

The angel met the king on his way, and the king—seeing that his face was handsome and radiant—bowed to him and said: "Peace be unto thee, stranger!" And the angel replied: "Peace." The king asked: "From where do you come?" and the angel replied: "To where are you going?" The king did not want to confess his dream, because he thought that he was talking to a stranger. But the angel said: "Tell me everything, for I know you, and who you are, and what you are running away from, having left behind your throne and power. You are the king Anepsii. I implore you to return to your kingdom. Be not afraid of your night vision, for you cannot leave your throne because of a mere dream. There will be no harm done to your kingdom. What you saw in your dream is not going to happen now, but before the Second Coming."

And the angel said this: "This is how the Devil contrived to lead the men from sobriety to drunkenness. There was a nun named Jezebel who had sinned and gave birth to a daughter. When the girl reached twelve years of age, she became possessed by the Devil, who flared up lewdness in her. She acted upon the Devil's wishes ever since, and lived in carnality for thirty years. God gave her a chance to repent, but she did not. Then God sent His angel and he made the earth divide, and the rift was thirty cubits wide. Then the earth swallowed that wanton woman, with the Devil in her belly and the cesspool of filth in her bosom. And then it rained over her grave, and on the very same spot the dirt spewed a weed. The Greeks, in compliance with the Devil's plan, will adopt this weed and plant it in their gardens, and call it 'tobacco.' And those who have partaken of this weed will become delirious, and will experience extraordinary coldness in their limbs, and fainting spells, and tremors. This intoxication will cause their death. After they are dead, they will head straight to Hell. You are going to see it for yourself soon." And Anepsii asked: "When am I going to see this?" And the angel replied: "In twenty years you will see crowds of drunk-ards before the very gates of your palace, and they will shake and pass out. The secret and venomous weed will cause many deaths. You will under-stand that the minute a lascivious person begins to rule the world, the Devil starts to kill with his rod. For nothing is more maddening and harmful for man than lewdness and drunkenness." And, having said this, the angel be-came invisible.

The legend, as far as we have read it, contains much that can tell us about Old Believer ideology. The story employs many biblical references, lending it an air of authority. When King Anepsii meets the angel, for example, he speaks as Jesus did to the apostles after the Resurrection and frequently quoted in the Orthodox liturgy: "Peace be unto thee" (Luke 24:36). Almost immediately the angel describes the end of the world: "What you saw in your dream is not going to happen now, but before the Second Coming." To explain, the angelic messenger develops a theme found in the Book of Revelation. In Revelation, according to Christian tradition, Jezebel represents all those who might claim to believe in Christ but whose actions belie their beliefs. In its prologue, the legend quotes the relevant passage from the biblical text:

> Saint John the Theologian wrote this to the angel of the church in Thy-a-ti'ra in the second chapter of the Book of Revelation: "Notwithstanding I have a few things against thee, because thou sufferest that woman Jez'e-bel, which calleth herself a prophetess, to teach and to seduce my servants to commit fornication, and to eat things sacrificed unto idols. And I gave her space to repent of her fornication; and she repented not. Behold, I will cast her into a bed, and them that commit adultery with her into great tribulation, except they repent of their deeds. And I will kill her children with death [Revelation 2:20–23].". . . . Hear ye and comprehend that the Holy Ghost said this about that obscure and vile weed, tobacco, which has existed from time immemorial.

Of course, the Bible story never mentions tobacco. The Old Believ-ers used the idea of ingesting unclean things (as Jezebel did in Revela-tion) to include "that vile weed." By connecting a book of the Bible to tobacco, the legend also links the Old Believers' taboo against tobacco to divine Scripture, thus giving the taboo more power. Likewise, the leg-end slyly introduces Greece (not America) as the source of tobacco. Al-though long revered as the foundation of Eastern Christianity, Greece had lost its luster among Old Believers when it sent emissaries to defend Nikon's ritual changes. Who would inaugurate a practice designed to lead believers to Hell? Who else but the Greeks, the root of all errors introduced by Nikon?

According to the legend, tobacco had existed from the beginning of time, but its widespread use did not come immediately. Instead, the poisonous plant was cultivated as weak people learned of its power to make them feel good:

> The king Anepsii returned to his kingdom. He did not tell anybody what the angel revealed to him. For twenty years he kept silent, waiting for the prophecy to be fulfilled. And then a certain physician named Tremikur, a Greek, went to the fields to look for medicinal herbs. He found an unknown plant on the same spot where the angel struck the lewd woman. He saw the plant, and the Devil prompted him to pluck it and smell it. And, having done so, Tremikur became very merry and forgot all his troubles. He then took the weed and planted it in his garden. He took to plucking the weed, and smelling it, and appeared to be merry, as if he were drunk. People asked him: "Where did you get the wine?" He then showed them the weed in his garden, and sold it for silver. Soon all Greeks had this plant in their gardens. Some started to burn it and inhale the vapors. And soon they felt extraordinary coldness in their limbs, some fainted, some shook violently, some became insane, and some died. The deranged men boasted that they had this weed instead of wine. All these intoxicated people, fainting and shaking, some dropping dead, gathered at the king's palace.
>
> The king saw his people in this sorry state and marveled at this news. He thought they were drunk. He then asked some of the Greeks: "How did it happen? Why are these people fainting, and shaking, and paralyzed? Why are they dying? Where did you get the wine?" The Greeks replied that they had not imbibed any wine or beer. The king Anepsii ordered them tortured, and under torture they confessed that they had a plant in their gardens, a certain strange weed that caused this state of intoxication. The king asked: "Where did you get this plant and its seeds?" They replied that Tremikur the Greek physician had sold them this weed. The king ordered Tremikur brought to his palace and proceeded to interrogate the physician about this plant, asking where Tremikur had obtained the weed and whether it was its root, blossoms, or seeds that was used to prepare the intoxicating substance. He also had Tremikur point out the exact spot where the tobacco was first found. Tremikur led the king to the place, and it was the very same place where the angel struck the whore, and where the earth swallowed her corpse, and buried it thirty cubits deep. The king recognized the place and brought people there, and ordered them to dig the pit thirty cubits deep. The diggers then discovered the putrid corpse, which had almost completely decomposed, except for the skull and anal bones. The king asked: "Who knows if this corpse belongs to a man or a woman?" Tremikur answered: "I don't know for certain, but twenty years ago a whore lived here."

In this portion of the legend the king's dream finally comes true, just as prophesied by the angel. Trying to keep their intoxicant a secret, the Greeks have to be tortured before they confess their use of tobacco. Once he learns of its origin, Anepsii wastes no time in searching his land for the wellspring of tobacco—the putrid remains of Jezebel's daughter, a latter-day Eve who had forsaken God and seduced countless men. Anepsii realizes that both the prophetic dream and its angelic explication had come to pass in his own times and contemplates the truth of Christianity. Comprehending the power of a Christian God who would send a prophetic dream and angel, Anepsii seeks out an erudite and pious Christian girl. He is impressed by her and learns that she has been taught by a Christian bishop.

> At night, the king fell asleep while thinking about the Christian faith and he had a vision. An angel came down to him and said: "I command thee to send for the bishop that the maiden told you about. The bishop will be your way to salvation." And the king asked the angel: "Who are you?" And the angel replied: "I am the one that you met twenty years ago, when you were running away from your kingdom, and I am the one who commanded you to return and rule your realm."
>
> The king woke up and sent for the bishop. . . . The king then felt the balm of the divine Word, and accepted the holy baptism in the name of the Father, and the Son, and the Holy Ghost, and his Christian name was Aleksii. And many princes, and aristocrats, and people were baptized, too.
>
> The bishop prayed and fasted for forty days, and he was blessed with a vision. An angel came to him and said: "Condemn this loathsome plant, for it had been planted by Satan over the rotten body of a filthy and accursed harlot. God will ban anybody who smells this weed from His heavenly kingdom and condemn him to the eternal torment. Satan wants to fulfill his burning desire to drown the world in corruption. . . . Whoever neglects my admonition and defies the will of God shall be forever the enemy of Our Lord. His name shall be wiped out from the Book of Life, and he shall be cast to Hell, with hands and legs tied, and the Devil will cast him in a pit full of burning brimstone.

Finally, having been baptized a Christian, the king helps his bishop to understand the implications of tobacco use. The legend's central message is not subtle—tobacco is Satan's tool to corrupt humanity, and those who use it "shall forever reside with the Fiend and demons in the fiery river." Although the king's vision shows tobacco's deadly effects, the bishop's dream illustrates the eternal damnation promised to those who use a plant spawned from evil. By indulging in pleasures of the flesh, tobacco addicts align themselves with Satan and forswear the path to godliness. Even Christians are subject to the temptation of tobacco, and the Old Believers' legend reasoned that its power of corruption would multiply as did its number of users.

> In the ages before the Last Judgment callous knaves, hypocrites, drunkards, and apostates will abandon the faith and start acting upon their own wishes and desires [rather than the will of God]. This evil plant will spread and multitudes of people will be consuming it and, in their intoxication, will forget how to repent. And God will turn His face away from them, and love will end among people. They will hate each other, and fathers will turn against their sons, and sons against their fathers, and people will defy the Holy Scriptures. God will impose a merciless government upon them, which will not care for people in distress, and the poor will hate the rich, and the humans will forget how to get along with each other. Nation will

fight against nation, and kingdom against kingdom, and a great catastrophe will befall the earth. This is why God commands thee to condemn this evil and filthy plant." And, having said this, the angel became invisible.

Tobacco use, according to the legend, heralds the reign of the Antichrist and the end of the world. This conclusion dovetails neatly with Old Believer ideology—as they endured persecution from the church and state, the faithful asserted that they were experiencing the end times. In Old Believer accounts, Nikon's reforms were acknowledged by a council of Greek and Russian prelates in 1666—the Year of the Beast [Satan]—and all the traditions held sacred to traditional Russian Orthodoxy seemed to be turned on their head. Foreign influences, first from Greece and later from across Europe, introduced new substances into Russian life (not only tobacco but also potatoes, new clothing styles, and new kinds of alcoholic beverages). Who was to say that these were not tools of the Antichrist to wrestle pious Russians away from God?

The legend provides an Old Believer synopsis of tobacco's export, showing that the Western nations had forced the substance on Russians, here simply called "Christians." Old Believer woodcuts and manuscript illuminations amply illustrated their belief that the world was soon to end, brought on by the forces of Nikon's reforms and foreign vices. Yet, was all lost? Was it possible for a Christian to fight against the anti-Christian pagan tide stretching out across Russia? The legend provides the antidote to tobacco use and a path back toward salvation in the church.

The faithful Christians, men and women, then banished this plant from their gardens. But pagans, who did not obey God's law, exported tobacco to other pagan lands. The accursed Greeks brought it to Germans, Turks, Tartars, and the Ukrainians, and from these lands tobacco came to us Christians. Many people, having inadvertently tasted tobacco, kept smoking it, and thus have left the faithful to join the pagans. Consumed by the desire for the stench and putrid taste of tobacco, they condemn themselves to the eternal torment. God saw men who, afflicted with this deadly addiction, were falling into the Devil's trap and condemned themselves to the eternal torturous abyss. . . . Should someone not want to denounce tobacco, he should be banned from the Church for seven years, as befits a harlot, and then he is welcome to come back to the Church, and he should be treated as a beloved friend rather than an enemy. He then should live in repentance, lamenting day and night his sins, and live not according to his own will, but the will of God, and praise the loving Father, Son, and the Holy Spirit.

And so ends the legend's story but not its influence. As Old Believers faced the rapid modernization of the late Imperial period, they often retold the legend and interpreted its relevance in terms of their own changing lives. Manuscripts dating from the late nineteenth century copied or quoted from the legend, using it to defend Old Believers' views that tobacco use had condemned Russian society. One manuscript claimed that Satan was trying to steal Russia from God and, in turn, rule it for himself: "I will take the evil seed and plant it in the ground and from it will sprout the tobacco weed, and many people will eat it and [smoke] it," writes the anonymous author, "and they will be stolen from the Lord God, and in stealing them I will fill [my] hellish womb, and with them will begin to rule."

Tobacco thus became an Old Believer symbol for all the ills of Russia, an emblem for the purity of the Old Belief versus the degradation of society. When Old Believer writers began to publish (after persecutions ceased in 1905), they did not need to convert their brothers and sisters to an antismoking point of view. The legend had already done that for them. Instead, Old Believer authors could use the centuries-old abhorrence of tobacco as a weapon against their foes.

No one was spared criticism for smoking—especially the clerics of the state-sponsored church. An Old Believer writer almost gloated over the death of one Father Joseph, abbot of Russia's most revered monastery, the Trinity Saint Sergius Lavra. According to newspaper accounts, the abbot "loved to smoke." Father Joseph, intoned the Old Believer, was just one of many monks who embraced tobacco use. More scandalous, according to this source, was the death of Seraphim of Sarov, a saint canonized by the state-sponsored church in 1905. Published reports claimed that Seraphim had died while at prayer, and a novice later found him still standing but dead in his cell. Nonsense, intoned the Old Believer press—in fact, Father Seraphim had suffocated from a smoldering fire lit when he dropped his pipe onto a heap of rags. The author was almost conspiratorial: "that Father Seraphim passed away from this cause is a generally known legend among those close to Sarov and in various places, and confirmed in the circumstances of his death." Although no official would admit it, "to speak truthfully is to say that he died from tobacco, which began the fire." For an Old Believer audience who knew the legend, this rumor damned the holy man and condemned his church.

Nevertheless, Old Believers themselves sometimes yielded to the temptation of tobacco. In the words of the legend: "many people, having inadvertently tasted tobacco, kept smoking it, and thus have left the faithful to join the pagans." More concretely, Old Believers realized that the rapid changes in society produced people more likely to fall into the trap. "In the remote countryside and villages, where the folk are whole and religious," claimed one author, "smoking among these Old Believers is really rare." When people left the village to work in the factories, however, they fell prey to satanic influences that told them smoking was urbane and civilized. Even young children became addicted, thus ensuring the debauchery of a future generation of Russian society.

Worried about sickness and damnation from the evil weed, Old Believers sought ways to insulate themselves from its influence. In the most extreme cases, Old Believer families packed up their possessions and fled farther into Russia's hinterland; at the beginning of the century, one could easily still hide from society by homesteading in Siberia or central Asia. Setting off on such a dangerous adventure had become part of Old Believer lore—the faithful had fled persecution by the thousands in previous centuries, and the thought of a pure life in some pristine forest held great allure to those who were afraid of society's ills. Like King Anepsii after his vision, these Old Believers ran away from society, "committing themselves to fasting and labor."

Most Old Believers, however, sought a more temperate response to outside society's sinfulness than outright flight. When they prayed, many Old Believers first asked forgiveness for interacting with anyone who had fallen into sins such as tobacco use. Fortified with prayer, these Old Believers sought at least to limit their interaction with *tobachniki* (tobacco users). In one part of the legend, Christians are enjoined to "ban [tobacco users] from kissing icons, the Holy Cross, or the Bible, forbid them to receive the Holy Communion, prohibit them from attending the divine service until they abandon this accursed weed. Should somebody approach you, do not give them your blessing, for their putrid lips and filthy heads are abomination to the Holy Spirit." By keeping their own religious life pure from tobacco's influence, these Old Believers hoped to find their way through the maze of modern temptations and hold off the Devil's attacks.

The legend demanded that holy objects be kept safe from tobacco. While the smoke of incense purified icons, homes, and the faithful, tobacco would defile holy things. Many Old Believers therefore kept their icons behind glass doors in a case they called an "ark," referring to the Old Testament's Ark of the Covenant. Likewise, tobacco smokers were banned from holy places, thus keeping unclean people from corrupting godly things. In this way, the remnant of faithful might be kept pure from the spread of the Antichrist's power as embodied in tobacco.

Some Old Believers, however, viewed science as a way to justify their own traditional taboos. "Present day science," wrote one Old Believer, "shows that smoking is no better than heavy drinking." Although scientific evidence against tobacco had not achieved critical mass (no official health proclamation on smoking would appear in Russia until the late twentieth century), some scientists did claim that smoking endangered health. Of course, declared the Old Believers, we knew it all the time! We have always called that "filth in the mouth" a poison, an extraordinary sin, a form of suicide! Indeed, according to the Old Belief, science was simply beginning to catch up to the wisdom passed down by generations of Old Believers. Instead of fearing modern science, they could embrace it as a corollary to their own teaching.

All of these strategies—flight, purification, and science—helped the faithful Old Believers to interact in the inconstant world of nineteenth- and twentieth-century Russia. The legend on tobacco provided a foundation for Old Believer views of the world. As life changed rapidly, some Russians might decide to jettison tradition and embrace modern life. Old Believers hoped, on the other hand, that their traditional beliefs would give them the tools to interpret the world around them, describe their place in society, and point the way toward salvation.

SUGGESTED READINGS

The text published here is the only English version of the legend in print. Olga Tsapina, of Moscow State University, provided an excellent translation from archaic Russian usage. Although it is somewhat abridged, the text closely follows the first published version, *Legenda o proiskhozhdenii tabaka* [Legend on the appearance of tobacco], which appeared in *Pamiatniki starinnoi russkoi literatury* [Monuments of ancient Russian literature] (St. Petersburg, 1860), pts. 1–2, 427–34. Other quotations from Old Believer writers come from various magazines that appeared from 1905 to 1917.

After many years of neglect, many scholars have turned their interest toward Russia's Old Believers. The most influential article in English on the Old Belief is probably still Michael Cherniavsky's "The Old Believers and the New Religion," *Slavic Review* 25 (1966): 1–39. The most prolific writer, however, has been Robert Crummey, whose *Old Believers and the World of Antichrist* (Madison, 1977) is a classic. More recently, he has published articles analyzing Old Believer culture; see, for example, "Old Belief as Popular Religion," *Slavic Review* 52 (1993): 700–712. A collection of articles edited by Stephen K. Batalden entitled *Seeking God: The Recovery of Religious Identity in Orthodox Russia, Ukraine, and Georgia* (DeKalb, Il., 1993) contains a number of good pieces on the Old Belief, as does Samuel H. Baron and Nancy Shields Kollman, eds., *Religion and Culture in Early Modern Russia and Ukraine* (DeKalb, IL, 1997). There are a few books that analyze the Old Believer experience in modern Russia; see Roy R. Robson, *Old Believers in Modern Russia* (DeKalb, IL, 1995), and James L. West et al., eds., *Merchant Moscow: Images of Russia's Vanished Bourgeoisie* (Princeton, 1998). These publications contain complete bibliographies of works in Russian, English, and other languages.

CHAPTER 3

An Epidemic of Possession in a Moscow Rural Parish in 1909

CHRISTINE D. WOROBEC

It would be difficult to find a more contentious issue in a modernizing society than demonic possession. When science begins to pose direct challenges to traditional beliefs—and medical professionals start to compete with clergy, sorcerers, healers, witches, and others who mediate between humans and the supernatural as purveyors of fundamental truth—the attribution of any causation or behavior to demonic influence is bound to generate skepticism and controversy. Where scientific progress brings forward new professions and actively promotes the value structures on which they rest, previously sacrosanct elements of the nonmaterial world come under scrutiny. Such a confrontation between established ways and modernity inevitably gives rise to philosophical differences writ large, but it also produces tensions in more personal ways. This conflict could be particularly troublesome in the rural villages of late Imperial Russia, where stability and the subordination of the individual to the whole were necessary for community harmony and, indeed, survival. Any disruptive clash between traditional belief and science therefore became the concern of everyone, and those at the margins of both the old and new values—women, for example—often experienced these frictions most intensely and fashioned the most extreme responses. Such was the case when an epidemic of possession broke out in the village of Troitskoe in 1909.

Even those who did not believe in demonic intervention had to take it seriously as an element that could influence social existence. The population of premodern Russia had seen direct supernatural agency in virtually all human events of any consequence. Contrary to canon law and the wishes of church hierarchs, Russian Orthodoxy at the level of popular religion therefore did not preclude a belief in witchcraft, sorcery, and magic. Depending on size, every village had at least one resident prepared to intervene between the spirit world and the local population, a situation that lasted into the 1920s and beyond. Moreover, this phenomenon was not solely a rural one. Russians of all classes viewed their environment as inhabited by a combination of benign and evil spirits who participated constantly in human affairs and with whom daily negotiation was mandatory. As the twentieth century arrived, demons and spirits still occupied a place in the framework of social discussion. And for those who could not cope with new thinking, the refuge of the supernatural beckoned.

Christine Worobec's examination of the epidemic of possession in Troitskoe raises provocative issues pertinent to any discussion of the resilience of Russian traditionalism. Since most people who fell victim were female, was this a specifically feminine response to change or possibly just a manifestation of uncontrollable conduct? Was possession a feminine tool to receive public sympathy and even a kind of redemption? And how did the medical professionals react when they came into contact with beliefs they considered irrational? In addressing these questions, Worobec uncovers important insights about Russia in the early twentieth century: villagers responded to medical professionals not just as purveyors of a different truth but also as outsiders; exposure to "modernizing" influences such as life in the city did not necessarily reduce the peasants' propensity to believe in the supernatural; and members of educated society may have been relatively free of belief in demonic spirits, but they also could be ambivalent about modernity. These factors make tidy resolutions impossible and, in fact, open the village to an avenue of scrutiny that challenges previous conventional wisdom.

Christine D. Worobec, associate professor of history at Northern Illinois University, received her Ph.D. at the University of Toronto. Her publications include Peasant Russia: Family and Community in the Post-Emancipation Period *(1991) and, as coeditor,* Russia's Women: Accommodation, Resistance, Transformation *(1991).*

During the 1909 Lenten services in the parish of Troitskoe,[1] Moscow province, a strange event occurred that subsequently gripped the parish and surrounding villages for the entire spring and summer. It all began with the experiences of the married peasant woman Klavdiia Fadeeva of the village of Khomutovo, located about a kilometer from the parish church. Whenever she came to church services in the latter part of Lent that year, she began to scream in a frightening voice. As time went on, her shouting fits intensified, and on Good Friday she disrupted the solemnity of the liturgy by imitating the sounds of cocks, dogs, cows, and sheep. Thereafter, when she was not making cacophonous animal noises in the presence of holy objects or during a religious service, she uttered vulgar and blasphemous words in a voice not her own. Frightened witnesses became convinced that Klavdiia was possessed by one or more demons. They labeled her a *klikusha* (shrieker), using a term that referred to a woman who believed herself and was believed to be possessed or bewitched. Before they knew it, three other women began to imitate the physical symptoms of *klikushi* and likewise to experience possession fits repeatedly during church services and whenever they were in the proximity of icons, incense, and holy crosses.

The threat of a widespread epidemic that would disrupt the tranquility of the countryside prompted nervous government officials, even more anxious and cautious after the rural disturbances that had accompanied the Revolution of 1905, to dispatch police and a psychiatrist to the affected villages. What appeared to be uncontrollable and unruly female behavior became defined as pathological and thus under the purview of medical specialists who enjoyed unprecedented prestige as purveyors of scientific truth. When the investigating outsiders arrived on the scene, they were assured by parishioners, who undoubtedly wished to deflect attention away from themselves, that Troitskoe and its neighboring villages had until then never experienced an epidemic of possession. As it turned out, possession was not unknown; one of the victim's relatives, her mother-in-law, believed that she had been possessed for twenty-five years.

Was the epidemic in Troitskoe an isolated phenomenon, an anomaly in a European Russia that was rapidly industrializing and modernizing? Did it, as M. Lakhtin (the examining psychiatrist) thought, result from the anxieties produced by the 1905 Revolution? In other words, was it a manifestation of typical female resistance to revolutionary change? Or did it serve as a metaphor for uncontrollable disorderly conduct? And were beliefs in possession and bewitchment an integral part of Russian Orthodoxy and Russian peasant culture? Did possession provide a public forum in which women could express their pain in an acceptable fashion and receive sympathy, relief, and even redemption? And what happened when the scientific rationalism of psychiatrists came into contact with what they perceived to be superstitious and irrational beliefs on the part of unenlightened peasants? Did the older acceptability of the public display of anxiety clash with more modern ideas of individual self-discipline and self-control, and conformity to bourgeois values? The following discussion will attempt to answer these questions.

As the investigating psychiatrist was well aware, the possession epidemic in Troitskoe was far from unique. Lakhtin's scientific analysis of the epidemic's victims, which he presented to a meeting of the Moscow Psychological Society on December 5, 1910, began with a historical discussion of beliefs in demonic possession that extended back to the time of the ancient civilizations and moved forward to the early centuries of Christianity, then the pagan era of the ancient Eastern Slavs, the centuries of Kievan Rus, and finally the medieval period of Muscovy. In this regard, Lakhtin was following in the footsteps of his European medical counterparts. By delving into the past and uncovering the universal laws of nature, psychiatrists could display their ability to make retrospective diagnoses that would ultimately lead, they thought, to effective treatment. Russian psychiatrists also hoped to wrest control from Orthodox monks and clerics to whom victims of possession turned for exorcism. While, according to Lakhtin, cases of actual possession were rare in the Russian lands before the sixteenth century, they had become fairly common in that century and increased in number during the seventeenth century, a time of crisis throughout Western Europe. The psychiatrist ended his historical narrative with examples of eighteenth- and nineteenth-century Russian laws that made possession and sorcery crimes against the state, noting that as of 1868 so-called shriekers came under the purview of circuit courts.

By providing the historical context for possession in the Russian lands, Lakhtin was sensitive to the cultural and religious underpinnings of the belief as well as the phenomenon's consistent features over several centuries. Throughout the medieval and modern periods, individuals who believed themselves to be possessed acted out a highly ritualized drama. During Mass, in the midst of an icon procession, or in contact with relics and other holy objects, they convulsed uncontrollably, tore at their hair and clothing, uttered animal sounds, swore, and blasphemed. These actions were all believed to be caused by the demons who inhabited these individuals' bodies and who could not tolerate holy symbols. Before falling into an unconscious stupor and with the encouragement of witnesses, the possessed sometimes shrieked out the name of the individual who they thought had bewitched them and planted the demons inside their bodies. Possession could result directly from God's wrath with a sinful soul. Or, more often, Russians believed that possession stemmed from the malefic powers of a sorcerer or witch who consorted with the Devil and hexed or cast a spell on them.

While the manifestations of possession remained constant over time, the victims of possession changed, as did the elements of Russian society who believed in the veracity of the possession. Beliefs in possession and possession's intimate ties to sorcery were widespread among members of Russian society in the medieval period and even the eighteenth century, at the dawn of the Enlightenment and secularization. Only gradually did they become the preserve of the peasants and peasant migrants to the cities in the period after the 1861 emancipation of the serfs. By the end of the nineteenth century, upper-class members of Russian society who retained strong beliefs in Orthodoxy could accept the rare existence of possession even if they no longer believed in the powers of sorcerers and witches. On the other hand, skeptics, including physicians and psychiatrists, dismissed even the possibility of possession and preferred to label shriekers hysterics, a designation that bespeaks of a pathological manifestation to which women, because of their dangerous sexuality, are prone but which defies precise definition. Interestingly, as possession came under attack from the state and scientific rationalism, its victims became almost exclusively women.

While setting the historical and cultural scene for possession, the psychiatrist Lakhtin did not include in his report examples of possession in the nineteenth- and early twentieth-century Russian countryside. Such an omission may have been conscious on his part as Lakhtin wished to stress the 1905 Revolution's negative impact on popular consciousness, noting that not only had the number of possessed women increased in its aftermath but so too had rumors about the existence of witches in individual villages. By sounding the tocsin of primitivism, he confirmed educated society's fear of uncontrollable masses who were ready to spill the blood of anyone whom they considered malevolent. It is also possible that he thought a catalog of pre-1905 eruptions of possession unnecessary, given his medical audience's familiarity with recent examples, including an 1898 epidemic in the Smolensk village of Ashchepkovo. The latter had gained notoriety, thanks to a 1900 book written by N. V. Krainskii, the psychiatrist sent out to Smolensk by the government to curtail the outbreak.

Had Lakhtin cited the Ashchepkovo epidemic, he might have commented on the similarities shared by that village and the parish of Troitskoe, and in so doing imparted more explicitly the ambivalence that educated Russians had toward modernity and their unease about entirely repudiating the past, especially with regard to the Russian peasantry. Reading between the lines of both Lakhtin's and Krainskii's texts, however, can elicit some of that disquiet. On the positive side of the modernity coin, Ashchepkovo and Troitskoe were fairly close to railway stations and enjoyed higher-than-average literacy rates. Krainskii attributed the absence of alcoholism in Ashchepkovo and the villagers' successful opposition to the opening of a tavern in their midst to their literacy. Khomutovo peasants, according to Lakhtin, not only read newspapers regularly but had also discussed establishing a reading room where villagers could read books and newspapers as well as participate in discussions and lectures. Scientific enlightenment of the peasants through schooling and dissemination of secular texts constituted a major goal of Russian psychiatrists, which they believed would turn villagers away from their superstitions and beliefs in possession.

Krainskii, however, voiced a word of caution in assuming that enlightenment and literacy signified a triumph in rationalism and the vanquishing of peasant superstitions. He described the chief instigator of the Ashchepkovo epidemic, Vasilisa Alekseeva, whom he believed to have been shamming her possession, as appearing to be an urban woman.

Having spent considerable time in Moscow with her migrant husband, "she wears city clothing, she is fairly advanced for her circle, she speaks in a fairly witty fashion and knows how to justify her beliefs. She is literate and learned some things in Moscow so that she gives the impression of an intelligent and fairly enlightened woman."[2] Under that veneer, however, Vasilisa still subscribed to popular notions about witchcraft and followed the example of her mother, who reportedly was also a shrieker. In a note of antimodernism, Krainskii infers that Vasilisa, in having a taste of city life and prized individualism, had appropriated traditional beliefs in order to corrupt her village.

Here on the debit side, modernity brought with it economic and moral changes that, according to members of the Russian intelligentsia, had a negative impact on the village. While continually referring to the peasants as the "dark" or unenlightened masses, they clung to populist notions of the countryside that idealized the collective nature of communal life and the moral purity of peasant women. The lure of that paragon of modernity, the city, they argued, destabilized rural society by fostering individualism, which in turn weakened patriarchal relations and led to the breakup of the extended peasant household. Nowhere was that individualism stronger than in economically mixed villages such as Ashchepkovo and Khomutovo, where a significant portion of their male populations went off to the city of Moscow for considerable chunks of the year to ply various trades or work in industry. Women and the elderly, left behind in the villages, had to work the land and fulfill communal obligations. Tensions between married women and their in-laws sometimes drove the former to set up nuclear households at the expense of extended households, which the intelligentsia considered to be more viable economically. Finally, the city—that hub of depravity, in the eyes of educated society—infected the village with syphilis. It is not accidental that some of the victims of possession in both Troitskoe and Ashchepkovo had syphilis.

In spite of the proximity of Troitskoe to Moscow and the peasants' relatively high literacy, beliefs in demonic possession and bewitchment among villagers and their migrant male relatives remained strong in the early twentieth century. An examination of the lives of the victims of possession of the Troitskoe parish will illuminate aspects of village life and culture that made such beliefs relevant to villagers' lives on the eve of World War I. The four sufferers of possession were typical of *klikushi* elsewhere in European Russia: they were married peasant women in their twenties and thirties, the prime childbearing ages. They also had husbands who worked in Moscow, a not uncommon phenomenon in central Russia at the turn of the century. While their life stories are filtered through the lens of a psychiatrist experimenting with the new therapy of psychoanalysis and asserting dominion over his patients, these women were encouraged to talk about themselves and infused the narratives with their own understanding and desires. Eyewitnesses also shaped the stories' contours.

The life experiences of three of the possession victims indicate the prevalence of marital tensions. Tatiana Ezheva had been married only two years but did not get along with her husband's family, with whom she lived. Not having her spouse there to protect her from her in-laws' recriminations, she returned to her natal parents' home, once temporarily until her father sent her back, and then again on a permanent basis; at least the latter was her intention when the epidemic of possession gripped her and the parish. Klavdiia Fadeeva, however, was estranged from her husband. Notwithstanding, once she became possessed, her husband became more solicitous of her needs, advising her to come to Moscow for treatment and sending her a copy of a religious icon to aid her recovery. Another of the shrieker's spouses had a volatile personality, as a result of which Vasilisa Fedorovna Bolshakova, on the one hand, undoubtedly benefited from his lengthy absences from the village. On the other hand, the husband's absenteeism meant that she was pestered by other men. The independence and freedom that some women enjoyed as a result of being married to migrant laborers did not accrue to these women. Not only had their economic burdens increased, but they also enjoyed little protection against in-laws and neighbors who cast aspersions on their family loyalty, work habits, and sexuality.

Both Klavdiia Fadeeva and Vasilisa Bolshakova attributed the beginnings of their personal problems and their initial experiences with evil forces that ultimately led to their being possessed to strange occurrences at their weddings. In rural Russia, weddings were vulnerable times for newlyweds and their guests as peasants believed that sorcerers or witches sought revenge for having been wronged either before or during the marriage festivities or, worse yet, for not having been invited. Revenge in the form of a hex or implanting the bride or groom with demons might adversely affect an individual's sexual performance or fertility. In the end any community member, either invited or uninvited to a wedding, could conceivably become a witch or sorcerer. While various precautions were taken against evil spirits, celebrations of nuptials increased stress levels among the wedding party and guests as they expected misfortune to befall them. Matters were not helped when a betrothed couple's families, as in the case of Klavdiia and her fiancé Vasilii, continually quarreled over the details of the multiday revelries. Brides believed themselves to be especially prone to the invasion of evil spirits because of the dramatic change taking place in their lives and their liminal position of being neither maiden nor wife.[3]

In reconstructing the events at her wedding seven years after the event, when she experienced her fits of possession in Troitskoe and Khomutovo, Klavdiia noted that she had her first premonition that evil forces were at play during the religious ceremony when the marriage crowns on her and her husband-to-be's heads began to shake. The ensuing headache prevented her from attending the postceremonial tea. Klavdiia's husband also became quite ill. According to Klavdiia's reconstruction of the day's events, there was a scandal on the wedding night, the time set aside for the public celebration of a marriage's consummation. When the bride and groom were led to their bed, the groom was so sick that Klavdiia thought that the attendants had plied him with liquor in order to make him a laughingstock. Initially the couple could not consummate the marriage, a fact that became the subject of derision among the wedding guests. Fortunately, by morning, the couple had successfully engaged in sexual intercourse. All was not well, however; Klavdiia remembered experiencing a dreadful pain in her stomach when she awoke. On the second and third days of the celebrations, the pain shifted to her legs and forced her to take to her bed.

Klavdiia's memory also served up a third portent of sorcery. She recollected that shortly after the wedding, three chickens suddenly died as a result of mysterious ruptures that she ascribed to the malevolent skills of her husband's sister. Only later did she remember yet another sign: after the ceremony she recalled discovering pins that someone, no doubt her husband's sister and sister-in-law, must have stuck in her wedding crown, presumably in an attempt to make her barren. Vasilii confirmed Klavdiia's recollection of the pins by noting that he too had found pins in his shirt after the nuptials. In spite of the early signs of bewitchment, Klavdiia did not exhibit the manifestations of possession until seven years later, in 1909.

Like Klavdiia, thirty-seven-year-old Vasilisa Bolshakova used the past to understand her present predicament as a shrieker by attributing the start of her difficulties to her marriage at age twenty. She recollected that her stomach began aching immediately after the ceremony. Disaster awaited her on her wedding night when her mother-in-law and another woman became embroiled in an argument just as she and her husband were escorted to the marital bed. The groom reacted with such anger that he jumped out of bed and boxed the two women in the ears. Vasilisa was, however, able to coax her husband back to bed, and the marriage was consummated. Her problems appeared to be over. Fifteen years later, Vasilisa had another brush with bewitchment, this time during a village wedding, when a woman reputed to be a witch crossed in front of her carrying a milk pail. In view of the fact that witches were infamous for stealing milk from other people's cows and making cattle barren, Vasilisa interpreted the pail as proof of the woman's identity as a witch.

Her foreboding that she was under some kind of malevolent spell came to fruition two years later when during Lent of 1909 she was accused of engaging in an extramarital affair with the blacksmith Petr and was attacked in public by Petr's wife. Having been humiliated as an adulteress in the village and subsequently the victim of a theft, Vasilisa became depressed and ill. When Klavdiia began to experience her fits of possession and shrieked out at Easter that Vasilisa had been bewitched at a wedding two years earlier, Vasilisa herself came to believe in the veracity of the claim. In other words, Vasilisa had to be prompted by Klavdiia's assertion that she was bewitched to reconstruct her life experiences with malevolence and piece together the above story. Her case was helped by the recollection of unpleasant experiences on her own wedding day.

Once convinced that she too might be bewitched, Vasilisa accompanied Klavdiia to the district around Moscow's Presnenskaia Gate to seek the help of Brother Iakov, whose fame as a spiritual leader and successful exorcist was widespread in the province, especially among migrant male workers in Moscow. In the end, all four victims of possession in the parish of Troitskoe would seek his services.

Reluctantly, Klavdiia had previously gone to Iakov by herself, having been advised to do so by her mother, husband, and neighbor Tatiana Ezheva, who also believed herself to be possessed and had felt considerably better after she had seen the healer. On Klavdiia's initial visit in the spring of 1909, Iakov's ministrations appeared to have exorcized the demon possessing her. The demon had responded to the healer's prayers that Iakov had vanquished him and that he would come out in pieces, rather than stay in Klavdiia's body for ten years, as he had originally planned. Klavdiia's release from her demon turned out to be temporary, however. Shortly upon her return to Khomutovo, her fits increased in intensity until her demon began to imitate the sounds of various animals. Soon she was back at Iakov's Moscow apartment and this time she, or her demon, attacked Iakov, who gave her holy oil to drink and ordered her to cough. As she began to cough, Iakov grabbed her by the waist and commanded his helper Sergei to put his hand on her waist in order to make Klavdiia divulge who had bewitched her. She complied, naming her husband's sister and sister-in-law, Katka and Varka, as her tormentors. On still another visit, Klavdiia brought her neighbor Vasilisa Bolshakova, fully expecting that Iakov's treatment would force Vasilisa to reveal the name of the person who had bewitched her during her attacks. When that presumption proved incorrect, Iakov answered that eventually Klavdiia's devil would provide the information that Vasilisa's demon was unwilling to divulge. He also counseled Vasilisa to take Communion more frequently, which she did. But every time she did so, she experienced fits of possession anew. Not satisfied with Brother Iakov's treatments, Klavdiia and Vasilisa began to visit local monasteries that ministered to the possessed.

Informed by word of mouth about successful exorcisms and religious publications that recorded miraculous cures of the possessed at specific holy places or before miracle-working icons, victims of possession left the security of their villages and traveled with relatives or friends to neighboring and distant monasteries. As important social occasions during which friendships were forged and gossip was exchanged, pilgrimages themselves were part of the healing ritual. While Lakhtin's report does not detail the experiences of Klavdiia and Vasilisa at the monasteries they visited, other sources provide us with clues as to what occurred there.

We know for a fact that after Epiphany 1898 the shrieker Vasilisa Alekseeva of Ashchepkovo made the rounds of numerous holy sites, where monks confirmed that she was possessed and chanted special prayers and Masses for her. Her demons refused to leave her body, however, because Vasilisa left each of the monasteries before the full regimen of exorcisms had taken hold. This pattern of early departure made clear her unconscious desire to prolong the liminal status that being possessed provided her. As a confirmed shrieker, family and neighbors relieved her of household and family responsibilities, and she enjoyed a certain notoriety. Unlike Klavdiia Fadeeva of Troitskoe, however, she did not acquire the skills of a clairvoyant through possession. Vasilisa's shrieking may also have reflected her frustrations at being an urbanized woman accorded the diminished status of daughter-in-law in her husband's household and larger community.

As a final resort, Vasilisa turned to the Simonov monastery in Moscow, which housed between thirty and forty shriekers at any one time. There Father Mark, like others before him, affirmed Vasilisa's belief that she was possessed and advised her to stay at the monastery for six weeks, during which time she was to attend special services from 3 A.M. until 1 P.M. each day and take his treatment of grasses, oils, and Communion bread. Another woman, thirty-three-year-old Maria Fedorova of the village of Zhikharevo (located just three kilometers from Vasilisa's village of Ashchepkovo), described the monk's therapeutic method in the following manner: "I went to see him [Father Mark] in his cell. When he initially came to me, I could not control myself; I fell down, cried and sobbed and was not conscious. . . . After some time I came round. . . . He brought Communion bread to me, and once again I could not control myself. Then he asked if he could hold me; he smeared me with tree sap and put a piece of Communion bread in my mouth."[4] Maria commented further that when Father Mark administered a mysterious substance to the shriekers, they would begin to screech out the names of the individuals who had bewitched them.

Russian psychiatrists, including Lakhtin and Krainskii, opposed the monks' ministrations to *klikushi*. By offering special prayers, holy water, oil, and herbs as well as by performing exorcisms, these spiritual confessors, according to the medical specialists, convinced shriekers that the monks possessed exceptional God-given powers to drive away their demons and relieve their suffering souls. Perhaps most galling from the psychiatrists' point of view was the fact that peasants did not hold the monks accountable for their actions. When the latter worked, the healers and healed ascribed the cure to God's infinite mercy; in the event of unsuccessful exorcisms, the possessed blamed their own sinfulness rather than the failure of the holy individuals who tried to purify them.

Iakov, the self-proclaimed spiritual healer who treated both Klavdiia and Vasilisa of Khomutovo, came under special attack from Lakhtin. The psychiatrist portrayed him as a severe cripple, a feeble-minded old man who throughout his life had gone from monastery to monastery and mixed with beggars and the lame. To Lakhtin, Iakov can only imitate those rites and prayers that he heard in church. Those who go to him do so for help and advice and they receive both from him, since Iakov's words are so quiet and imprecise but so benevolent that everyone finds in them what they want to hear.

If Iakov only prayed and gave advice, his actions would be beneficial; but he tried to treat the illness and instruct others. He only affirms the people's superstitious belief in the strength of the Devil, Lakhtin continued. It is obvious that it is not enough to fight a psychopathological epidemic with a police investigation of individuals. There will always be paranoiacs, maniacs, and the mentally ill, and another or several individuals will replace the one who has been removed. The fight must be directed toward those conditions that allow for the existence of such phenomena as the activities of Brother Iakov, and before anything else the broad enlightenment of the masses.[5]

Lakhtin thus was ready to leave theology and praying to clerics, monks, and nuns as well as to self-appointed religious figures such as Brother Iakov—but certainly not medical and psychological treatments. Like psychiatrists in the rest of Europe, Lakhtin and his medical colleagues refused to acknowledge or failed to understand the psychological comfort that monks and lay healers offered the population at large and railed against the superstition that they believed to lie at the root of faith healing. They were not amenable to sharing the stage with these individuals and their unscientific cultures. Rather, they sought to extend the authority of modern science over care of the body and the mind, in spite of abysmally low cure rates in insane asylums and wards.

In the case of the shriekers, expanding the role of scientific treatment meant isolating them from rural culture and either hypnotizing them or, in the case of Lakhtin, subjecting them to the psychoanalysis that involved leading questions about their sexual practices and fantasies. Little did they understand that the triumph of scientific rationalism and psychiatrists' control over what they deemed to be mental illness would in turn result in the codification of hitherto tolerated behaviors as aberrant and new illnesses. It should not be surprising that psychiatrists enjoyed only fleeting luck with hypnosis and later psychoanalysis on *klikushi* who did not see any redemptive value in such therapies and who furthermore distrusted the psychiatrists as outsiders and emissaries of the state.

Orthodoxy and popular beliefs were remarkably benevolent toward and accepting of a variety of behaviors that in the age of scientific rationalism and the advent of psychiatry were labeled psychological in nature. The veneration of "holy fools in Christ" (*iurodivye*), individuals imbued with the grace of God who through unconventional behavior criticized the political and social status quo in medieval Muscovy, provides a compelling example of this benevolence. Shriekers in some ways were the converse of holy fools but in other ways shared similarities with them. Unlike holy fools, they did not enjoy spiritual powers. Neither shriekers nor holy fools, however, bore responsibility for their actions: demons guided the behavior of *klikushi*, while God instructed holy fools to do His bidding. Like holy fools, the possessed blasphemed and created public disorders within religious settings, although holy fools were just as likely to act in the nonreligious domain. The source of the *klikushi*'s ailments, however, were negative life experiences (barrenness, postpartum depression, familial tensions, abusive or unfaithful spouses, and rape) rather than a divine command to warn humans of their foibles. And like holy fools, the possessed enjoyed a place within the popular belief system and folk idioms. Released from their responsibilities during the course of their possession, they were free to seek the help of popular and spiritual healers. But by forsaking their social and economic obligations, if only for a time, shriekers were also unconsciously saying that they were no longer willing, at least temporarily, to cope with the adversity that life placed before them.

Possession may have been a catchall spiritual and cultural outlet for women whose emotional burdens needed release of some kind and hope of redemption. It was expressed in a feminine idiom of passions, uncontrollable bodily contortions, and immobility that did not ultimately challenge the patriarchal hierarchy. Through possession, women's relationships with family and neighbors were significantly altered. While those who experienced miraculous cures became the subject of community memory and pride, others achieved greater respect and social status as a result of rooting out or neutralizing evil within the community. Still others remained shriekers for several years. Once having played out their emotional anxieties through possession, they found their new roles of an elevated suffering preferable to returning to their everyday positions.

In Imperial Russia, clergy and peasants subscribed to a myth of possession. Their cosmic world view had a place for spirits and malevolence that needed to be driven out so that possession victims could be cured and reincorporated into their societies. While all subscribed to the same cosmology and idioms of possession, obviously not everyone experienced possession. Indeed, it was the rare individual who became possessed. Nevertheless, possession was both a personal and public experience; the ritual of possession occurred in a public setting in which the numerous and necessary witnesses understood the symbols of possession and acted swiftly to neutralize the spirits before they caused greater harm. Community participation remained critical to the integrity of the ritual drama that had the potential of resolving, or at least relieving, personal and community tensions and reinforcing religious values. By allowing women's suffering to be publicly expressed, Russian peasant society participated in their social healing.

NOTES

1. In the Russian countryside only fairly sizable villages had churches that served smaller villages in the outlying area. The village and parish of Troitskoe drew parishioners from such villages as Khomutovo and Roshchino.

2. N. V. Krainskii, *Porcha, klikushi i besnovatye, kak iavleniia russkoi narodnoi zhizni* (Novgorod, 1900), 98–99.

3. "Liminality" is a term used by anthropologists to describe the transitional stages that occur in rites of passage—such as those between adolescence and adulthood for males, and maidenhood and wifehood for females—among peoples in the developing world. Being transitional rather than concrete, these stages can be fraught with danger.

4. Krainskii, *Porcha*, 144.

5. M. Lakhtin, *Besooderzhimost v sovremennoi derevne: Istoriko-psikhologicheskoe izsledovanie* (Moscow, 1910), 45–46.

SUGGESTED READINGS

Engel, Barbara Alpern. "The Woman's Side: Male Outmigration and the Family Economy in Kostroma Province." *Slavic Review* 45 (1986): 267–71.

Frank, Stephen P. *Crime, Cultural Conflict, and Justice in Rural Russia, 1856–1914.* Berkeley, 1998.

Gilman, Sander L., Helen King, Roy Porter, G. S. Rousseau, and Elaine Showalter. *Hysteria beyond Freud.* Berkeley, 1993.

Kivelson, Valerie. "Patrolling the Boundaries: Witchcraft Accusations and Household Strife in Seventeenth-Century Muscovy." *Harvard Ukrainian Studies* 19 (1995): 302–23.

Krainskii, N. V. *Porcha, klikushi i besnovatye, kak iavleniia russkoi narodnoi zhizni.* Novgorod, 1900.

Lakhtin, M. *Besooderzhimost v sovremennoi derevne: Istoriko-psikhologicheskoe izsledovanie.* Moscow, 1910.

Ryan, W. F. "The Witchcraft Hysteria in Early Modern Europe: Was Russia an Exception?" *Slavonic and East European Review* 76 (January 1998): 49–84.

Worobec, Christine D. *The Bedeviled Village: Hysteria, Shrieking, and Witchcraft in Russia.* Forthcoming.

———. "Witchcraft Beliefs and Practices in Prerevolutionary Russian and Ukrainian Villages." *Russian Review* 54 (April 1995): 165–87.

Zguta, Russell. "The Ordeal by Water (Swimming of Witches) in the East Slavic World." *Slavic Review* 36 (June 1977): 220–30.

PART II

THE COMMUNIST EXPERIMENT

No decade of Russian history surpasses the period from the Bolshevik Revolution of 1917 to the beginning of the Cultural Revolution in 1928 for drama and importance.[1] The Bolshevik Revolution changed Russia from a long-standing autocracy into the world's first viable Marxist state. As part of this transformation, the Soviets nationalized the country's resources and then moved toward their development in planned, centrally directed five-year increments. Certainly no less momentous for the long term, the Bolsheviks also attempted to create a society and citizen of a new type—the so-called New Soviet Man or New Soviet Person[2]—as a model for the global reconfiguration of the human condition. To this end, the revolutionary state tried to recast existing social institutions fundamentally (itself a daunting undertaking in what was still largely an agrarian country plagued by widespread poverty and illiteracy) and to alter the predominant values that governed the character and rhythms of daily life. In short, the Russian experiment in communism encompassed but was by no means limited to politics and economics, nor were its aspirations confined only to the Soviet Union.

Basic to any such attempt to integrate political, economic, and social change was the issue of state power and popular support. Unless the party could establish itself as a viable national presence and governing institution, the range of what the Bolsheviks could attempt, not to say accomplish, would be limited. Success did not come easily. The Russian civil war of 1918–1921, during which the defeat of the revolution at times appeared imminent, involved the use of force in military conscription and grain requisitioning. Such measures generated mass discontent, and by the beginning of the 1920s the Bolsheviks faced opposition not only from their enemies but also from the workers and peasants in whose name they had seized power. Then, just as the party was transforming itself from an underground revolutionary cadre into a governing organ, Vladimir Lenin, the only leader the Bolsheviks had ever known, fell ill in late 1922 and in January 1924 died. Even as he lay incapacitated, a struggle for political succession began. By the time Joseph Stalin emerged as party leader four years later, fierce political infighting had left important members of the revolutionary leadership—Grigorii Zinoviev, Lev Kamenev, Leon Trotsky, Nikolai Bukharin, and others—discredited and their supporters disillusioned. In short, during its first decade the fledgling Soviet state was in no way the powerful dictatorship that it would later become.

The prerevolutionary opponents of Bolshevism continued to exercise influence after 1917, and the regime endured broad-based unpopularity throughout the 1920s. All of these factors limited its actual authority in society, where the sway of tradition proved persistent, while serious factionalism in its own ranks compounded the party's predicament on all fronts.

A significant part of this political dilemma derived from the condition of the national economy. General shortfalls and shortages of consumer goods undermined public confidence and eroded patience. In response, the leadership implemented the New Economic Policy (NEP) in March 1921, which restored a limited market in the hope of reinvigorating supply and distribution. NEP, however, was far from universally popular. In addition to those in the party who saw its tolerance of market mechanisms to be a betrayal of Marxist principles, a large number of ordinary citizens resented the newly enriched entrepreneurs it created in what was still an economy of shortage. NEP thus became a leading issue of contention during the political succession struggle, and the party reversed itself more than once during the 1920s on its implementation. Factional struggles within the party therefore wreaked havoc in a economy already destabilized by famine, high unemployment, shortages of consumer products, and unreliable food supplies.

Despite such formidable political and economic obstacles, however, the Bolsheviks did not delay their social revolution. Even as desperate peasants streamed into the cities—where already deteriorating infrastructures were strained beyond their limits—and the countryside reverted to much of its prerevolutionary insularity, the Bolsheviks did not contract their social vision. On the contrary, in an attempt to inculcate a new world view, they launched far-reaching reforms in virtually every sphere of human endeavor. They reconceptualized law and criminal justice in ways that took the social preconditions of crime into account; promoted science, health, and public sanitation; set up literacy programs; sought to eliminate religion; recast education and established the Komsomol (Young Communist League) to kindle new thinking among the young; singled out issues such as alcohol abuse, prostitution, and homelessness among juveniles; challenged bourgeois ethics in matters ranging from sexuality to gender relations to the structure of the family; and generally worked to construct a proletarian culture in both an aesthetic and sociological sense. In these endeavors, party members were far from unanimous in their opinions. In practice, the lessons of experience joined with the dictates of political pragmatism to refine these various enterprises as they moved forward.

In this broad effort to create a new social ethos, issues of family and the individual received special emphasis. Operating from the belief that the patriarchal, religiously sanctioned family represented tsarist society in microcosm, the revolutionary state moved quickly to make divorce more easily available, stripped fathers of their extensive legal authority over wives and children, gave official recognition only to civil marriages, and legalized abortion. The party declared the full equality of women and even gave an equivocal endorsement to free love. These were not ends in themselves, but part of a broader intention to redefine family and gender roles writ large. Ideally, the emerging socialist society would ultimately assume greater responsibility for child rearing, preparation of meals, and social welfare, although during the 1920s these were plans and not realities. And the Soviet state employed additional techniques of social engineering. Under experimental programs, youth underwent rehabilitation rather than punishment for juvenile crime. These citizens of the future also experienced a revolution in education, where a proposed new pedagogy was to transcend traditional academic subjects and teach an integrated approach to life and labor. Moreover, the Bolsheviks approached the promotion of literacy as the equivalent of fostering Soviet values, followed the same thinking in their efforts to popularize science and technology, and enabled state institutions to become innovators in painting and sculpture, poster art, architecture, film, music, and literature.

Consistent with this spirit, the Bolshevik assault on traditional society made the eradication of religion another early priority. Karl Marx had labeled religion "the opiate of the masses" in the old world, and religious belief was to have no place in the new. Soviet power regarded it as a cumbersome superstition that benefited the elite of the old regime and would only impede the society of the future. In January 1918 the state therefore issued its decree on the separation of church and state, which nationalized church land and property, removed religious instruction from the schools, and forbade the use of religious oaths and symbols in public institutions. Under the separation decree, citizens enjoyed the right of religious observance, and both church and state could promote their respective positions. Outside the law, however, antireligious militants desecrated places of worship and assaulted clergy, which alarmed those party leaders who feared the political repercussions of alienating religious believers. In 1925 the League of the Godless therefore formed in an effort to eradicate religious influences through nonviolent means, and its publications mixed verbal attacks on the church with the promotion of science, public health, literacy, and even the improvement of personal hygiene. When these efforts failed to produce the desired results and, in fact, led to the perception that religious belief was actually increasing during the second half of the decade, the state turned to stronger measures. The Law on Religious Associations, issued in April 1929, restricted religious activity only to registered congregations and banned all religious instruction and proselytizing.

Citizens readily made known their reactions to these various Bolshevik initiatives. In general, most peasants who came to the cities did not, as the state anticipated, quickly acquire a new identification with socialism but instead reconstructed a village subculture in urban settings. In rural areas, the peasants exploited the weaknesses of the new order to reestablish communal authority in the villages, where traditional practice governed the countryside more strongly than Soviet law. And on the level of specific reforms, Bolshevik programs frequently led to unanticipated and undesired consequences. Easing the divorce law, for example, not only contributed to a general atmosphere of emancipation for all citizens, assailed patriarchal authority, provided women with new social latitude, and undermined a key prerogative of the Russian Orthodox Church, but it also produced acute family instability. In addition to a dramatic rise in the urban divorce rate—the world's highest during the 1920s—women had difficulty in collecting alimony and child support, and by the end of NEP many married women equated ease of divorce with ease of desertion. To cite another example, in the realm of entertainment the public preferred imported adventure and romance fare to the silent film masterpieces produced by Sergei Eisenstein, Vsevelod Pudovkin, and Alexander Dovzhenko.

The Bolshevik social revolution of the 1920s therefore led to mixed reactions. Rapid transformation had its supporters, to be sure. But the Bolshevik ranks also included many less ready to discard existing conventions too rapidly, and in the second half of the 1920s their influence increased. In addition to a moralistic voice that made itself heard in spheres such as battling alcoholism and prostitution, party leaders backed away—in practice, if not in propaganda—from women's rights, sexual liberation, artistic experimentation, and other assaults on bourgeois values. Both the party and Komsomol intervened in the personal morals of members, and in society at large anger as well as enthusiasm greeted sexual permissiveness, assaults on religion, and experimentation in education. In sum, by 1928 advocates of rapid social transformation had made their influence felt, but there were also many Russians who wished for stability, a return to rigorous standards, and conventional morality.

NEP therefore constituted not only an economic program but also a laboratory for social experimentation. The influences that prevailed there ran the gamut of the anticipated and unanticipated. Party leaders recoiled from a popular culture that championed images and ideals antithetical to the revolution (Chapters 4 and 5), traditional elements in society continued to pursue nonrevolutionary agendas openly (Chapter 6), and at the grassroots the population had their own ideas about what they needed to know in the new society (Chapter 7). Lacking the power simply to impose its will, the state was forced to accommodate much of what it could not control.

NOTES

1. The Russian Social Democratic Workers' Party, founded in 1898, split into Bolshevik and Menshevik factions that became separate political parties in the twentieth century. When the Bolsheviks seized power in October 1917, they did so in the name of the All-Russian Congress of Soviets, which essentially became the government of the revolutionary state. The Bolshevik Party subsequently changed its name to the Communist Party of the Soviet Union. In this work, therefore, "Bolshevik," "Communist," and "Soviet," following common practice, will be used interchangeably.

2. The Russian word *chelovek* translates as "man," "person," or "human." "Person" is more in keeping with contemporary American speech, but "man" better reflects Bolshevik usage of the 1920s, which promised far more than it delivered in the area of female emancipation and sensitivity to issues of concern to women.

CHAPTER 4

The Roots of Golden America in Early Soviet Russia

ALAN M. BALL

The prevailing mass perception of America in the Soviet Union during the 1920s was strongly positive. This view was not true, of course, among Bolshevik leaders, who largely deplored America's crassness and lack of "culture" while at the same time grudgingly admiring its technological expertise and prosperity. Lenin stridently criticized the "capitalist" and "exploitative" principles used to maximize the efficiency of American as-sembly lines by reducing the latitude of each worker and thereby increasing labor discipline. At the same time, he searched for similar "rational" and "scientific" techniques to accomplish the same in Soviet factories. But among Soviet commoners, America's reputation fared much better. Indeed, to a majority of Russian workers and peasants, America appeared as a land of individualism and economic opportunity as well as the home of technologi-cal wizardry and universal affluence.

The explanation for such widespread admiration for the world's most conspicuous embodiment of capitalism within the first Marxist society tells us far more about Russia than America. In reality, the myth of "golden America" actually took root during the late tsarist period. As Alan Ball shows in this essay, popular literature available to the Russian masses after the 1870s promoted America in adventure stories and accounts by Russian travelers and emigrants. The expansion of literacy in Russia at the time gave these writings far wider distribution than would earlier have been the case, and the largely positive images they presented reached a consider-able audience. Moreover, emigration itself polished the image of America, as those who left home sent glowing descriptions and money back to rela-tives and friends in the Russian Empire. After the revolution, America's relief efforts during the famine of 1921–22 further reinforced its preex-isting reputation as a country at once affluent and generous. And above all, the wide distribution of Hollywood films during the 1920s reached every corner of the USSR and spread images of prosperity that even the illiterate could understand.

Alan M. Ball is the author of Russia's Last Capitalists: The NEPmen, 1921–1929 *(1987) and* And Now My Soul Is Hardened: Abandoned Children in Soviet Russia, 1918–1930 *(1994). He received his Ph.D. from the University of North Carolina at Chapel Hill and is associate professor of history at Marquette University.*

"Never was one country technically or materially, or both, more over-awed by another than is Russia to-day by the United States," concluded Theodore Dreiser after his journey through the Soviet Union in 1927.

> Indeed, I have stood in amazement at times at the childlike naïveté and wonder with which grown Russians (men and women who have been in China and all over Europe), to say nothing of the untraveled youth of the land, will listen to any exaggeration relative to the wealth or splendor or technical equipment of America. . . . "Everybody is well-dressed in America; no one is poor. Every one, including all workingmen, has a car, an apartment or a little house, a telephone, a radio, a victrola, electric lights, a gas stove, and time and means wherewith to travel." "Oh, yes, we know—it is perfect in America."[1]

While American technology dazzled members of the Soviet intelligentsia and political elite, Dreiser's description applied most of all to peasants and other members of the general population. American mass-production techniques might impress Lenin and Stalin, in other words, but popular imaginations made room for much more to admire in the New World.

Not only were Americans efficient and competent, they were thought capable of feats that could only be miracles elsewhere. Fabulous wealth, medicines, entertainments, and opportunities—anything one could dream of—abounded across the Atlantic. Such faith, complained an article in *Pravda* a year before Dreiser's visit, gripped peasants most tightly during hard times. In the spring, with food reserves depleted and scarcely any strength left to work, "they talk about America." Stories circulated about "America's heavenly miracles," about the enormous yields surely enjoyed by every farmer, who "harvests his grain with his own machinery and drives home in his own car." The peasants were convinced that Americans lived "on farms—though it's unknown exactly what a farm is—better than any *sovkhoz* [state agricultural enterprise], and very easy to buy. You just work a couple of years in a factory and save a little American money."[2] The poet Vladimir Mayakovsky also sensed an idealization of this prosperity among ordinary Russians. Our peasants, he told a New York audience in 1925, think of America and see "endless fields on which graze huge herds of plump cattle."[3]

One may safely conclude that two or three decades before the Revolution of 1917, millions of Russians had already developed a favorable impression of America—with no encouragement from the tsarist government. What, then, gave rise to their images of the United States? The absence of public opinion surveys and other individual testimony from most of the vast population bars mathematical precision, but a number of developments doubtless contributed. During the Romanov dynasty's last half century, for example, the spread of literacy helped to disseminate glimpses and fantasies of American life. Rural primary schools multiplied from roughly 23,000 in the early 1880s to 108,000 in 1914. Although most peasant children attended for no more than a year or two, and 60 percent of the population was illiterate on the eve of World War I, the schools reached far more of the young than ever before. Thus, in 1913 two-thirds of the army's new recruits were literate, compared to only one-fifth in 1874. Among children twelve to sixteen years of age in European Russia, a census in 1920 found that 71 percent of the boys and 52 percent of the girls could read.

As the number of readers expanded in these decades, so did the volume of publications. More to the point, amid this surge of Russian printing, a variety of sources encouraged a positive, if often fanciful, view of America. Translations of James Fenimore Cooper's stories about Indians, for example, fascinated Russian schoolchildren throughout the period, as did the tales of Mayne Reid and other authors of adventures in the New World. Anton Chekhov described two boys who plotted an "escape" to America, where they expected to "get gold and ivory, kill their enemies, become sea pirates, drink gin, and end up by marrying beautiful ladies and owning big plantations."[4] Although the lads' venture collapsed shortly after they left home, one of them continued to fantasize about America. So did other youths, including the future author Leonid Andreyev. "When I was a child I loved America," he confided in 1908. "Perhaps Cooper and Mayne Reid, my favorite authors in my childhood days, were responsible for this. I was always planning to run away to America."[5]

Cooper's frontier America, of course, did little to nurture *modern* images of the United States. Readers of the *Leather-Stocking Tales* might find exotic settings and much to sustain an impression of resourceful American individualism, but where did the Russian popular mind acquire its vision of American material comfort and technical wizardry? For those with more than rudimentary literacy, accounts by Russian visitors to America served this purpose. Despite the scathing comments on America by prominent Russian intellectuals, including Fyodor Dostoevsky and Maxim Gorky, a larger number of more favorable assessments from less renowned pens reached the common reader. These articles, books, and stories, written to be widely accessible, have attracted the scholarly attention of Hans Rogger and helped him to "explain the friendly fascination with America that was found among Russians of all classes" at this time. In a study of twelve Russian publications about the United States, intended for the general public around the turn of the century, Rogger encountered sweeping hostility in only two. The remaining works, while not oblivious to America's shortcomings, devoted more effort to portraying a land of opportunity and wealth unattainable for most of the tsar's subjects.[6]

Augmenting the dozen texts in Rogger's sample, several additional narratives written late in the tsarist era offered similar conclusions from a diverse corps of observers that included Peter Demens, an Imperial Guard officer. Unlike other Russian authors, he settled in the United States and even pursued a number of business ventures there during the last quarter of the nineteenth century and the early years of the next. Thus, his descriptions of America, published in Russia as a book under the pen name Tverskoi in 1895, drew on first-hand experience beyond that acquired by other visitors. For some years thereafter, Tverskoi continued to supply reports on America to a Russian periodical, and he may well have reached more readers than any other Russian commentator on the United States of his day.

He did not relish everything he saw. Pervasive advertising, speculative excesses, and powerful monopolies that seemed immune to legislatures and courts—these numbered among the hues in Tverskoi's American portrait. Yet no one could doubt that rosy tones predominated and matched many components of the ideal America rooting itself in Russian imaginations at the time. There, in the New World, technology made life better: "The so-called heavy work of day laborers is incomparably lighter in America than in Russia or in other European states. Machines have taken the place of this hand labor to a significant degree." Wages rose; prices of numerous basic goods did not, and banks proliferated to accommodate the savings of a prosperous society. "While in Great Britain in 1890 out of every thirty-nine inhabitants one was a beggar, in America there was only one out of every eight hundred and fifty-seven in this category," and even the humblest born might make a fortune. Philip Armour, "who now is one of the wealthiest people in America, began his life fifty years ago as a butcher in Wisconsin." He along with Jay Gould, Andrew Carnegie, John D. Rockefeller, and others "all began with a few coppers and now reckon their annual income in the tens of millions."[7]

Tverskoi's reports would likely have been too difficult or too expensive for marginally literate readers, who turned most often to the new mass-circulation newspapers and cheap serialized adventure stories. Here, scenes from American life appeared in a light that was often positive, if at times improbable, as demonstrated in the serial detective tales of the early twentieth century. These escapades appeared as complete stories in fewer than fifty pages and cost less than 10 kopecks. Well-known Western sleuths, especially Nick Carter and Nat Pinkerton (both American) and Sherlock Holmes, found themselves recruited in Russian adaptations to star in countless adventures, sometimes presented to the reader as fact: "Nick Carter is alive. He is an inspector of the New York secret police and there are daily descriptions of the feats of this man, the greatest American genius, in all American newspapers."[8] Carter and Pinkerton dashed around the United States (and even the globe), availing themselves routinely of cars, airplanes, telegrams, and other modern technology. In the process, as they sped from Florida to New York and from Chicago to San Francisco, they left their Russian readers with images of a thoroughly modern America.

The stories were wildly popular for several years before World War I, with millions of copies published in Russia—6.2 million Pinkertons, 3.1 million Carters, and 3.9 million Holmes—over a nine-year period beginning in 1907. As late as 1915, well past the peak of demand for the adventures, street sales in Petrograd (as the capital was renamed at the beginning of the war) totaled 288,225 Pinkertons and 72,380 Carters. Individual testimony corroborated the impression left by these numbers regarding working-class literary tastes. "They read Nat Pinkerton and are satisfied with that," complained a trade unionist in 1910, while the literary critic Kornei Chukovskii observed: "For a long time I could not believe my eyes when I saw the way the workers were gobbling up Nat Pinkerton."[9] While most sales of detective serials occurred in cities, they also made their way to the peasantry through a variety of channels. A study of St. Petersburg schoolchildren found that one-fifth of those familiar with the stories had first encountered them in the countryside. Peasants could purchase the tales at train stations or from workers and soldiers returning to the villages, and even from city children vacationing in the district.

Historian Jeffrey Brooks observed that when Russian "popular journalists and the authors of cheap fiction wrote of America for newly literate readers" around the turn of the century, they often produced a "moral fantasy" featuring "notions of success and self-improvement that gained wide currency."[10] Throughout the period of peak European emigration to the United States, from roughly the middle of the nineteenth century to the eruption of World War I, similar conceptions of America guided waves of people hoping for something better across the Atlantic. These images of bounty required no literacy for propagation—among peasants in particular, they commonly circulated by word of mouth, growing ever more remarkable in the process. According to a Swedish newspaper in 1846, a beggar girl roamed through villages spreading visions of America "in far more attractive colors than Joshua's returned spies portrayed the Promised Land to the children of Israel. 'In America,' the girl is reported to have said, 'the hogs eat their fill of raisins and dates that everywhere grow wild, and when they are thirsty, they drink from ditches flowing with wine.' " Naturally, observed the journalist, "gullible *bondfolk* draw the conclusion from such stories that it is far better to be a hog in America than to be a human being in Sweden."[11] In such ways, word spread in numerous countries and tightened its hold. A researcher discovered that among peasants in southern Italy, "along with the traditional and inevitable concept of America as the land with streets paved in gold," there developed such a strong "affection for . . . this strange and distant land, that they seem tied to it by bonds stronger than the tenuous ones that link them with the capital of their own country, Rome."[12]

Emigration to America from the Russian Empire (and from eastern and southern Europe generally) occurred quite late in Europe's exodus to the New World. For most of the nineteenth century the overwhelming majority of America's European immigrants—approximately 80 percent as late as the 1880s—came from northern and western Europe. But during the next decade the tide of people from southern and eastern Europe surged as sharply as it ebbed from countries to the west; and by the first decade of the twentieth century, such nations as Italy, Austria-Hungary, and Russia supplied three-quarters of Europe's immigrants to the United States. From Russia alone, roughly 3.2 million passengers crowded ocean liners to America during the period 1880–1914, some 2.8 million of them in just fifteen years beginning in 1899.

What finally loosed this torrent in the twilight of the Romanov dynasty? Certain pressures, including a population growing too large in some regions to be supported by traditional occupations, resembled developments in many countries during periods of mass emigration. Other considerations owed more to Imperial policies, especially measures taken against non-Russian minorities. In 1882, for instance, a year after the assassination of the comparatively liberal tsar Alexander II, the government announced new laws restricting Jews' opportunities to conduct business, worship, participate in local government, or enter a university. Over the next twenty-five years, sporadic pogroms terrified Jewish communities with violence at the hands of anti-Semitic mobs who were ignored, or even encouraged, by authorities. At the same time, the government's Russification campaign attacked religious, administrative, and cultural practices common among Poles, Lithuanians, Finns, and other non-Russian subjects of the tsar. These measures alone go far in explaining why 44 percent of the immigrants to America from Russia in the years 1899–1910 were Jews, 27 percent Poles (from the portion of Poland absorbed by Russia in the eighteenth century), nearly 10 percent Lithuanians, and 8.5 percent Finns.

According to Merle Curti and Kendall Birr, "America was almost an unknown name to the vast untutored masses" in southern and eastern

Europe as late as the middle of the nineteenth century. Only in the century's later decades did America begin to dazzle many eastern European peasants with visions "of wealth, of bigness, of opportunity"—and emigration played a part in this change.[13] If not through the pages of cheap popular newspapers and fiction, stories about America reached people in Russia's western provinces from Czechs, Germans, and other neighbors whose relatives or acquaintances had already ventured to the New World (as, later, Russians, Ukrainians, and Belorussians would hear about America from Jews or Poles). Thereafter the "news" spread rapidly through diverse conduits, including peddlers and beggars, as previously mentioned. It seems scarcely coincidental that this dawning sense of a bountiful America coincided with the deluge of voyagers arriving in New York at Ellis Island from Russia by the turn of the century. Whatever it was that triggered decisions to emigrate, belief in "golden America" often governed the choice of destination. Immigration figures themselves suggest the rapid diffusion of this consciousness. During the 1870s only 13 percent of the 367,000 emigrants from the Russian Empire traveled to the United States. After jumping to 48 percent by the following decade, America's share of Russian emigration reached 61 percent in the 1890s and approached 90 percent only ten years into the twentieth century.

European steamship companies depended heavily on a sustained current of transatlantic passengers, and during the 1880s these firms became energetic solicitors of potential immigrants. They hired agents who fanned out in the target regions and built up networks of subagents (including such local notables as mayors, innkeepers, and clergymen) that could number hundreds of people. These agents earned a commission on the sale of steamship tickets, which moved them to glorify America without restraint. They put up posters, distributed translations of articles from the American press, and at times took more enterprising measures, as in Italy, where some stood at church doors handing out cards printed with hymns and poems extolling the United States. When eastern and southern Europe emerged as a fecund source of immigrants in the 1880s, Russia's western provinces became familiar turf for steamship agents within a decade. While scholars have questioned whether these recruiters managed to sell tickets to many people whom poverty or persecution had not already convinced to emigrate, the agents did at least help spread the "American myth." No one had a greater incentive to portray the United States in glowing hues, and their pictures helped shape the impressions of America formed by those who remained in Russia as well as those who departed.

An agent, of course, was a salesman, and his enthusiasm for America might arouse skepticism. More credible were emigrants already in the

United States whose letters advertised the New World to relatives and friends in Europe. The correspondence also demonstrated another way in which rising literacy rates served to spread the word. Between 1900 and 1906, over five million letters traveled from America to Europe (with roughly three million mailed in the opposite direction), and while some naturally lamented the authors' misfortunes abroad, sources agree on the generally enthusiastic tone of this testimony. According to a U.S. congressional commission studying emigration in 1911, these letters to friends back home "have been the immediate cause of by far the greater part of the remarkable movement from southern and eastern Europe to the United States during the past twenty-five years."[14] A Russian official noted the letters' persuasive power and complained: "As the result of a natural desire to boast, the letters of emigrants always exaggerate considerably the attractive side of the life and the various wonders of America."[15]

Praise arose from more than a desire to boast. Workers in the United States could often earn, and save, hundreds of dollars more per year than in Europe, and when they sent some of this money to relatives back home, they enhanced the image of wealthy America. The sums involved clearly totaled tens of millions of dollars, although much escaped the attention of officials. In the form of money orders alone, $70 million traveled from America to Austria-Hungary and Russia during the period 1902–1906—and it took very little of this traffic to impress a peasant community. The congressional commission on emigration received reports from inspectors in Europe regarding the effect on a village of letters containing less than $100: "The cottage of the recipient becomes at once the place to which the entire male population proceeds, and the letters are read and reread until the contents can be repeated word for word."[16]

Meanwhile, roughly one-third of America's European immigrants in the first decade of the twentieth century later sailed back to the Old World. The figure was lower for people who entered the United States from Russia, 15 percent of whom subsequently departed for their homeland. The comparatively low rate of return was owed to the prevalence among Russian immigrants of Jews, who remained in the United States at a much higher rate than did any other significant category of European newcomers. Of the 1.2 million people entering America from Russia between 1908 and 1913, approximately 93 percent of the Jewish contingent came to stay, compared to 74 percent of the Poles and only 59 percent of those identified as Russians (Great Russians, Ukrainians, and Belorussians taken together). All told, 233,000 immigrants returned to Russia during this six-year period. Some did so in despair or bitterness over their experiences in the United States, but a larger number apparently never intended to stay. As ocean travel grew faster, safer, and less expensive during the second half of the nineteenth century, increasing numbers of workers from southern and eastern Europe sought to take temporary advantage of the higher wages in America to accumulate savings sufficient to live more comfortably back home. They might repeat this cycle and even collect their families eventually and move permanently to the United States. Most important for our purposes, during their return visits in Europe, they often served as live affirmation—even more convincing than letters—of America's treasures. Better dressed than their neighbors, with suitcases of gifts and money to improve their households, they regaled friends and neighbors with stories that gave substance to the "American myth."

In 1917 revolutionary waves sweeping over Russia left the nation with a new socialist government by the end of the year, but they did not wash away the attitude toward America that had crystallized earlier among ordinary Russians. Indeed, numerous manifestations of the United States soon appeared on the Soviet landscape and reinforced prevailing notions of America, despite the Kremlin's Marxist orientation. In 1921, for example, representatives of foreign organizations arrived to offer assistance to millions of people facing starvation in a region centered among provinces along the Volga River. Dozens of relief campaigns in different countries collected food and other supplies for the victims, but one organization overshadowed them all. The American Relief Administration (ARA), established in 1919 to provide assistance in war-torn Europe, reached an agreement with the Bolshevik government in 1921 and furnished over 90 percent of all famine relief sent to the Soviet Union between 1921 and 1923. At its peak, the ARA's staff numbered 200 Americans, who directed 80,000 Russians in operating 35,000 aid stations that distributed nearly a million tons of food, seed, clothing, and medical supplies. More than 7 million people received inoculations and vaccinations, and close to 11 million were fed during the famine's most ominous period.

Various American and Soviet officials expected (although in the Soviet case they did not desire) that the ARA's assistance would impress its recipients with the United States. While the accuracy of their hopes and fears cannot be measured statistically, there seems no reason to doubt that the ARA strengthened some aspects of the popular image of the United States evident before 1917. Millions of people had direct contact with the ARA and received food, clothing, and medicine for themselves and their children. Sixty years later, U.S. visitors to the Soviet Union found survivors of the Volga famine who still retained grateful memories of this assistance. Like the money or gifts that a relative brought back from America, although now on a larger scale, the ARA's relief operation implied a bounteous America and, perhaps, an efficient and generous one as well.

Among the factors mentioned so far, those associated with emigration and popular publications before 1917 appear to have nudged the most people toward radiant impressions of America. Famine relief from the ARA perpetuated certain features of the "American myth," but only among a portion of the population. The millions of beneficiaries assisted by the ARA were concentrated mainly in the famine-stricken provinces, while residents of Moscow, Minsk, or Petrograd had little opportunity for contact with relief efforts. However, another mechanism emerged after the revolution to advertise America as vividly as anything had before 1917, and it enthralled millions of Soviet citizens from one end of the country to the other.

American movies swept around the world in the decade after World War I and soon dominated the global market that French and other foreign distributors had controlled just a few years before. Once the Bolshevik government began importing foreign films in quantity by the mid-1920s, America's offerings drew enthusiastic audiences as readily in the Soviet Union as elsewhere. In 1922 only seven American feature films appeared in the Soviet Union, compared to 41 selections from Germany and 15 from France. In the next year, Hollywood's contribution jumped to 101 features (35 percent of the Soviet market) and then soared in 1924 to 231 titles (57 percent of the market). In every remaining year of the decade, American movies reached Soviet screens in quantities greater than all other foreign films combined, and larger than the number of Soviet films produced until 1928. Hollywood's exports provoked controversy on a number of fronts during the 1920s—including the role that these movies played in promoting certain images of the United States.

Observers in many countries had no doubt that the films heralded the United States in one way or another. Will Hays, the powerful president of the Motion Picture Producers and Distributors of America, wrote in 1924 that "steps have been taken to make certain that every picture which is made here shall correctly portray American life, opportunities, and aspirations to the world." When Hays concluded that "we are going to sell America to the world with American pictures," it sounded like a global public service. Foreigners who recognized the marketing clout of American films often found it difficult to share Hays's enthusiasm. "The fact is," observed a member of the British House of Lords in 1925, "the Americans realised almost instantaneously that the cinema was a heaven-sent method for advertising themselves, their country, their methods, their wares, their ideas, and even their language, and they have seized upon it as a method of persuading the whole world, civilised and uncivilised, into the belief that America is really the only country which counts." Four years later Horace Villard, a senior officer in the U.S. State Department, produced a memorandum grounded in the assumption that American movies influenced opinions formed about the United States. Alas, he argued, Hollywood's pictures featured crime and "scenes of wealth, fast living or immorality." Under this influence, more foreigners would soon regard America as "the land where everyone achieves financial or industrial success" and seek to emigrate, with the unrealistic expectations that Villard predicted would result in "disillusion and resentment."[17]

No one doubts that American movies entranced audiences in the Soviet Union during the 1920s and that many of these films portrayed a luxurious, fast-paced life in which the fruits of modern technology figured as routine accessories. More difficult to confirm is the plausible assumption that Hollywood's fare helped to shape Russian images of the United States. Nothing from this period enables the statistical exercises performed in surveys of American television's international impact in the second half of the twentieth century, but the findings of these recent studies lend support by analogy to hypotheses regarding an earlier generation of Soviet movie audiences. Farfetched as the plots of some U.S. television programs might be, for instance, foreign viewers commonly assume them to be taking place against a largely accurate background of American life. Thus, most respondents to a study in Thailand declared American shows a reliable window on life in the United States and often cited the program "Dallas" in this regard, as did viewers in Taiwan and Mexico. American comedies and other shows diversified somewhat the television diet of foreign audiences and contributed to the impressions they formed of the United States. The key point is that the power of television on their imaginations suggests a parallel role played by Hollywood movies during the Soviet Union's first decade.

Indeed, while the impact of American television varies from country to country, the programs have conveyed some of the same impressions that movies made sixty years before. When asked to describe Americans, respondents in the television studies supplied clusters of adjectives that included terms with which many Russians could have agreed in the 1920s. "Individualistic," "ambitious," "practical," "industrious," "efficient," and "materialistic" all figured in lists compiled by researchers in Taiwan, Mexico, and Thailand. Often American television presented arrogant, treacherous, self-centered, and violent characters who left troubling impressions of the United States, but even they cavorted in sumptuous settings that misled foreign viewers about America's prosperity. Little wonder, then, that another study in Israel reported American television contributing to exaggerated opinions of the wealth possessed by most people in the United States. The heavier an Israeli's diet of American programs, a researcher concluded, the greater the overestimation of American affluence.

These studies also noted that television's influence increased among people who had little direct contact with Americans and that the programming's most pronounced effect was to reinforce opinions of the United States already formed by viewers from other sources of information. Much the same might be said of American movies in the Soviet Union during the 1920s. Few among the millions of viewers there could have relied on personal experience for impressions of America, while the substitute received from Hollywood corresponded well with popular images of the United States that had been widespread for decades. Testimony from the likes of Peter Tverskoi, tales of Nat Pinkerton, letters from countrymen in the New World, and American famine relief all pointed to a thriving nation and sometimes encouraged the vision of workers living like kings amid technology that bordered on the magical. Theodore Dreiser discovered Russians convinced of this vision with a certainty that owed much to Hollywood: "And, oh, if each could only get to America, melt (as each is sure he would) into all the joys and glories he sees depicted in the American movies! Oh! Oh! Oh!"[18]

Dreiser may have been exaggerating, but he drew on fact rather than fiction, and he described an effect of popular culture still evident in Russian notions of American life at the end of the twentieth century. In 1991 a *Baltimore Sun* correspondent found himself talking with a small group of bankers and government officials in Vladikavkaz, the capital of North Ossetia in the Northern Caucasus. As one of the bankers ran through some American movies on his office videocassette recorder, the correspondent noticed from remarks made by the viewers that they "were looking beyond the violence, sleaze, and corruption of the plot at sleek cars, designer apartments, glittering high rises, and well-stocked stores. Whatever happened up front, the background was the promised land."[19] In the years thereafter, quite apart from widespread apprehension regarding American foreign policy, Russia's own social and economic distress has prepared the ground on which visions of rich America have flourished as abundantly as they did among the tsar's peasants and Lenin's workers.

NOTES

1. Theodore Dreiser, *Dreiser Looks at Russia* (New York: Horace Liveright, 1928), 52–53.

2. *Pravda*, April 3, 1926.

3. Quoted in Charles Rougle, *Three Russians Consider America: America in the Works of Maxsim Gorkij, Aleksandr Blok, and Vladimir Mayakovskij* (Stockholm: Almqvist and Wiksell International, 1976), 11.

4. Anton Chekhov, *Boys* (Moscow: Progress Publishers, 1979), 15.

5. Quoted in Richard Ruland, *America in Modern European Literature: From Image to Metaphor* (New York: New York University Press, 1976), 71.

6. Hans Rogger, "How the Soviets See Us," in Mark Garrison and Abbott Gleason, eds., *Shared Destiny: Fifty Years of Soviet-American Relations* (Boston: Beacon Press, 1985), 115 (for the quotation); idem, "America Enters the Twentieth Century: The View from Russia," in Inge Auerbach, Andreas Hillgruber, and Gottfried Schramm, eds., *Felder und Vorfelder russischer Geschichte* (Freiburg: Rombach, 1985), 169 (regarding the study of twelve publications).

7. The translated quotations from Tverskoi's book are contained in *This Was America*, comp. Oscar Handlin (Cambridge, MA: Harvard University Press, 1949), 355, 366, 368.

8. Quoted in Jeffrey Brooks, *When Russia Learned to Read: Literary and Popular Literature, 1861–1917* (Princeton, NJ: Princeton University Press, 1985), 147–48.

9. Quoted in ibid., 152.

10. Jeffrey Brooks, "The Press and Its Message: Images of America in the 1920s and 1930s," in Sheila Fitzpatrick, Alexander Rabinowitch, and Richard Stites, eds., *Russia in the Era of NEP: Explorations in Soviet Society and Culture* (Bloomington: Indiana University Press, 1991), 236.

11. Quoted in George M. Stephenson, "When America Was the Land of Canaan," *Minnesota History* 10, no. 3 (September 1929): 238–39.

12. Ruland, *America in Modern European Literature*, 31.

13. Merle Curti and Kendall Birr, "The Immigrant and the American Image in Europe, 1860–1914," *Mississippi Valley Historical Review* 37 (September 1950): 229.

14. U.S. Congress, Senate, 61st Cong., 3d sess., *Senate Documents*, vol. 12, Document 748: "Emigration Conditions in Europe" (Washington, DC: Government Printing Office, 1911), 57.

15. "Konsulskaia doneseniia: Russkaia emigratsiia v Soedinennye Shtaty. Sovetnik Posolstva v Vashingtone st. sov. Shcherbatskogo," in *Izvestiia ministestva inostrannykh del 1914 g.*, 1914, kniga VI (Petrograd: Tipografiia V. O. Kirshbauma, 1914), 128.

16. "Emigration Conditions in Europe," 57.

17. All quotations are from Ian Jarvie, *Hollywood's Overseas Campaign: The North Atlantic Movie Trade, 1920–1950* (New York: Cambridge University Press, 1992), 111, 305, 326.

18. Dreiser, *Dreiser Looks at Russia*, 53.

19. Scott Shane, *Dismantling Utopia: How Information Ended the Soviet Union* (Chicago: Ivan R. Dee, 1994), 207–8.

SUGGESTED READINGS

Bailes, Kendall E. "The American Connection: Ideology and the Transfer of American Technology to the Soviet Union, 1917–1941." *Comparative Studies in Society and History* 23, no. 3 (July 1981): 421–48.

Brooks, Jeffrey. "The Press and Its Message: Images of America in the 1920s and 1930s." In *Russia in the Era of NEP: Explorations in Soviet Society and Culture*, edited by Sheila Fitzpatrick, Alexander Rabinowitch, and Richard Stites, 231–52. Bloomington, IN, 1991.

Curti, Merle, and Kendall Birr. "The Immigrant and the American Image in Europe, 1860–1914." *Mississippi Valley Historical Review* 37 (September 1950): 203–30.

Dreiser, Theodore. *Dreiser Looks at Russia*. New York, 1928.

Hindus, Maurice. "Henry Ford Conquers Russia." *The Outlook* (June 29, 1927): 280–83.

Jarvie, Ian. *Hollywood's Overseas Campaign: The North Atlantic Movie Trade, 1920–1950*. New York, 1992.

Rogger, Hans. "America in the Russian Mind—or Russian Discoveries of America." *Pacific Historical Review* 47 (February 1978): 27–51.

———. "How the Soviets See Us." In *Shared Destiny: Fifty Years of Soviet-American Relations*, edited by Mark Garrison and Abbott Gleason, 107–45. Boston, 1985.

Tan, Alexis S., and Kultida Suarchavarat. "American TV and Social Stereotypes of Americans in Thailand." *Journalism Quarterly* 65 (Fall 1988): 648–54.

Tan, Alexis S., Sarrina Li, and Charles Simpson. "American TV and Social Stereotypes of Americans in Taiwan and Mexico." *Journalism Quarterly* 63 (Winter 1986): 809–14.

Weiman, Gabriel. "Images of Life in America: The Impact of American TV in Israel." *International Journal of Intercultural Relations* 8 (1984): 185–97.

CHAPTER 5

Moscow Chic

Silk Stockings and Soviet Youth

ANNE E. GORSUCH

Youth will inevitably be a primary focus of any social revolution. According to conventional wisdom that seems to cut across cultures, the young are still in their formative years and consequently not fully socialized in the ways of the Old World being swept aside. Energetic and idealistic, they are yet to be corrupted by experience and still have the potential to raise society and even humankind to a higher level. And through channels of formal and informal education, new ideas and messages can reach the young more easily than any other demographic group. The Bolshevik leadership certainly subscribed to these assumptions. When Soviet youth displayed a highly visible affinity for Western fashions and popular culture during the 1920s, it was therefore a cause for serious concern. In the environment of NEP, however, the official reaction to "Moscow chic" was not, in the first instance, repression. The revolutionary regime promoted its own ideals vigorously, but it also accommodated what it was powerless to eradicate.

A discussion of youth culture therefore offers insights into the early Soviet regime that are often surprising. State propaganda, to be sure, idealized a Communist youth who dressed in modest and functional clothing and spent leisure time in the pursuit of personal betterment. This ideal had its adherents, but many other young women and men elected to imitate the fashions and behavior that they encountered in imported films and magazines. Clad in the attire of their movie heroines and heroes, they made socializing a higher priority than political enlightenment, often at great financial sacrifice. Undoubtedly aware that it risked losing the allegiance of this generation if it resorted to heavy-handed repression—Komsomol music patrols designed to prevent the dancing of the tango and foxtrot ended disastrously—the regime resorted to pragmatism. While in no way abandoning its own views, Soviet power incorporated Western fashions into its own publications; and rather than banning the use of lipstick, for example, the state made its production a government monopoly. Such an approach entailed no official endorsement of the individualism that the young were expressing through their choices of clothing and behavior, but, conversely, a preference for fashionable attire over Soviet sartorial utilitarianism did not in all cases signify a nonrevolutionary attitude. As Anne Gorsuch demonstrates in this essay, issues of popular culture in the USSR during the 1920s therefore cannot be reduced to simplistic dichotomies—fashion versus the Komsomol, Communist ideals versus bourgeois decadence—but have to be studied in terms of the internal logic of the situation. And unraveling these riddles offers important insights into Soviet society during its pivotal formative period.

Anne E. Gorsuch is assistant professor of history at the University of British Columbia. She is the author of Enthusiasts, Bohemians, and Delinquents: Youth, Popular Culture, and Politics in Revolutionary Russia *(2000), and her articles on Soviet youth have appeared in* Russian Review *and* The Carl Beck Papers. *She received her Ph.D. from the University of Michigan.*

𝒜 cartoon in the early Soviet satirical magazine *Rowdy* showed a young couple dressed in flapper fashions and dancing the Charleston. One asked the other: "So, Vasia, what class do you consider yourself coming from?" Vasia responded, "Frankly speaking—the *dance-class!*" This cartoon reflects the cultural contradictions of a still un-Communist Soviet Russia. With the introduction of the New Economic Policy (NEP) in 1921, expensive food and clothing stores, flashy nightclubs, gambling casinos, and other manifestations of the changing economic climate resurfaced in Soviet Moscow for the first time since before the Revolution of 1917. One of the most visible, and to the Bolsheviks some of the most troublesome, expressions of this "bourgeois" culture were the young Russian bohemians who adopted the flapper fashions of Paris and New York and danced to the seductive rhythms of American jazz. Taking their cue from Hollywood movies playing in Soviet theaters and from fashion magazines such as *Mody sezona* (Fashions of the season), young Russians—including many young Communists—spent their factory wages on silk stockings, makeup, and manicures.

The changing atmosphere of the 1920s resulted in part from the legalization of private trade that accompanied the introduction of NEP. With it came the resurgence of entrepreneurs (NEPmen). Some peddled goods on the street, and others opened clothing and food stores, cafés, and restaurants. Private traders lined the streets selling everything from furs and velvet dresses to Singer sewing machines and Kodak cameras. Even the government daily newspaper *Izvestiia* ran advertisements for corsets, fashion magazines, and pianos next to notices about the latest books on problems of everyday life and contests for the best factory. However, although the Bolsheviks legalized private business to rescue a foundering Soviet economy, there were many Communists who tolerated NEP and NEPmen as a necessary, but temporary, evil. Private trade in food and clothing restored a population on the brink of death, but some wondered if the price was too high. They worried about what one observer called the sinister "grimaces of NEP," the dirty underbelly of a society feverishly trading, eating, and drinking as a last lurid display of material consumption before the crackdown.

Party leaders and activists were concerned not only about the economic contradictions of NEP but also about the implications of continued exposure to what they considered "bourgeois" attractions. The relatively relaxed cultural borders of NEP permitted an influx of mass media images from the West that showed to young people in the Soviet Union what their European counterparts were dancing, watching, and wearing. The bodies of these flappers and foxtrotters—the Western clothes they wore and the exotic movements they made—were visible reminders of threats to a healthy Communist body politic. Their playful forms of personal expression and entertainment appeared to challenge the serious and more puritanical aspects of Bolshevik culture. Committed to penetrating and transforming intimate areas of everyday life, Bolshevik moralists saw the pleasures of dress and dance as evidence of deviance and opposition. Instead of dressing up, the good young Communist was supposed to be involved in "healthy" diversions: going to the Communist youth club, attending lectures on political topics, and participating in antireligious activities, all of which would presumably protect his or her physical and ideological "cleanliness." For worried Bolsheviks, the popular pleasures of flapper fashions ran counter to their more serious, sober, and collectivist ideals for the new generation of Soviet youth.

In this period of transition and great cultural confusion, appearance was a quick indicator of character and political affiliation. According to Soviet Commissar of Health Nikolai Semashko, the simple, hygienic dress of the revolutionary should be functional (allowing for the proper regulation of body temperature), neat, and clean. Semashko condemned any interest in "bourgeois" fashion as too extravagant, elegant, and Western. With the introduction of NEP, however, there was an explosion of interest in flapper fashions in the latest Western styles. Some of this interest echoed the prerevolutionary period when Paris and London were considered the major arbiters of style. From the early nineteenth century, the Russian upper classes had emulated French and English dress; and by midcentury, fashion journals had contributed to the beginnings of a Russian consumer culture. Turn-of-the-century magazines such as *Zhenskoe delo* (Women's world) carried illustrations of European fashions with articles on fine art exhibitions, while *Modnyi svet* (Fashionable set) had articles on "What One Should Be Wearing" with illustrations of elegant clothing for women and girls and sewing instructions.

The most important influence on fashion-conscious young women and men, after 1917, was the sophisticated dress of the American movie star. The favorite movies of this period were foreign, with the great early silent film stars: Douglas Fairbanks, Harold Lloyd, Charlie Chaplin, Buster Keaton, and Mary Pickford. "American films dominate, inundate, glut, overwhelm the Russian motion picture houses today," wrote a troubled American observer. "Clara Kimball Young has a theater devoted solely to her in Moscow. In the Arbat, centre of the workers' quarters of the Russian capital, a new building celebrates the glory of Douglas Fairbanks in electric letters three feet high."[1] Leningrad's Nevsky Prospekt was lined with commercial movie theaters with alluring European names: "Soleil," "Nirvana," "Piccadilli," and "Parisian." In early 1928 a major Moscow theater on the Arbat showed twenty-two foreign films and only seven Soviet ones. Posters advertising the latest foreign film could be found all over the streets and public squares, obscuring the political notices. The ads for commercial theaters were often blatantly erotic and violent: a poster for *Life for a Life* portrayed a woman with tousled hair dressed only in her bathrobe, while an advertisement for a detective film depicted two menacing men with revolvers and a third man wearing a black mask. To attract patrons, some commercial theaters resorted to expensive and well-stocked buffets, free coatrooms, and even orchestras that serenaded moviegoers with the latest European dance music.

Famous costume designers such as Adrian of Hollywood created the screen images of innumerable Hollywood stars, who then served as role models. Young women "cut back on everything else, so that they can 'look like their screen heroes,' " complained Bolshevik moralist Ivan Bobryshev.[2] One young man who had been told he looked like the actor Gary Pil took to calling himself after the actor, and he grew side whiskers to look a part of the *beau monde*. Young women were said to admire Mary Pickford because she made even rags look like a princess's dress: "She was enchanting . . . although she wasn't especially pretty, she made us believe that she was very beautiful."[3] In contrast to the rough-and-ready young working-class revolutionary who wore a leather jacket, shock boots, and a worker's cap, fashionable young women in Soviet Russia wore bright red lipstick and narrow-toed high-heeled shoes, bobbed their hair, and shortened their skirts, while young men wore ties and tight double-breasted jackets.

Some of the urban population's information on the latest styles came directly from Russian fashion magazines, which provided European images for the Russian reader and were sold in Moscow stores such as "Fashion World." Two popular examples were *Mody sezona* and *Mody* (Fashions), both of which were published monthly in Moscow. Other than the quality of paper and printing, there was little to differentiate these magazines from their equivalents in the West such as *Fémina* or *Vogue*. That the Bolsheviks criticized much of Western fashion but permitted Russian fashion magazines to be published is a vivid example of the kinds of cultural conflicts that flourished during NEP.

The images of the fashionable young woman and man found in *Mody* and *Mody sezona* were at odds with the modest, working-class life-style advocated by many Bolsheviks. A 1924 issue of *Mody* showed models in soft, full dresses that were very feminine—a far cry from the functional clothing advocated by Commissar Semashko. The young women wore wide-brimmed hats, often trimmed with feathers or flowers, and leaned languorously against elegant balconies or strolled in the park holding fancy parasols. There were models in beaded gowns that were clearly meant for elegant evening parties, not for the Communist youth club. In one picture, immaculately groomed children played in a ballroom overlooking a large garden, evoking the leisurely, pastoral life-style of Russia's own former nobility. In another there were models attired in elegant dressing gowns made of the latest in Chinese fabrics, suitable only for the wealthy aristocrat with plenty of leisure time on her hands. By 1928, *Mody sezona* showed the type of clothing more typically associated with our images of the modern young flapper. The lean, boyish figures wore short dresses whose hems fell just below the knee, and their bobbed hair was covered by close-fitting cloches set with ribbon or rhinestones. In the Winter issues they were shown in sleek fur-trimmed coats, and in the summertime in simple dresses with abstract patterns influenced by the artistic avant-garde. As pictured in these pages, the adventurous and independent young woman of the postwar years had a busy social life and needed the clothing appropriate for every occasion. In Summer 1928, *Mody sezona* described "the kind of dresses that Parisian women take with them when they go to their summer houses," and the proper outfits for a game of tennis or a drive in the car. The daring young flapper might even make an airplane flight, for which she needed the leather aviator's cap and goggles shown in the Spring issue of *Mody sezona*. Men and boys were not immune from efforts to dress Russians in the latest European fashions. The boys, who in these drawings looked like proper British boardingschool pupils, wore shorts, knee socks, and sailor hats. The men were dressed in double-breasted plaid suits, with dapper bowlers and boaters. They carried gloves and walking sticks or posed cigarette in hand.

Although the images found in Russian and European fashion magazines showed a life-style that few, if any, Soviets could achieve, they encouraged young consumers to buy certain kinds of clothing by making an association between clothing and life-style. Advertising of this type evoked dreams of adventure and a carefree life far removed from the daily burdens of revolutionary Russia. The magazines, and the consumer products described therein, appealed to the fantasies of the new Soviet consumer. The question, of course, is how to understand and interpret the persistence of such desires in a postrevolutionary environment.

Some youth drawn to imitate these "decadent" Western fashions were the wealthy children of private entrepreneurs who feverishly shopped and traded, knowing that the right to do so was temporary and subject to increasing restrictions. The interest in flapper fashions, however, was not limited to the children of NEPmen or their poorer cousins, the Soviet shop girl or office boy. Many of the young people who were attracted to the Western fashions pictured in magazines and in Hollywood films were working-class youth. Once the war ended and wages went up, some factory girls, "avid followers of fashion and primpers," donned "stylish checked caps, and coquettish yellow shoes, and beige stockings." Even those who did not make much money wore "nice dresses specially made for them, and always carefully ironed."[4] When they could not afford to buy the new luxuries, they did their best to imitate them. Young women used Russian fashion magazines to reproduce the styles of New York and Paris at home with whatever hard-won materials they could find in public markets or Soviet stores. Journals such as *Home Dressmaker* printed patterns "necessary for every family and every woman." Unable to afford expensive imported items, young women bought "imitation silk stockings, lipstick and Soviet substitutes for Coty products—made by the Chinese."[5] By the late 1920s, girls could buy Russian lipstick, still considered a "bourgeois vice," but so popular that it was now produced by a government monopoly. Hungry for the fancy goods denied them, young women envied the clothing of Western visitors. As one visitor noted: "Some have developed an almost pathological desire for the good-quality clothes they have so long been deprived of. I have had them feel feverishly my foreign clothes, hat, frock, sample the material, stroke the silk, almost pull my underwear from under my blouse in their frenzied hunger."[6]

While young people in Paris or London could shop in the latest *grand magasin* or department store, Soviet youth who could afford to buy clothes were limited to small, privately run shops such as the popular Moscow stores "Paris Fashions" and "Viennese Chic." In contrast to the noise and flamboyance of European department stores, many of the choicest shops in postrevolutionary Russia were to be found in out-of-the-way apartments. As one observer described:

> To reach the millinery shop we left our sleigh one evening in the courtyard of an immense white house which was once the residence of a nobleman. We skirted the corner of the house and at the rear turned into a tiny door. My guide led me up the two dark flights of stairs, and pushed [open] a door.

We literally fell into a lighted corridor, and picked our way down between a few broken chairs, an old mattress, a bicycle, and a pile of old hats. The milliner herself answered our knock on one of the doors at the end of the passageway.[7]

Some members of the Komsomol (Young Communist League) kept the leather jackets, crumpled skirts, and patched shoes of the Civil War period, thinking that this demonstrated their revolutionary devotion. But other Communist youth succumbed to the lure of fashion, and they sacrificed to do so. One young Komsomol woman, who made 65 rubles per month working in a factory, was said to spend two-thirds of it on manicures, cosmetics, and dance parties. Komsomol activists in one factory reported that there were many cases of female workers who literally starved because they spent all of their wages on silk stockings, makeup, and manicures, while *Komsomolskaia pravda* (Komsomol truth) described young working women who wore "fashionable" low-cut dresses and "scanty shoes that pinched their toes."[8] Worried observers condemned the girls' efforts to "make their bodies more beautiful, draping different bows and scarfs around their necks, and striving not to wear boots, like the likes of us, but little half boots with very high heels."[9]

It seems likely that by imitating the clothing and manners of wealthy West Europeans, even as they toiled away in the heat and dust of the factory floor, young Russians hoped to appropriate some of the modern independence, chic, and sophistication associated with flapper fashions. Silk stockings and red lipstick can be understood as a manifestation of some young people's desire for easy and enjoyable forms of everyday life and must have served as a release from the dreary realities of a working-class existence. On a deeper level, however, imitation of upper-class clothing can be seen not only as a search for chic and sophistication but also as a devaluation of certain "traditional" forms of working-class culture. It seems that fashion-conscious factory youth had internalized the message implicit in some commercial culture that suggested that their own forms of dress, behavior, and language were not as good as those of the middle and upper classes. To this end, up-and-coming young Communists used "bourgeois" clothing to segregate themselves from the "masses." Some Communist university students wore the same peaked cap and jacket as the prerevolutionary intelligentsia, for example, to distinguish themselves from "uncultured" and uneducated youth. Contemporary observers noted that many young people not only tried to dress in the latest styles but also made an obvious effort to reproduce "aristocratic manners" in everything they did. *Komsomolskaia pravda* described a young Komsomol member named Boris Kliuev who tried to escape the world of workers by leading a double life—honest young Communist by day, bourgeois dandy by night: "In the evening after work this young Communist can no longer be considered your colleague. You can't call him Boris, but imitating a nasal French accent you must call him 'Bob.' If you meet him somewhere in the park 'with a well-known lady' . . . and start to talk to him about something related to the factory, he will cautiously glance back at the 'madam' and without fail change the conversation."

According to the author of this article, Kliuev did not want to call himself a worker but imagined a more "picturesque" appellation: *elektrotekhnik* (electrical engineer), or *elektrik* (electrician).[10] Similarly, there were working-class girls who refused to go out with factory boys, looking "condescendingly at their comrades at work." Instead, "they moved about in 'high society,' with the children of specialists, . . . NEPmen, and so on";[11] some still dreamed of marrying young naval officers. This "vice" was not limited to young women; Komsomol newspapers also complained about Komsomol men who preferred to go out with "the made-up daughters of NEPmen" rather than the supposedly less attractive, but more Communist, Komsomol women. One frustrated Komsomol woman from Kiev complained about the impossible luxury and sophistication that attracted these young men and described the "typical" scene in which the daughter of a NEPman "with delicate hands" played "some romantic piece" on the piano while the young worker sat on a "deep, soft sofa."[12]

Flapper fashion was a mark of urbanity and as such became a part of the whole ritual of gender relations and efforts at upward mobility in the countryside as well as in the city. Before the revolution, the peasant girl hoping to attract attention sewed herself a fashionable skirt in the latest style "all covered with flowers." After the revolution, she wore gloves and carried a parasol, and instead of typical peasant bast shoes and work boots, she wore leather half boots. Such aspirations to city sophistication were reflected in some traditional four-line *chastushki* (topical songs in rhyme), such as this one:

> Don't refuse me money, Papa,
> Twenty-five rubles
> To buy a parasol and leather boots,
> Just like cultured people have.[13]

Makeup was also very important, and observers noted that in some peasant trunks one could find "a whole battery of boxes with various greasy materials: powder, rouges, pomades, cream and other cosmetics."[14] For peasant youth and urban youth, nice clothes and an attractive appearance were likely associated with an easy life. The occasional piece of finery or tube of bright lipstick transported these young women from their difficult lives into an imagined world of sophistication. Peasant girls in the 1920s enriched their vocabulary with a whole range of "fashionable" words borrowed from the formerly French-speaking upper classes: "merci," "pardon," and "s'il vous plaît."

We should not overemphasize the purposefulness of this emulation of the upper classes. Dress might be seen instead as a way to "play" with elite culture. The pleasure that some youth derived from dressing up may have had little explicit political significance. Young people did not always see clothing in the same way as their elders did, either. "Modern" clothing may have been a way to look up-to-date, but it did not necessarily mean nonrevolutionary. At the same time, post-1917 Soviet Russia was clearly a very different place from either prewar Russia or New York, and official discourse encouraged the "respectability" of Semashko's neat and functional clothing, not the costumes of the elite or the far-out fashion of the flapper. In this environment, flapper fashion did have political significance, no matter what the intent of the wearer, and some youth were conscious of the politics of dress. Non-Communist university students in the traditional institutes of higher education such as Moscow State University "paraded about" in jackets with white silk linings. Before the revolution, students who wore these coats were called *belopodkladochniki* (those who wear white silk linings). After 1917 this term described students who were considered "political aliens." That some students continued to wear these jackets despite the approbation suggests that they deliberately used the language of clothing to express their resistance to Communist norms and to define themselves as anti-Bolshevik.

Many Bolsheviks saw the Soviet flapper's open identification with "bourgeois" culture as a threat to the successful socialization of youth. In contrast to the socially aware young Communist who was supposed to sublimate her own desires for pleasure to the wider concerns of society, the fashion-conscious individual seemed to emphasize her rejection of the socialist agenda through her choice of clothing. The focus on fashion signaled a rampant individualism of personal and cultural expression that threatened the collectivist mentality that many party and Komsomol leaders thought was necessary to build a new society. They worried that for some youth the culture of clothing had become more important than any other question. Bolsheviks condemned the sacrifice, both literal and figurative, of Soviet youth on the altar of fashion and warned them to protect themselves against its dangers.

Indeed, some stories about youth and fashion might best be understood as cautionary tales. In one such story, the protagonist, a young Komsomol worker named Olga P., is said to be "consumed" with clothing. As Bolshevik moralist Ivan Bobryshev describes it, "Class, revolution, construction—these ideas didn't exist; there was a different 'sun'—a skirt." When Olga discovers one day that her favorite velvet skirt is missing, she cries to a friend: "I have no life . . . they stole my skirt . . . In my velvet skirt I looked like the daughter of a nobleman."[15] She then commits suicide by drinking a bottle of vinegar essence. This story bears a notable similarity to prerevolutionary morality tales told to and about young peasants who were also condemned for attempting to emulate the petty bourgeoisie. In one story from 1910, a young woman goes without food to save money to buy a dress in a shop window. Like Olga, she too dies because of her "unhealthy" desires.

In the morality tale about Olga P., we can see two apparent sources of youths' "decadent" behavior. The first is the dangerously polluted "alien" culture of the bourgeoisie. By labeling flapper fashions as bourgeois, party and Komsomol leaders helped create the image of a decadent "other" against which the Communist "self" could be developed and defended. In their view, "real" Communist youth were not excessively interested in clothing or cosmetics. If they were, it was assumed that they had been diverted from their "normal" path and influenced by the bourgeoisie. To claim otherwise would have suggested that Communist youth were themselves interested in fashion and external appearance, and in this way not so different from the very youth and youth culture that they were expected to oppose.

Femininity was the second source of this "decadence." The overly fashion-conscious "bourgeois" youth was frequently, though not exclusively, female. An article entitled "The Girl in the White Scarf" described the appearance and shallow life of the "typical" daughter of a private entrepreneur who "loved her body" and "valued her physique."[16] Superficial and self-absorbed, she and young women like her were thought to be dangerous because of their ability to distract others (men) from the more serious tasks of Communist construction. The linking of females and fashion suggested a shocking independence among women and a proclivity toward excessive eroticism. Cosmetics, which were still associated with a kind of moral ambiguity, the new shorter dresses, and bobbed hair suggested degrees of sexual liberation (that is, the liberation of women and the liberation of sexuality) which may have made some Bolshevik moralists uncomfortable. Despite a rhetoric of gender equality, many male Bolsheviks and Communist youth were still uncomfortable with women's equal participation in the cultural sphere or elsewhere.

Western films, fashion magazines, and traveling artists and performers helped to structure a consumer mentalité similar to that of Western Europe and the United States. Although this alternative culture was in conflict with many ideals for Soviet youth, it is not surprising that so many young people enjoyed the lively, imaginative, and exotic aspects of the new culture industry. The beauty, fun, and adventure of slipping on a pair of silk stockings apparently answered a need that was not filled by the disciplined, and sometimes puritanical, leisure activities prescribed by Bolshevik moralists. A minority of young people purposefully used the language and gesture of bohemian culture to disrupt the fragile boundaries of Bolshevik control, but many seemed simply to enjoy the fantasies of dress and dance available to them in this transitional era.

Young people did not need to be consciously resistant to have a political effect, however. Dress had particular political meaning in the unsettled and contentious environment of NEP. The policies of NEP were supposed to provide an increase in material well-being; NEP was meant to bring recovery, even prosperity, to Soviet citizens. Even more to the point, factories in Soviet Russia made lipstick, and Russian magazines printed dress patterns for the young flapper. But the objectives of NEP, and the relative economic freedoms that it permitted, were clearly problematic in that they allowed (and even encouraged) behaviors and beliefs that ran counter to other, more serious ideals for youth. Flappers were anxiety-provoking because they exemplifed aspects of NEP (prosperity, material pleasures, even luxury) that made many committed Communists uncomfortable. Flapper dress violated multiple cultural and political ideals—it was "frivolous," interfering with the development of rational and disciplined forms of recreation; it was "uncivilized," threatening Bolshevik conceptions of proper public behavior; and it was "immoral," sparking fears of uncontrollability. Soviet discourses about dress defined these pleasures of the body as dangerous and, by doing so, tried to discipline them. In this period of great anxiety about social transformation and social control, the popular (particularly when tied to material pleasure and prosperity) could be threatening.

NOTES

1. Paxton Hibben, "The Movies in Russia," *The Nation*, November 11, 1925, as cited in Jay Leyda, *Kino: A History of the Russian and Soviet Film*, 3d ed. (Princeton: Princeton University Press, 1983), 185.

2. Ivan T. Bobryshev, *Melkoburzhuaznye vliianiia sredi molodezhi* (Moscow-Leningrad: Molodaia Gvardiia, 1928), 105.

3. M. M. Rubenshtein, *Iunost: Podnevnikam i avtobiograficheskim zapisiam* (Moscow: Izdatelstvo Vysshikh pedagogicheskikh kursov, 1928), 222.

4. Ekaterina Strogova, "Womenfolk: Factory Sketches," in *An Anthology of Russian Women's Writing, 1777–1992*, ed. Catriona Kelly (Oxford: Oxford University Press, 1994), 282.

5. Dorothy Thompson, *The New Russia* (New York: H. Holt, 1928), 46.

6. Ella Winter, *Red Virtue* (London: Victor Gollancz Ltd., 1933), 48.

7. Edwin Ware Hullinger, *The Reforging of Russia* (New York: E. P. Dutton, 1925), 255.

8. M. Rafail, *Za novogo cheloveka* (Leningrad: "Priboi," 1928), 50–51; Bobryshev, *Melkoburzhuaznye vliianiia*, 68.

9. Vladimir Kuzmin, "Pismo o novom byte," in Izrail M. Razin, *Komsomolskii byt* (Moscow-Leningrad: Molodaia Gvardiia, 1927), 320.

10. T. Kostrov, "Kultura i meshchanstvo," *Revoliutsiia i kultura* 3–4 (1927): 27.

11. Bobryshev, *Melkoburzhuaznye vliianiia*, 68–69.

12. Kostrov, "Kultura i meshchanstvo," 27.

13. Yuri Sokolov, "Chto poet i rasskazyvaet derevnia," *Zhizn: Zhurnal literatury, byta i obshchestvennoi zhizn* 1 (1924): 306.

14. V. A. Murin, *Byt i nravy derevenskoi molodezhi* (Moscow: "Novaia Moskva," 1926), 82–83.

15. Bobryshev, *Melkoburzhuaznye vliianiia*, 104–6.

16. Evgenii Iukon, "Devushka s belym sharfom," in *Obyvatelshchinu na pritsle!* (Leningrad: Krasnaia gazeta, 1928), 89–90.

SUGGESTED READINGS

The study of popular culture is by nature interdisciplinary, and the material used in this article comes from Soviet archives, libraries, newspapers and magazines, fiction and autobiography, sociological and ethnographic works, travelers' accounts, interviews, and visual sources such as film, posters, and photographs. In other words, my "texts" have been not only written ones but also social practices such as dance, dress, ritual, and language. For journalistic and literary accounts translated into English on the climate of NEP see Ilya Ehrenburg, *First Years of Revolution, 1918–1921*, trans. Anna Bostock (London: MacGibbon and Kee, 1962); N. Ognyov, *The Diary of a Communist Undergraduate*, trans. Alexander Werth (New York: Payson and Clarke, 1929); and Vladimir Lidin, *The Price of Life*, trans. Helen Chrouschoff Matheson (Westport, CT: Hyperion Press, 1973). Good historical treatments on culture in the 1920s include Catriona Kelly and David Sheperd, eds., *Russian Cultural Studies* (New York: Oxford University Press, 1998); Frederick Starr, *Red and Hot: The Fate of Jazz in the Soviet Union, 1917–1980* (New York: Oxford University Press 1983); Richard Stites, *Russian Popular Culture and Society since 1900* (New York: Cambridge University Press, 1992); and Denise J. Youngblood, *Movies for the Masses: Popular Cinema and Soviet Society in the 1920s* (New York: Cambridge University Press, 1992). For more on the theoretical issues involved in studying youth culture see two classics: Dick Hebdidge, *Subculture: The Meaning of Style* (London: Methuen, 1979); and Stuart Hall and Tony Jefferson, eds., *Resistance through Rituals: Youth Subculture in Post-War Britain* (London: Hutchinson, 1975). An excellent recent study is Ken Gelder and Sarah Thornton, eds., *The Subcultures Reader* (New York: Routledge, 1997).

CHAPTER 6

Russian Orthodoxy and the Tragic Fate of Patriarch Tikhon (Bellavin)

EDWARD E. ROSLOF

The February and October revolutions of 1917 raised special problems for the Russian Orthodox Church. The end of the Imperial Government fundamentally redefined the church in institutional terms. The rise of Bolshevism forced a far-reaching reassessment of the identity of Orthodoxy in society, and the collapse of traditional authority brought the internal differences in the church to the surface. On the level most obvious, the status of a church that had been subordinate to the state but also under its protection changed dramatically after 1917. During the two previous centuries, Orthodoxy had come extensively under state authority. The Spiritual Regulation enacted by Tsar Peter the Great early in the eighteenth century replaced the Patriarchate with the Holy Synod, a committee of twelve with a lay Procurator as its head. This change certainly impinged on independent church governance, but it also granted Orthodoxy the status of a quasi-official religion and extended to it special protections. Under the Holy Synod, the church actually pursued its interests with remarkable effectiveness, but by the beginning of the twentieth century there was a perceived drop in its influence in society at large, and religious reformers sought ways to alter the church from within. Thus, when the collapse of tsarist power in February 1917 ushered in eight months of rule by the liberal Provisional Government, the favored status of Orthodoxy was already in jeopardy. The Provisional Government attempted both to remove the privileged status of Orthodoxy and to intervene directly in its affairs in matters such as the political composition of the Holy Synod and self-government of parishes and dioceses. For its part, the church seized the opportunity to reinstate the Patriarchate in October 1917, with Vasilii Ivanovich Bellavin—who took the name Tikhon—as the first Patriarch of Moscow in more than two centuries. But the Bolshevik seizure of power in October 1917 led to new and even greater problems (see Chapter 10). Ideologically opposed to religion, the revolutionary government employed a vast array of resources to attempt to eradicate it, and with the rise of the Soviet state the Russian Orthodox Church entered a period of prolonged repression.

In this examination of the career of Patriarch Tikhon, Edward Roslof demonstrates that the battle between Orthodoxy and Bolshevism was multilayered and nuanced. First, from their strongly contrasting points of view, the two sides often spoke past one another. The church had come to view its status in relation to other denominations as well as the state as a divinely inspired natural order. It viewed every challenge to its position as sin, which robbed it of some of the flexibility that it might have used productively in the circumstances surrounding the revolution. Second, in guiding the faith through these troubles, Tikhon had to take the various faces of Orthodoxy into full account. The influence that the monk Rasputin had exercised over Empress Alexandra had tarnished its reputation, as did the internal splits that came into public view in 1917 and thereafter. One such fissure was opposition to Tikhon in the form of so-called Renovationism, which the Bolsheviks were able to exploit. Third, and above all, the logic of events forced Orthodoxy to reach some accommodation with Soviet power, which Tikhon attempted alternately with policies of political neutrality, defensiveness in the face of Bolshevik aggression, symbolic resistance, and, finally, pragmatic cooperation. As Roslof shows, Tikhon's efforts ultimately created the foundation for the survival of Orthodoxy within the Soviet system.

A specialist on the Renovationist movement in the Russian Orthodox Church, Edward E. Roslof is assistant professor at United Theological Seminary. He received his Ph.D. from the University of North Carolina at Chapel Hill, and his articles have appeared in Slavic Review *and other leading journals.*

The revolutionary turmoil that gripped Russia in the first quarter of the twentieth century had an enormous impact on that country's religious culture. The rush to transform Russia swept away old social rules that gave order to Orthodox life by telling what was permitted and forbidden for all believers. Russian Orthodox clergy experienced the effects of this revolutionary transformation most directly. Two centuries of Imperial governance had formed a closed clerical estate (*soslovie*) that formed a cocoon around clergymen and their families. This cocoon protected the rights of priests and their children—especially their sons—even as it limited their choice of occupation and life-style. The state exacted a price for its protection by expecting priests openly and directly to enforce public morality and support the government's policies. While the clergy often negotiated with the state over the specifics of those expectations, they generally remained loyal to the system itself.

The 1905 Revolution marked the beginning of the destruction of the clergy's cocoon. During the political upheaval, the clergy demanded an end to tsarist restrictions on their life-style but soon found that their rights were attacked as well. Freedom of religious confession led many Orthodox faithful to abandon the church of their ancestors. New groups competed for the religious loyalty of the population. The brightest and best sons of the clergy rejected the traditional path of church service for secular professions. During the revolutions of 1917, revived social turmoil fed anticlericalism and radical political ideologies that advocated the complete separation of the church from both the state and the public education system. To the dismay of most church leaders, the radical Marxists, led by Vladimir Lenin, came to power in October 1917 and immediately implemented policies to end Orthodoxy's privileged position in the new Soviet Russia. A struggle began between church and state leaders for the support of the Russian people, with newly elected Patriarch of Moscow Tikhon (Bellavin) becoming both a target for religious opponents and a rallying figure for supporters of Orthodoxy.

The first fifty years of Patriarch Tikhon's life gave few clues that he would play the pivotal role in that struggle. He was born in January 1865 in Klin, a village located in northwest Russia's Pskov province. Vasilii Ivanovich Bellavin was the son of a parish priest and his wife. His family had lived in the region for at least five generations, during which time all his paternal direct male ancestors had served as clergy—the result of Peter the Great's Ecclesiastical Regulation of 1721, which required education for Orthodox clergymen. Only the sons of priests had access to seminaries, so the priestly vocation became hereditary. The Bellavin family took their spiritual responsibility seriously, as evidenced by generations of regional church records that praised their good nature, peacefulness, humility, thrift, and strong morality.

Family tradition and social expectations shaped Vasilii's early life. When he was only four, his father was appointed priest at Transfiguration of the Savior Church in the prosperous town of Toropets. Materially comfortable, the young boy was inclined to participate in the rich spiritual life of his father's parish. He reportedly avoided secular amusements, such as the local puppet theater, in favor of church services, religious processions, and devotional readings. At the age of nine, Vasilii began his elementary education at the ecclesiastical school in Toropets. Four years later, he left home to study at the seminary in Pskov, still following the traditional path laid out for boys in the clerical estate.

In Pskov, the young Bellavin continued to display a religious maturity that made him the pride of the seminary and the object of curiosity among his peers. He refused to engage in frivolous activity and dedicated himself to his studies. His classmates later remembered Vasilii's brilliant answers, especially to questions of dogmatic theology, coupled with his love of languages. He finished seminary at the top of his class and in 1884 began graduate study at the theological academy in St. Petersburg.

Moving to the capital exposed Vasilii to a wider range of theological disciplines and positioned him for rapid promotion within the Orthodox church. There he received the nickname "the Patriarch" from his fellow students because of his piety and personal bearing. He wrote his candidate's thesis (the equivalent of a Master's thesis) on Pasquier Quesnel, a seventeenth-century French Catholic theologian whose views were condemned by the pope. In 1888, Bellavin took his first step into the church's hierarchy with his appointment to the faculty of the seminary in Pskov.

At this point, the Russian church required Vasilii Bellavin to make a decisive and irrevocable choice between the "white" and "black" clergy. He could marry and join the ranks of "white" parish priests. His education undoubtedly would have brought a promotion to the rank of archpriest and possibly an appointment to the faculty of a theological academy, but further advancement would have been impossible as long as his wife remained alive. Vasilii instead chose not to marry, thereby entering the ranks of the monastic "black" clergy and becoming nearly assured of elevation into the episcopacy. He took monastic vows at the end of 1891 and adopted the name "Tikhon" in honor of Saint Tikhon of Zadonsk, a famous Russian Orthodox missionary. Ordination as deacon and then priest came immediately thereafter.

Following standard practice, the Holy Synod of the Russian Orthodox Church moved Tikhon into a series of posts as a monastic priest and then bishop in the years preceding the 1917 revolutions. In March 1892 he became inspector of the seminary in the city of Kholm (now Khelm, Poland). After only three months, Tikhon was promoted to the position of dean of that seminary. Five years later he was consecrated as suffragan bishop of Lublin (also part of present-day Poland), and in 1898, less than a year later, Tikhon became bishop of Alaska and the Aleutians in North America. Following a promotion to archbishop of the Aleutians and North America in 1905, he lived in San Francisco and New York until 1907. For seven years (1907–1914), Archbishop Tikhon held the episcopal see located in the old Russian cities of Yaroslavl and Rostov, 175 miles northeast of Moscow. He then served as archbishop of Vilnius in Lithuania from 1914 to 1917.

Tikhon's career as a member of the monastic clergy before the Bolshevik Revolution fit the typical pattern. A promising candidate for the episcopacy usually worked in seminary administration until he was thirty-two years old, the minimum age required by church law for ordination as bishop. He then served as suffragan or assistant bishop for several years and later moved into his own episcopal area. The Holy Synod re-assigned bishops frequently for both ecclesiastical and political reasons. Tikhon was transferred to North America after he gave his archbishop a negative report on the abbess of a women's convent in the countryside outside Lublin. The abbess, a countess by birth, used her political connections with the Imperial court in St. Petersburg to have Tikhon moved. Similar circumstances led the Holy Synod to transfer Tikhon from Yaroslavl to Vilnius in 1914, reportedly because he refused to participate in promonarchist organizations and had run afoul of the provincial governor.

Although typical in many ways, Tikhon's rise within the church hierarchy also had two distinctive elements. First, he spent long periods outside the Russian heartland. His many years of service in Poland, North America, and Lithuania were unusual, and the reasons for his appointments to these regions are not explained. Perhaps it was his own preference—as reflected in his choice of a monastic name from a missionary saint—combined with the Holy Synod's assessment of Tikhon's personal strengths. They certainly would have been aware that the Bellavin family had deep roots in Pskov province, an area known for its multiethnic population. Tikhon's accomplishments in dioceses where the Russian population was the minority validated the Holy Synod's assessment of his suitability for such appointments.

As a bishop in the Imperial Russian church, Tikhon also displayed extraordinary pastoral skills and humility. These proved to be the keys to his success but were not the usual qualities for Orthodox bishops in Tikhon's time. The simple, clear speech that he gave on the day of his consecration as bishop reflected this aspect of his personality. The church newspaper *Tserkovnye vedomosti* (1897, No. 43, pp. 1560–61) recorded Tikhon's words: "Sometime in my early youth, episcopal service was presented to me as honor, respect, strength, and power. Now, I understand that the episcopacy is first and foremost not strength, honor, and power but administration, work, and self-denial." The biographical sources on his thirty years as a bishop indicate that Tikhon never reveled in the prestige of the episcopacy, nor do these later sources emphasize the academic brilliance that marked his elementary and seminary education. Instead, contemporaries praised Bishop Tikhon for his attention to duty. He traveled constantly throughout his dioceses, visiting churches and leading long liturgical services. The Orthodox tradition places great value on ritual and images (icons), and Tikhon seemed to have an inner quality that made him a traveling icon within the jurisdictions entrusted to his oversight. That quality elicited enormous popularity for him from the parishioners of his dioceses, who flocked to church services whenever he was present.

Popularity among the Orthodox laity did not, however, transfer automatically into power in the ecclesiastical hierarchy. Under usual circumstances, Tikhon's career would have stalled after his demotion from Yaroslavl to Lithuania, although he showed no concern about this setback during his first seven months in the new post. As before, he kept a relentless schedule of visiting churches, celebrating the Divine Liturgy, and blessing parishioners. He also inspected the diocese's monastic and agricultural holdings, examined church schools, and preached. Unlike his predecessors, he refused the trappings of episcopal power and traveled in an ordinary carriage. Once again, he refused to expect and encourage the deference that Russian society usually accorded those of high ecclesiastical rank. Indeed, his refusal to act like a typical bishop might have hindered his further advancement with the Orthodox church of the Russian Empire under ordinary circumstances.

The rules for religious behavior changed dramatically when World War I began, however, and Tikhon benefited directly from that change. When the Germans invaded Lithuania in July 1914, his diocese was on the front line, and Tikhon directed his energies to support the war effort. He traveled to the front, offering physical and spiritual comfort to the soldiers. As the Germans advanced on Vilnius, Tikhon left for Moscow with relics from the first Lithuanian martyrs for Orthodox Christianity. In 1916, Tsar Nicholas II awarded Archbishop Tikhon a diamond cross for his work in defense of the Fatherland. During the war, Tikhon gained further national visibility when he was appointed to the Holy Synod.

Social unrest and revolution in 1917 pushed Tikhon to the pinnacle of ecclesiastical power in three stages. During the first, immediately after the abdication of Nicholas II in March 1917, confusion and hesitancy seized the church. For many Orthodox leaders, the fall of the tsar and the rise of the Provisional Government meant that the church had lost its very basis for existence. They could not accept a new political order based on "the will of the people" instead of "the grace of God." Their opposition to this new political order became focused on L. N. Lvov, the new Procurator of the Holy Synod. After being named to this post by the Provisional Government, Lvov began changes that reflected the political mood of the times. He cleaned house at the Holy Synod, removing those who had gained office through the influence of the "mad monk," Grigorii Rasputin, and retiring conservative bishops. He then implemented a series of measures to decentralize power in the church. The theological academies were granted academic freedom, and the Holy Synod was reorganized with new members and more open rules for debate. Most important, a new law was passed that aimed to renew the church by allowing self-governing parishes and dioceses.

In the confusion that followed the February Revolution, Tikhon solidified his position as a defender of traditional Orthodox values and episcopal rights. Joining with five other bishops who were also members of the Holy Synod, Tikhon took the bold step of withdrawing from that body. The six church leaders issued a statement on March 8 explaining their decision. They rejected the right of Lvov and the new government to make changes in the church without the consent and participation of all Russian Orthodox bishops. Thus, Tikhon showed his solidarity with those who wanted less state interference in Orthodox church affairs. He also made clear his support for a model of church governance based on a council of bishops as the primary decision-making body.

Ironically, Lvov's reforms provided the means for Tikhon's second step to the patriarchal throne. Using the Holy Synod's new law on self-governance, believers throughout Russia met and voted on the fitness of their clergy. A handful of dioceses and several hundred parishes removed their respective bishops and priests. In June, representatives from the dioceses in and around Moscow chose Tikhon to fill the vacancy created by their removal of their bishop. Tikhon was promoted to the rank of Metropolitan, the second highest episcopal office (after Patriarch) in the Orthodox tradition. Overnight, Metropolitan Tikhon moved into one of the most important positions in the Russian church.

In the final stage of his advancement, Tikhon became the first Patriarch of Moscow since the early eighteenth century, when Peter the Great abolished the office and replaced the Moscow patriarchate with the Holy Synod. Nicholas II's abdication during the February Revolution had removed the last obstacle to calling a national council of the Russian Orthodox Church. After several months of preparation, including the election of 563 lay and clergy delegates from all dioceses, the first Russian church council in 250 years opened in Moscow on August 15, 1917. Increased radical activity in the countryside throughout the spring and summer had raised fears of anticlericalism among ordinary believers. Delegates to the national church council gathered with the hope that they could stem the tide of social unrest. One of their first official actions was to elect Metropolitan Tikhon as presiding officer of the council by an overwhelming majority; he received 356 of the 430 votes cast.

For the next eleven weeks the council's debates deadlocked over the best course for the church, even as the threats of revolution in Russia grew. Initially, the diversity of council delegates brought elements of national discord into the conclave. Some council members wanted to modernize church life, while others defended traditional Orthodoxy. The rules governing the deliberations gave the bishops a modified veto power over all of the council's decisions; three-fourths of the eighty bishops had to agree to any proposal before it could even be considered by the nonepiscopal majority. This regulation, combined with the fact that liberal and radical delegates began to withdraw from the council, prevented any revolutionary proposals from being adopted.

Plans to restore the Moscow Patriarchate provoked the greatest disagreement among the delegates. Some argued against restoration on democratic principles, observing that the Patriarch would be associated with tsarist power in the popular mind. They preferred a revised Holy Synod that would be guided by periodic church councils having substantial representation from the parish clergy and ordinary believers. Those arguing in favor of a Patriarch said that he would defend the church's material and spiritual interests. The latter argument gradually won over most delegates, in large part because the plan for restoration was modified to place limits on the powers of the new Patriarch. When Lenin and the Bolsheviks seized control of the government in late October 1917, the council reacted by quickly voting to reinstate the office of Patriarch. He was described as "first among equals" in relationship to other Russian Orthodox bishops, but the highest authority of the church remained in the hands of periodic all-Russian church councils. Between councils, the delegates agreed, the Patriarch would share administrative responsibility with a revised Holy Synod dominated by senior bishops. Both Holy Synod and Patriarch would be directly accountable to the periodic councils. This arrangement ensured that bishops held the reins of power in the church.

On October 30, 1917, as the sounds of constant gunfire reverberated in the main streets of Moscow, the council began the process for selecting the eleventh Patriarch of Moscow and All-Russia. The initial ballot was open to all candidates, laymen, and parish clergy and monastic clergy alike. On the next day, when military cadets and Bolsheviks fought one another for control of the Kremlin, the council narrowed the field to three men: Archbishop Antonii (Khrapovitskii) of Kharkov, Archbishop Arsenii (Stadnitskii) of Novgorod, and Metropolitan Tikhon. Although Tikhon had been overwhelmingly elected as president of the council, he only became eligible for the patriarchal throne on the third ballot of the day. More than half of the council delegates had left Moscow for their homes at the outbreak of the revolution; most of those who remained preferred either Antonii or Arsenii because of their stronger theological credentials and more forceful personalities. In a strictly elective process, the council would never have chosen Tikhon. The body had decided, however, to follow the ancient custom of the Alexandrine church and allow God to indicate which candidate was most worthy through a process of drawing lots. The Bolsheviks had gained control of the Kremlin and prevented the council from using the Cathedral of the

Assumption for the traditional service. Instead, the council gathered for the Holy Liturgy at the Cathedral of Christ the Savior on November 5. After an exceptionally elaborate ceremony, an elderly revered hermit called Aleksii came out of seclusion to draw the lot bearing Tikhon's name.

On the day that he was elevated to the patriarchal throne, Tikhon reached the height of his power and stature in the church. Across Russia, Orthodox believers greeted him as the one who was "divinely chosen." Archbishop Evlogii (Georgievskii)—an eyewitness at the service in the cathedral who wrote about these events in *Put moei zhizni* (The path of my life), his memoirs recorded in Paris thirty years later—recalled, "Many people had tears in their eyes. They felt the election of the Patriarch was a source of joy for everyone in those days of Russia's troubles. He was their defender, a representative and intercessor for the Russian people. . . . Everyone wanted to believe that, with a Patriarch, dissension would somehow disappear" [*Put moei zhizni* (Moscow: Moskovskii rabochii, 1994), p. 303]. Despite these hopes and his own best efforts, Patriarch Tikhon could not end Russia's turmoil in society at large or even within the church.

One of the main reasons for his failure was that the conservatism of most church leaders put them in opposition to the momentous changes in Russia. Council sessions continued until September 1918, although the number of delegates participating in deliberations shrank significantly. The remaining delegates displayed a strong conservative bent and pushed their new leader to confront the government. The council also continued to implement changes that strengthened episcopal power, including creating five new posts for Metropolitans and filling them with archbishops strongly opposed to Bolshevism. Both Antonii and Arsenii were made Metropolitans and given seats on the new Holy Synod. Tikhon followed their advice throughout most of 1918 even as competing political factions began their preparations for civil war.

Tikhon's policy was not to incite the Orthodox faithful to a holy war against the government; instead, he asked them to band together against attacks on church property and Orthodox religious rights. His strongest response came after the Bolsheviks nationalized all property, including the church's holdings, in November 1917 and announced in January 1918 their intention to separate the church from the state and the state from the schools. On January 19, 1918, the Patriarch issued a proclamation that anathematized "the confessed and secret enemies of Christ" who were sowing "anger, hatred and destructive accusations instead of brotherly love." Although not mentioning the Bolsheviks by name, Tikhon left no doubt that the new rulers of Russia were the targets for his prophetic wrath. He instructed believers to avoid contact with those being anathematized and to use all their strength "in the defense of our insulted and oppressed Holy Mother Church."

This call to action reflected the deep concern of Orthodox leaders such as Tikhon over Orthodoxy's role in Soviet society. They witnessed a dramatic shift in the relationship between political and spiritual power in Russia's religious culture. The council was inclined toward militant protection of Orthodox privilege even though ordinary Orthodox believers greeted most of the council's appeals with indifference. For example, Tikhon's anathema was reportedly not read even in the churches of Moscow, much less in those in the provinces. The separation decree made clear that state power would no longer be used to support any religious group. An editor at the newspaper *Bednota* (Poverty) emphasized this point in an article on April 12, 1918, when he wrote: "The church, that is, the spiritual leadership, now does not have political power. It does not command any politicians or soldiers who had formerly helped enforce its orders. Spiritual power is now simply that and nothing more." These words reflected the initial Bolshevik goal to form a nonreligious society; later Soviet rulers launched an antireligious drive to enforce atheistic culture.

Tikhon failed in his search for Orthodoxy's place in the new revolutionary order. Throughout 1918, with only trial and error to guide him, he developed a policy of strict political neutrality combined with public statements in support of Orthodox Christian values. During the spring, he led huge rallies for Orthodox believers in Petrograd and Moscow to show the strength of the church. That summer, when his close adviser, Prince G. I. Trubetskoi, requested a patriarchal blessing for an anti-Bolshevik military leader in the south, Tikhon refused. Upon receiving the news of the execution of Nicholas II and his family, however, the Patriarch immediately organized a requiem prayer service. On the first anniversary of the Bolshevik Revolution, Tikhon distributed an open letter to the government condemning both the terms of the treaty that ended Russian participation in World War I and the state's use of violence against its political enemies. He framed his condemnations in terms of concerns for religious rights and Christian morality, not political opposition.

The Bolshevik leadership rejected Tikhon's explanation that religious belief, and not politics, motivated his actions. In particular, his letter on the anniversary of the revolution crossed the line into politics for government leaders, undoubtedly because it was printed in massive quantities—perhaps as many as five million copies were produced. The government ordered the Patriarch's arrest within a week after the letter appeared but soon received a wave of protests against this action from believers, religious leaders, and foreign governments. In response, the Bolsheviks released Tikhon less than seven weeks later, just in time for him to lead Orthodox Christmas celebrations on January 7, 1919.

Tikhon's relationship with the government continued to follow this pattern for the remaining six years of his life. The Patriarch reacted to changes in Soviet Russia with pronouncements that articulated both Orthodox values and political neutrality. The secret police responded with threats of arrest and public trial for counterrevolutionary activity. Repeatedly, they imprisoned the Patriarch and interrogated him about his conduct, supporters, and motives. The threatened trials never took place, but Tikhon's resolve and health weakened with each episode. In the final years of his life, the fate of his church weighed heavily upon him, and people commented on the weariness that had taken its toll on his face and the sadness they saw in his eyes.

As the years progressed, Patriarch Tikhon limited the social critique of his public statements in order to preserve the internal unity and doctrinal purity of Russian Orthodoxy. The church stood on the brink of schism, in large part because Bolshevik religious policy took power out of the hands of priests and bishops and gave it to members of parish churches. Some Orthodox believers wanted the church to reach an accommodation with the revolution and embrace socialism. Others even dreamed of modernization and revolution within the church itself. At the same time, domestic and émigré Orthodox groups argued for open resistance against godless Bolshevism. Members of Lenin's government wanted to exploit Orthodox factionalism in order to break up the church. Tikhon responded by avoiding confrontation with any of the factions as long as they accepted him as head of the church. He actively opposed those who attempted an open break with his administration or spiritual authority.

His approach worked until the government used its full resources to force both a split within the church and the Patriarch's political submission. The end of the Civil War in 1921 brought severe famine to the southern Volga region. Orthodox leaders led by Tikhon collected funds to relieve the human suffering. The disaster alarmed state officials, and they permitted the church to form a committee for coordinating Orthodox relief efforts. By the end of the year, however, party leaders grew increasingly concerned that the famine would be used by their political enemies as a tool for attacking Soviet power. Many of the Russians who fled the country after 1917 maintained social networks through the church, and the émigrés had begun to organize their own church administration abroad while maintaining ecclesiastical allegiance to Patriarch Tikhon. The government saw domestic Orthodox famine relief combined with émigré Orthodox anti-Bolshevik agitation as part of a conspiracy to foment counterrevolution. Their fears increased as anti-Bolshevik groups within Soviet Russia began to organize around the church.

When Tikhon decided to oppose the seizure of consecrated church valuables for famine relief, the Bolsheviks seized on his stance as an excuse to move against him and split the church. The Patriarch was willing to give up items made of precious metals and gems as long as they were not directly used in Orthodox rites. Violence erupted when believers tried to prevent state officials from confiscating valuables that Tikhon had ordered held back. Bloodshed gave the Bolsheviks an excuse for moving against church leaders. Metropolitan Veniamin (Kazanskii) of Petrograd was arrested, tried, and executed in the summer of 1922 for his attempt to follow the Patriarch's instructions. Tikhon was placed under house arrest, and a group of radical clergy used the covert backing of the secret police to set up a new church administration. Calling themselves "Renovationists" and "the Living Church," these parish priests and a handful of bishops embarked on a campaign to combine Orthodoxy with Bolshevism. Tikhon was helpless to stop their church revolution; in fact, they convinced him to give them temporary authority to handle church affairs and then used his acquiescence to form a new national church administration. The ensuing Renovationist schism in the Russian Orthodox church continued for almost twenty-five years.

By May 1923, Patriarch Tikhon's plans to maintain the unity and political neutrality of the church lay in total ruin. He was being held and interrogated in the notorious Lubianka prison, and the Soviet press gave every indication that he would soon be tried and executed for his "counterrevolutionary crimes." A national church council, controlled by the Renovationists under the direction of the secret police, had just stripped him of his ecclesiastical rank and abolished the Patriarchate. The schismatics claimed to control three-quarters of all Orthodox parishes in the country and proclaimed unswerving loyalty to the Soviet Union. Priests were prohibited under threat of imprisonment from including the Patriarch in liturgical prayers. Thousands of his supporters in the church had lost their positions and been exiled or arrested. The demolition of Imperial episcopal privilege was complete.

One month later, Tikhon emerged out of the ruins with renewed authority. The Bolsheviks released him from prison because they feared both the growth of Renovationism and international threats of armed retaliation should the Patriarch be executed. In return for his freedom, however, Tikhon was required to sign a statement repenting of his crimes against the Soviet state and condemning the anti-Soviet activities of foreign church leaders. Party officials in charge of antireligious policy calculated that this statement would cause further internal divisions within the church and prevent Tikhon from regaining his authority. They were mistaken. From the moment of his release, the Patriarch's standing among the majority of Orthodox believers grew. During his imprisonment, a Renovationist journal complained that Tikhon's very name had taken on a mystical quality among the faithful. After gaining his freedom, Tikhon was inundated with written statements of support from clergymen and their parishioners. The Patriarch was not discredited for his political submission. Instead, the Orthodox public expressed ecstatic support for their spiritual leader who had suffered at the hands of the godless but remained faithful to God. His very release was miraculous in light of the year-long publicity campaign that seemingly guaranteed his quick trial and execution.

For the last three years of his life, Tikhon issued statements in support of the government and attempted to implement Soviet restrictions on Orthodox activity. Despite these actions, most Orthodox continued to see him as a saint suffering for their faith. He was often interrogated by the secret police, who threatened him with new criminal charges. Tikhon watched "bandits" attack and kill his personal assistant in the middle of the night. The criminals, who were never caught, apparently had followed the orders of the secret police. When the Patriarch died on April 7, 1925, he left a testament that proclaimed the church's loyalty to the Soviet state, instructed Orthodox parishes to avoid involvement in politics, and condemned the activities of émigré churchmen. For the church, Tikhon's dying words—"Soon the long, dark night will begin"— came to be seen as a prophetic vision of Orthodoxy's fate under Soviet power.

The funeral for the eleventh Patriarch of Moscow and All-Russia on April 12, 1925, was the last major public Orthodox event in the Soviet Union for over sixty years. It was held on Palm Sunday, and the people gathered at Moscow's Don Monastery by the hundreds of thousands. Over thirty bishops and sixty priests participated in the funeral service. Government fears of demonstrations and disorder proved unfounded. At the urging of one of the bishops, the crowd regulated itself as a sign of love and respect for their departed Patriarch.

For most of the Soviet era, Patriarch Tikhon was the media symbol for religious counterrevolution. The details of his life after 1917 were distorted, and Soviet historians even changed the spelling of his family name (from Bellavin to Belavin) for reasons still unexplained. The rehabilitation of Tikhon's memory began in the waning years of Soviet power, as acceptance for the church's public role grew. In 1989 a church council canonized Saint Tikhon Bellavin, the "divinely chosen one" who remained faithful to Orthodox Christianity in the face of Communist repression.

The life of Patriarch Tikhon shows how Russian Orthodoxy adapted to Soviet rule. The church's position in society was totally reversed after

1917. The state no longer expected or desired Orthodox bishops to be moral leaders for the people. Government officials refused to use their power in support of church decisions. When the church's organization collapsed as a result of the new religious policy, Orthodox bishops lost crucial elements of their power in Russian society. Tikhon regained public support because he embraced traditional Orthodox virtues of humility and perseverance in suffering. He also gave Russian Orthodox believers an example for accommodating Orthodox Christianity with the new social order. Some rejected his example and chose greater or lesser accommodation with Soviet authorities, but these choices provided neither greater protection from persecution nor more support from Soviet society as a whole. Some of those who followed Tikhon's example shared his tragic fate and had their lives shortened by state action. Many others found that Tikhon's way was best for the difficult task of reconciling Soviet citizenship with Orthodox belief.

SUGGESTED READINGS

The Russian author Mikhail Vostryshev has written two recent biographies of Tikhon Bellavin. The first, *Bozhii izbrannik: Krestnyi put Sviatitelia Tikhona, Patriarkha Moskovskovo i vseia Rossii* (Moscow: Sovremennik, 1990), is a shorter, more factual account produced just after Tikhon's canonization, while the second, *Patriarkh Tikhon* (Moscow: Molodaia Gvardiia, 1997), reflects the demand for a hagiographic account of the saint's life. The Russian Orthodox Church's official history of Tikhon's patriarchate is found in Vladislav Tsypin, *Istoriia Russkoi Tserkvi, 1917–1997* (Moscow: Izdatelstro Spaso-Preobrazhenskogo Valaamskogo Monastyria, 1997).

The life of Russian Orthodox clergy before the revolution is described in Gregory L. Freeze, *The Parish Clergy in Nineteenth-Century Russia: Crisis, Reform, Counter-Reform* (Princeton, NJ: Princeton University Press, 1983). Church reaction to the 1905 Revolution is discussed in James W. Cunningham, *A Vanquished Hope: The Movement for Church Renewal in Russia, 1905–1906* (Crestwood, NY: St. Vladimir's Seminary Press, 1981). A succinct overview of the history of the church council is found in Catherine Evtuhov's article, "The Church in the Russian Revolution: Arguments for and against Restoring the Patriarchate at the Church Council of 1917–1918," in *Slavic Review* 50 (Fall 1991): 497–511. Detailed accounts of that council's proceedings are recorded in *Deianiia Sviashchennogo Sobora Pravoslavnoi Rossiiskoi Tserkvi 1917–1918 gg.*, 9 vols. (originally published in Moscow by Izdanie Sobornogo soveta, 1918).

Research on Tikhon and the Russian church during the early Soviet era continues to make important discoveries. N. A. Krivova, *Vlast i tserkov v 1922–1925 gg.* (Moscow: AIRO-XX, 1997), combines archival research with thoughtful analysis to present the political events surrounding the last years of Tikhon's life. Reactions against attempted changes in the church are described by Gregory L. Freeze, "Counter-Reformation in Russian Orthodoxy: Popular Response to Religious Innovation, 1922–1925," in *Slavic Review* 54 (Summer 1995): 305–39. William B. Husband's *"Godless Communists": Atheism and Society in Soviet Russia, 1917–1932* (DeKalb: Northern Illinois University Press, 2000) reveals the process by which belief systems changed in the first years of Soviet power.

CHAPTER 7

"Ask the Doctor!"

Peasants and Medical-Sexual Advice in Riazan Province, 1925–1928

Stephen P. Frank

Central to the Bolshevik desire to recast the predominant world view in Russian society during the New Economic Policy (NEP) was the promotion of philosophical materialism. As innovations grounded in materialism—the philosophy that all existence derives from matter and conforms to the physical laws that govern it—replaced traditional wisdom, the argument ran, new Soviet men and women would acquire a more enlightened understanding of their physical and, by extension, ideological environment. General political consciousness would inevitably rise, and the quality of life would improve. In order to promote materialism broadly, however, the revolutionary government had to demonstrate its superiority, since Bolshevik leaders knew well that they would not convince the masses with philosophical abstractions. Soviet power needed to marshal practical, professional expertise.

Work in Soviet society during the 1920s therefore did not include room for professional detachment, and the performance of duties and an activist role in mass enlightenment were inseparable. Soviet anthropologists eschewed "scholarly purism" in favor of trying to educate and uplift their rural subjects; academics sought to place the sciences, social sciences, and humanities on a Marxist-Leninist footing; and medical opinion did not flinch from delivering moral prescriptions as it addressed the physical well-being of the population. None of this was as exceptional as it appears from hindsight. During the nineteenth century, folklore in several European countries, for example, was sometimes altered to reflect contemporary political issues such as nationalism. Learning to justify prevailing social values and philosophy in terms of recent developments in science took place throughout Europe and North America, and medicine directly reflected the dominant mores and concerns of the society in which it was practiced. Examples abounded of doctors involved with the sex lives of patients beyond the limits of the health of the organism strictly defined—preventing masturbation in adolescent boys and shielding girls from knowledge of sex were widespread preoccupations.

As one of its many interventionist social strategies, the Bolsheviks therefore enlisted medicine in the task of creating new citizens. Party opinion held that the tsarist state had, in fact, manipulated mass ignorance and fears to ensure the political malleability of workers and peasants, and it counted on poor health and physical exhaustion to stifle unrest. Economic hardship, a limited understanding of technology and science, and primitive notions of health and sanitation had therefore not only been joined but also were self-perpetuating. Under the old regime, peasants felt helpless before illness and the elements, and they viewed misfortune as a punishment for sins. Their belief in the supernatural helped them mitigate these fears and even gave peasants a sense of empowerment, the party argued, but they were as equally likely to seek out the village sorcerer or faith healer as the priest or a medical professional. The poor state of rural medicine at the end of the tsarist period complicated this situation. Even if belief in traditional healers could be eliminated, there were too few doctors and medical facilities in the countryside to make much difference. As a first step, Soviet power therefore tried to extend medical knowledge in the village.

The message, however, could be no more viable than the messengers, and in this previously unstudied case Stephen Frank presents evidence that seriously questions our received assumptions about medical knowledge in rural areas. Letters on medical-sexual matters from peasants of Riazan province in 1925–1928 and responses in Dr. V. N. Voskresenskii's newspaper column demonstrate that the didactic approach that dominated Bolshevik thinking conformed poorly to observed experience. Rather than carrying out instruction broadly and unflinchingly in keeping with the Bolshevik ideal, Voskresenskii was selective in the issues that he addressed in print. Despite the many letters that requested information about sex, the doctor subscribed to the late nineteenth-century perception that the peasant was sexually innocent. Voskresenskii avoided sexual matters when possible or reconfigured questions to stress the lessons that he wished to impart. And as he differentiated "normal" from "abnormal" sexuality in his column, the doctor repeatedly contravened new Soviet ideas about female liberation and the family. For their part, the peasant letter writers did not display the innocence assumed in them by the intelligentsia. Popular healing may have continued to be strong in the village, but peasants also displayed a far-reaching medical curiosity about issues of sexual anatomy. Moreover, they could be insistent in their inquiries and not put off with misdirection or evasive replies.

Stephen P. Frank, associate professor of history at UCLA, received his Ph.D. from Brown University. His publications include Crime, Cultural Conflict, and Justice in Rural Russia, 1856–1914 *(1999);* Cultures in Flux: Lower-Class Values, Practices, and Resistance in Late

Imperial Russia *(as coeditor, 1994); and* The World of the Russian Peasant *(as coeditor, 1990).*

*W*riting from the provincial capital of Riazan in 1928,[1] local doctor V. N. Voskresenskii produced a lengthy official report about state-sponsored rural newspapers and their role in the important task of bringing hygienic and medical knowledge to the peasant population during the anxious period of the NEP (1921–1928).[2] Voskresenskii's report focused on a medical advice column that appeared in the largest rural news organ in the province, *Derevenskaia gazeta* (Village news), and on the hundreds of letters received from peasant readers who had responded to the frequently published advertisement: "Readers! What do you wish to know from the doctor? Send him your questions—he will answer."[3] Given the Soviet government's concern in these years with raising the cultural level of the countryside and especially with improving public health, Voskresenskii played a critical role not only as editor of the newspaper's advice column but also, more important, as the sole respondent to peasant inquiries and the "official" interpreter of their significance and meaning. His report and the letters on which it was largely based therefore provide insight into medical and official views about sex, as well as about the rural population in general, during the mid- to late 1920s. At the same time these sources allow us a glimpse—albeit a very fragmentary one—into the everyday concerns of Russian peasants over issues of family and private life that historians have not previously examined.

In addition to their better-known economic and social impact on the peasantry, the catastrophic events through which Russia had recently passed—World War I, the 1917 February and October revolutions, civil war and famine—devastated medical care primarily by stripping the countryside of trained physicians and paramedics (feldshers) and of funding for local medical stations and provincial hospitals. Although rural health care witnessed modest improvements during the last decades of the tsarist regime, it nevertheless remained grossly insufficient, and extremely primitive or nonexistent in many areas. In 1913 only about 7,000 physicians were employed in rural practice throughout the entire Russian Empire, serving a population of over 100 million. Some 35 percent of all Russian towns had no hospital beds in 1913, and only 21 percent of existing hospitals had more than twenty beds. Even when peasants did turn to professional medical practitioners, therefore, they usually saw either a feldsher or midwife rather than a doctor.

By contemporary estimates, one-half or more of the prerevolutionary peasantry continued to rely on traditional folk healers (*znakhari*), either because they mistrusted medical professionals as being outsiders or did not have ready access to modern medical assistance. With the decimation of the ranks of rural feldshers and especially physicians during World War I and the Civil War, even the slow progress of the late Imperial era was dramatically reversed. The 1920s saw a number of successes in efforts to reestablish an improved public health network, but despite the government's "Face to the Countryside" policy, by 1928 medical care for the peasantry remained far less available and of poorer quality than was the case for town dwellers. Over 40 percent of rural areas had no hospital beds in 1925, for example. In 1926 the entire countryside counted slightly fewer than 6,500 physicians—a figure that grew to only 8,937 by 1929. As a result, the Soviet government would ultimately be forced to rely, like its predecessor, on feldshers and midwives in rural medical practice, and the continued poor state of rural health care and lack of access to modern medical advice or treatment can best be seen during this period in the widespread revival of folk healers as the principal medical practitioners to whom peasants might turn for aid or advice.[4]

Forged from the Bolsheviks' firm faith in science, materialism, and "enlightenment" (understood primarily as education), early Soviet health policy focused on the science of "social hygiene," the practitioners of which, as historian Susan Solomon explains, "were to examine the social conditions within which disease occurred and spread and to propose social measures which would contribute to the . . . goal of preventing disease."[5] Preventive medicine, however, proved extraordinarily difficult to implement in the impoverished countryside, where it collided with limited state resources, the pressing need for immediate treatment, and the extreme reluctance of medical professionals and semiprofessionals to devote precious time to propaganda and educational campaigns against such problems as alcoholism. Still, this policy certainly influenced Dr. Voskresenskii's selection of peasant letters for his advice column, allowing him to discuss prevention above all else (the choice of questions about venereal disease stands out most prominently here). It also helped to shape the type of advice that he gave on matters of abortion or sex, although in this important area other elements came into play as well. Chief among these was a widespread and long-standing elite view of the rural population that saw peasants not simply as ignorant and backward but also innocent and nonsexual, still existing in a more "natural" state than members of other classes.[6] Only the continued strength of such views can fully explain how medical professionals such as Voskresenskii might ignore direct evidence to the contrary as it was presented regularly in his correspondents' own words (and in numerous contemporary studies of village life). Instead, as we shall see, he used peasant letters to reinforce prevailing opinion about sex and about the peasantry itself, often ignoring entirely the content of their requests for advice—requests that reflected the continued plight of rural health care, which left a substantial proportion of country people with no local, confidential recourse to trustworthy medical advice.

The newspaper *Nasha derevnia* (Our countryside), which served as an official organ of the Riazan Provincial Committee and the Provincial Executive Committee of the Russian Communist Party, began as a weekly in 1925 with a publication of just over 3,000 copies per issue. Renamed *Derevenskaia gazeta* at the end of that year, the paper's circulation grew to 12,800 in 1926, 17,400 in 1927, and reached 23,000 in 1928.[7] Unfortunately, the majority of questions sent by peasants to the paper's advice column was not published, and many of the original letters have not survived, making it impossible to provide a precise breakdown of the questions. Voskresenskii explained that most inquiries were answered by mail, with only a small portion printed in the newspaper. Nearly all of the questions demanded earnest attention, he stressed, with the exception of those that were "absurd, empty, or not serious."[8] In his opinion, the fact that peasants flooded the newspaper's advice column with questions was a clear indication of their "extreme need for medical advice" (and, by extension, the shortage of such advice). Indeed, it was the lack of sufficient medical assistance, especially in the many localities that did not have ready access to medical stations, that was abetting the universal revival and growth of folk medicine (*znakharstvo*).

Despite Voskresenskii's use of their questions as evidence of widespread ignorance, the peasants' letters often demonstrate at least a basic understanding of disease—a fact that would often contradict contemporary commentary on rural medical knowledge. Voskresenskii voiced his disappointment, however, over the fact that the letters expressed very little interest in matters of public or social hygiene. Rather, Riazan villagers appeared far more concerned with personal health and disease prevention. Not a few inquired about the possible effects of tobacco and alcohol: "Does tobacco act harmfully on the organism?" "What is the danger of vodka and tobacco?" "How does alcoholism affect children?" "Can mothers drink liquor?" for example.[9] "Is it possible to contract cancer from smoking and drunkenness?" asked one correspondent. "How does one recognize the beginning of cancer?" another wished to know. Yet most inquiries addressed the contagious diseases that remained widespread throughout rural areas during the 1920s. Some hoped to learn whether it was possible to prevent measles, and, if so, how. Many requested information about tuberculosis, including its symptoms, whether it was contagious or hereditary, how one contracted the disease if it was not passed on by one's parents, and if one could marry a woman whose husband had died of tuberculosis. Echoing long-standing beliefs that the communal shepherd was often a source of contagion, at least one peasant asked *Derevenskaia gazeta* which specific illnesses might shepherds transmit to others in the community. Individual peasants or groups of villagers sought out advice on matters of personal hygiene, including how to maintain healthy teeth and how to bathe properly. Others were interested in whether sports were good, whether fasting was useful (a clear reference to the frequent fast days in the Orthodox calendar that still influenced rural life), or "what can happen as a result of difficult work?" Finally, we might note certain questions that involved issues traceable to health concerns expressed by medical professionals as far back as the midnineteenth century, such as whether it was unhealthy or dangerous to keep livestock in peasants' cottages, or how to dry out the land upon which one's cottage stood.[10]

Dr. Voskresenskii left questions touching upon sexual life to the final pages of his report, although he admitted that they were the subject of many letters. Interest in questions about sex was growing rapidly, he noted, a fact evidently explained solely by the peasants' "complete ignorance and lack of education" about the most basic matters. This evident concern over sex did not rest simply upon assumptions of "ignorance," however, but drew from widespread worries during the 1920s over what many people perceived as a weakening of traditional sexual mores among the rural population, and especially the "freer forms" that "mutual relations between the sexes" had taken among village youths.[11] Perhaps as a direct result of such fears about "innocent" peasants sinking into what some social hygienists termed "disorderly sexuality," the thrust of Voskresenskii's replies to their letters was clearly intended to urge his village readers back on the path to "normalcy"—that is, to a more traditional and "natural" type of sexuality. His frequent emphasis as to what constituted "normal" and "abnormal" sex, like his advice concerning the fundamental purpose of sexual relations, repeatedly if only implicitly raised the distinction, held by many in the medical profession, between urban and rural sex. As one sexologist explained this difference based on a 1929 study of the sexual lives of Ukrainian village women, "rural sexual life was not characterized by the same 'lust' as in the city; it was more natural."[12]

Letter writers asked a broad array of questions on topics ranging from birth control and pregnancy to anomalies of the sex organs, prostitution, and sexually transmitted diseases. Although we cannot know the actual range for certain, among letters published in *Derevenskaia gazeta* and those discussed in Voskresenskii's report the most frequent subjects of peasant inquiry were birth control, masturbation, and venereal disease (specifically, syphilis and gonorrhea), each of which will be discussed below. As for other questions, some peasants requested information that we might have expected to be readily available in the village. Women sent in a number of letters about menstruation, for example: "When do 'the monthlies' happen?" "What is the right way to deal with menstruation?" or "If menstruation does not occur for several months in a row, is this harmful to a woman's health?" One Firsova, from the large commercial village of Beloomut, wrote in 1928 asking simply "about menstruation." In addition to telling Firsova when menstruation began among most Russian women and pointing out its temporary cessation during pregnancy and breast-feeding, Voskresenskii also stressed that sexual relations during menstruation could be dangerous for women.[13] Other letter writers, inquiring as to the age at which puberty or sexual maturity began, received surprisingly inconsistent answers. Among men, one correspondent was told in 1927, puberty usually began at age 19–20, "and therefore this will be the very youngest age at which normal impregnation is possible." Several months later, however, a reply to the same question stated that male sexual maturity began at about fifteen to sixteen years of age, while for women the onset of puberty "begins at 13–15 years of age, and is completely developed after age 15."[14] Some peasants even wrote to learn the best age to get married.

"Nocturnal emission" (spermatorrhea, or *polliutsiia* in Russian) concerned at least several peasants sufficiently to send letters to the advice column. Some merely asked what it was, while others sought treatment. To one such question in 1927, *Derevenskaia gazeta* explained that if nocturnal emission occurred rarely (only once or twice per month), then it was unnecessary to take any specific measures. But if it happened frequently, leading to weakness or other symptoms, the doctor recommended taking a half-hour walk before sleeping, washing or bathing in cold water, and not eating at night. One should sleep in a cool room, not covered too warmly, and it was best not to sleep with one's face to the pillow but instead on the side or back. Finally, and perhaps more difficult, "it is necessary to eliminate everything that might bring on sexual arousal."[15]

I. Makarov and M. Kriuchkov of Kamenets village wrote to *Derevenskaia gazeta* in September 1927 asking whether sexual intercourse affected one's intelligence; they were told that, for the most part, it did not, but only "when one does not have excessive, inordinate sexual relations." The doctor advised them to limit themselves to a "normal" amount of sexual intercourse—"up to two times per week." Here, peasant writers likely thought that they had not received direct or complete answers to their questions. Surely the female correspondent who asked, in 1926, "how often does [a man] need to have relations with a woman," could not have been fully satisfied with Voskresenskii's response, for he altered the question to focus solely on the "goal of impregnation," which could occur with a single act of copulation. Once pregnant, he added, returning readers to the regular theme of "normal" sex, "the woman's sexual attraction to the man disappears"; moreover, "sexual relations during pregnancy are abnormal and, for the woman, unpleasant." As long as a woman continued to breast-feed her child, sexual relations remained similarly "abnormal."[16] In short, peasants were being told repeatedly that conception was the fundamental, if not sole, purpose of intercourse.

It would appear that questions about sexual relations were much less likely to be published or to receive a direct answer. Among those not published, for example, were letters asking how one could know for certain whether a maiden was no longer a virgin, what was the danger in having sexual relations while standing, and "why is it that when a young man is close to the female sex organ, he gets an erection?"[17] Questions that could be interpreted in different ways were given the briefest of replies that ignored other possible meanings of what was being asked. R. V. Rogachev, for instance, wrote in early 1928 to ask: "Can a man be made into a woman?" Voskresenskii answered with a few terse sentences concerning various scientific experiments that had been conducted on transplanting sex glands from animal to animal, human to human, and animal to human, but explained that it was "impossible to completely change the sex of a person." In a reply to a question from I. S. Baron of Kiselevo village, the doctor explained: "Venereal diseases of humans cannot be passed on to livestock, and, likewise, people cannot contract sexual diseases from livestock or horses."[18]

Although few of their questions were published, peasants sought explanations and possible cures for impotence or other sexual afflictions which they obviously believed could not be discussed openly among themselves, or even within the family: "I read in *Derevenskaia gazeta* that they give doctors' advice about all illnesses," wrote "the Suffering One." "I have been afflicted for about two months with impotence and I therefore ask you to give me an answer about whether this can be cured and how it can be cured. Answer in *Derevenskaia gazeta* because I subscribe to it, and if you send a letter by mail it would lead to unpleasantness in the family." Among the more peculiar (and unpublished) questions asked— the reply to which is not known—was the following: "When I got married I had normal sexual relations, but after awhile things changed completely so that now during sex I have no desire at all, which I conclude is because of a curvature of my sexual organ which worries me a lot; and therefore I beg the editors to tell me how to cure this and why it happened, because my sexual organ does not fit into the vagina."[19]

Not surprisingly, a substantial portion of letters directed to *Derevenskaia gazeta* from women asked for information on how to prevent pregnancy. Here we find a particularly revealing exchange between peasants seeking knowledge and the often contradictory positions taken by medical officials on birth control. Doctors such as Voskresenskii were greatly concerned by a dramatic increase in the number of abortions during the early 1920s—a method that, for many rural women, served as the only available means of birth control. Most replies in the advice column therefore usually began with stern warnings about the danger of abortion, stressing the health risks that could result especially when the procedure was done by "nonspecialists" such as traditional healers or midwives. Voskresenskii also informed his readers, including a woman who wrote in 1926 to ask whether abortions were now performed in hospitals, about the laws pertaining to abortion. These procedures were to be carried out only in hospitals and only by doctors, he explained, underscoring the fact that it was illegal to perform abortions outside of hospitals. Among women who turned to a midwife or healer, he noted, more than one-half ended up as invalids unable to work, and many died from blood infections. In short, "you must go to your hospital to request an abortion."[20]

Still, rural women throughout Riazan province continued to "ask the doctor," sending letters (often signed by several villagers) throughout the years 1925–1929 that repeated over and again (and with growing frequency) the same request for advice on birth control "without having to turn to abortion." Primarily with the aim of fighting abortion, then, Voskresenskii advised correspondents of several birth-control options that might be tried, although he emphasized that, at the present time, there was no sure means of preventing pregnancy. Incorrectly, women were told to avoid sexual relations during the first week after menstruation. They might also use a douche solution of water and two tablespoons of pyroligneous acid (wood vinegar). Among "artificial" methods, the doctor noted that while protective coverings (usually metal) existed that fit over the cervix, these often caused irritation inside the vagina. By far the most "trustworthy" means of preventing pregnancy was to use a condom (commonly mispronounced *gondon* in the countryside) before copulation. Although already available for several decades in Russia, peasants still had limited or no access to condoms or else remained concerned about the possible harm that might result from their use, for at least one person wrote to ask whether it was dangerous for either the man or the woman to have sexual relations using a *gondon*.

Judging by the number of questions regarding its possible health effects, many Riazan peasants practiced "the withdrawal method" (*coitus interruptus*) but obviously were apprehensive about it. One peasant wrote: "When having sexual relations with my wife and being concerned with not making her pregnant, . . . I withdraw my sexual organ from my wife and everything that's there comes out onto the bedding, and I have used this method for two years and my wife hasn't gotten pregnant, but I am worried that [our] health might suffer from this so I beg you to reply." "Is it harmful to the health," another asked in 1925, "if, during copulation, the husband artificially ejects semen not into the sexual organs, but externally?"[21] Voskresenskii's replies could not have put his correspondents' minds at ease, for while he admitted that *coitus interruptus* was one possible means of preventing conception, it could have a serious impact on the health of both men and women. In one reply from late 1925 the doctor noted that medical opinion differed on the question of "such abnormal copulation": some specialists considered it not at all unhealthy, while others viewed it as harmful, "especially for the man or, in general, for people with weak nerves." In later replies, however, Voskresenskii spoke only in negative terms. *Coitus interruptus*, he told I. A. Naumov in 1928, could result in various maladies of the female sex organs and cause disorders of the nervous system among men. In another letter that same year he informed a group of peasants who had written for advice on birth control that the withdrawal method had a serious impact on women: "Not having received complete sexual satisfaction, nervous disorders can develop among women, and sometimes an inflammation of the internal sexual organs."[22] In other words, he told them, a woman could be fully satisfied only when a man did not withdraw before ejaculating inside her, and thereby completed intercourse in a "normal" manner (potentially leading to pregnancy).

One last, particularly revealing commentary recited to peasant women who asked about birth control emphasized their duty to bear children. The question of preventing pregnancy, after all, was no simple matter but a very grave issue, Voskresenskii wrote in 1926 when replying to "Citizen" (*grazhdanka*): "A woman should remember that her calling is to bear children," and for not wanting to do so "she will often pay in the future with a series of illnesses, especially in those cases when an abortion is carried out." Here, unlike in other replies, Voskresenskii did not even bother to answer the woman's question as to "how one protects oneself against pregnancy," but instead advised her to purchase the book by Dr. M. F. Levi entitled *The Prevention of Pregnancy as a Means of Fighting Abortion*, which was sold in Moscow for 20 kopecks.[23]

According to Voskresenskii, the subject of masturbation (*onanism*) appeared "completely unexpectedly" in a great many letters. As a "secret vice," the doctor explained, masturbation was not a matter of open discussion for the masses. But the guarantee of secrecy offered by his advice column had elicited this question, thereby leading outsiders like himself to speculate on the extent of masturbation among the peasantry. These letters, he stressed, were written without circumlocution and were clear requests for help and a cure from "this difficult misfortune." Given the symptoms about which correspondents wrote, moreover, it would appear that nearly all writers whose questions appeared in print were male. Certainly, letters published in *Derevenskaia gazeta* and those discussed in

Voskresenskii's report all speak of the harmful effects of masturbation on men rather than on both sexes. The only exception was a single query, written by a woman, asking whether female masturbators can bear children and whether male masturbators are capable of impregnating a woman.

Selectivity definitely played a major role in the nature of the questions published, for without exception all asked whether masturbation was harmful, how it affected penis size, and whether and how it could be cured. There was, then, a convenient match between the letters chosen for inclusion in the newspaper's advice column and prevailing official, medical, and traditional views on this topic.[24] In one of the most detailed (and thus unpublished) questions, a peasant signing himself "Interested" asked: "Is it possible to cure masturbation, which began at age 18 but hasn't been practiced too frequently, but which in my opinion has anyway affected the growth of my member (*chlen*) and my health [because] I have become very anemic and sluggish. In this condition can I have a wife and am I able to make her pregnant? I beg you to reply whether it is possible to hope for a cure of impotence and for the growth of [one's] member." The same worries were expressed in another letter, whose author wanted to know whether the results of masturbation could be cured without regard to one's age. Specifically, this peasant voiced particular concern about impotence and nervous disorders, which he attributed to masturbation, and also asked if it were possible to increase the size of his penis.[25]

In all replies to letters of this sort, Dr. Voskresenskii sought to emphasize the "unnatural" or "abnormal" nature of masturbation when compared to "natural sexual relations." To those peasants (including "Masturbator") who asked whether masturbation was harmful, the doctor told them that many men suffered from this "secret vice" and ruined their health in the process: "The *onanist* excites himself, forcing his imagination to paint a voluptuous picture. This is a great strain on the nervous system and the heart. The consequences of masturbation are extremely serious and often lead to impotence—that is, the inability to have normal sexual relations."[26] Commenting on another letter in 1928, Voskresenskii explained to K. M. Durov that "the artificial ejaculation of semen" (evidently his own definition of masturbation) was harmful, for it could result in a dramatic, negative impact on the organism. In the lengthiest response, given by the doctor to a question from N. Morgunov, he wrote that masturbation (also called, literally, "fornication by the hand," or *rukobludie*) was a disease that damaged a person's health: "Sexual stimulation during intercourse with women concludes more quickly than during masturbation. Masturbation is dangerous . . . , causing a series of disorders of the nervous system, the appearance of irritability, depression, loss of weight, and significant changes in sexual ability during intercourse. In the childhood years, masturbation influences growth and leads to obtuseness and the poor mastering of science."[27] We might underline here Voskresenskii's telling comment on the more rapid achievement of ejaculation during "intercourse with women," and the imbedded counterpoint suggesting the abnormality of lengthy self-stimulation. Once again, peasants read that "normal" sex was brief and that its implicit outcome was conception.

Rather than fulfilling its stated goal to provide "ignorant" peasants with an enlightened source of information on questions that concerned them the most, Voskresenskii's advice column served, above all, to disseminate traditional views (which remained strong during and after NEP) about sex, gender, and the very nature of the peasantry itself. These views could be seen most sharply in his writings on syphilis, for here he—as well as much of the Soviet health profession—continued to perpetuate the opinion, which originated in the prerevolutionary era, that the transmission of syphilis among peasants was primarily nonsexual. "Infection with syphilis," he explained in a 1925 reply, "takes place through both sexual and nonsexual means. In the countryside, nonsexual syphilis is most widespread." He stressed the same causation in 1927, writing that "common syphilis" had become prevalent in villages of Riazan province "not through sexual means." Instead, "crowded conditions, congestion, and lack of culture lead to mass infection. Syphilis is brought to the countryside by soldiers, and by peasants who go off to work in crafts and factories." The struggle against rural syphilis, he argued, should be fought by "increasing culture and literacy in the villages, by improving daily life and living conditions" as well as personal hygiene. In other articles, too, he emphasized strict observance of good hygiene as the main way to avoid infection by syphilis. Peasants were therefore advised to stop the dangerous custom of kissing as a common greeting ("conscious citizens should cease kissing people they do not know"), to not share cigarettes with others or drink vodka with "unknown people," to not use another's razor or towels, and to thoroughly wash the benches at the bathhouse. Only in 1928 did Voskresenskii begin telling his correspondents on a more regular basis that transmission of syphilis and gonorrhea also occurred during sexual relations, and that a man should therefore never have relations with unknown women, "especially when intoxicated."[28] But even when acknowledging infection through sexual intercourse, Voskresenskii continued to include lengthy information about nonvenereal sources of transmission.

As they had done before the 1917 revolutions, during the 1920s peasants sought beneficial knowledge and solutions to serious problems wherever they might find them. Given the poor state of rural health care and a lack of ready access to medical advice in the countryside, it is easy to understand why so many of them composed letters to *Derevenskaia gazeta*, sending their questions about disease or sex to the professionals in the provincial capital and waiting for knowledge to reach them either through the mail or in the "Ask the Doctor" column. The peasantry's willingness or eagerness to write to outsiders in the case of inquiries about more "delicate" or embarrassing matters of a sexual nature is especially evident, since these problems were not easily discussed at home or in the wider rural community.

What may appear remarkable at first glance, however, is the strikingly conservative tone of the replies, particularly in light of the radical views that pervaded early Soviet ideology on subjects such as social and personal life, or even sexuality. We might attribute this apparent contradiction between pronouncements and practice to the simple fact that so much of the historical study of the 1920s has focused on ideology and ideological struggles within the Bolshevik/Communist Party. Such works have emphasized the conflict of early Bolshevik utopianism or radicalism with the practical problem of reconstruction and ruling, a conflict that culminated in the Great Retreat to more conservative policies and approaches at the end of the decade. Yet, as Dr. Voskresenskii's advice column attests, and as more recent investigations of problems at the lower levels of administration have shown, in a vast range of areas of early Soviet life the utopianism of small segments of the social or political elite was not necessarily shared throughout the party apparatus, state administration, or especially society. The prerevolutionary cultural construction of the Russian peasants' "nature" and "sexuality" (or lack thereof), much of which carried over into the 1920s and was highly visible in *Derevenskaia gazeta*'s advice column, did not always correspond comfortably with theoretical or policy-oriented discussions of either village life or sex, since relatively conservative and paternalistic views of peasantry remained, to a great extent, dominant throughout and far beyond the era of NEP.

NOTES

1. Among the poorest and most agricultural areas in central Russia, Riazan province is directly to the southeast of Moscow.

2. The report, "Krestianskie gazety i sanitarnoe prosveshchenie," is located in the manuscript division of the Riazanskii Istoriko-Arkhitekturnyi Muzei-Zapovednik in Riazan (hereafter cited as RIAMZ), III/828, No. 315.

3. *Derevenskaia gazeta*, no. 9, February 1, 1926.

4. This information is drawn from Mark G. Field, *Soviet Socialized Medicine: An Introduction* (New York, 1967), p. 27; Samuel C. Ramer, "Traditional Healers and Peasant Culture in Russia, 1861–1917," in *Peasant Economy, Culture, and Politics of European Russia, 1800–1921*, ed. Esther Kingston-Mann and Timothy Mixter (Princeton, 1991), pp. 207–32; Samuel C. Ramer, "Feldshers and Rural Health Care in the Early Soviet Period," and Neil B. Weissman, "Origins of Soviet Health Administration: Narkomzdrav, 1918–1928," both in *Health and Society in Revolutionary Russia*, ed. Susan Gross Solomon and John F. Hutchinson (Bloomington, IN, 1990), pp. 121–45, 97–120.

5. Susan Gross Solomon, "Social Hygiene and Soviet Public Health, 1921–1930," in *Health and Society in Revolutionary Russia*, ed. Susan Gross Solomon and John F. Hutchinson (Bloomington, IN, 1990), p. 175.

6. Susan Gross Solomon, "Innocence and Sexuality in Soviet Medical Discourse," in *Women in Russia and Ukraine*, ed. Rosalind Marsh (Cambridge, MA, 1996), pp. 121–30, discusses this view of the peasantry. For its origins in the prerevolutionary period see Laura Engelstein, *The Keys to Happiness: Sex and the Search for Modernity in Fin-de-Siècle Russia* (Ithaca, 1992), pp. 165–211.

7. RIAMZ, III/828, No. 315, p. 28. A brief history of the rural press in Riazan province is provided on pp. 28–36.

8. Ibid., p. 7.

9. Ibid., p. 32.

10. Ibid., p. 33.

11. For one of many such commentaries see V. A. Murin, *Byt i nravy derevenskoi molodezhi* [Life and morals of rural youth] (Moscow, 1926), pp. 95–96.

12. Solomon, "Innocence and Sexuality," p. 124.

13. Ibid., pp. 39–40; *Derevenskaia gazeta*, no. 23, March 25, 1928.

14. *Derevenskaia gazeta*, no. 18, March 9, 1927; ibid., no. 65, September 4, 1927.

15. Ibid., no. 4, January 16, 1927.

16. Ibid., no. 63, August 22, 1926.

17. RIAMZ, III/828, No. 315, p. 39.

18. *Derevenskaia gazeta*, no. 7, January 26, 1928; ibid., no. 7, January 24, 1929.

19. RIAMZ, III/828, No. 315, pp. 38–39.

20. *Derevenskaia gazeta*, no. 96, December 23, 1926.

21. RIAMZ, III/828, No. 315, p. 37; *Derevenskaia gazeta*, no. 46, December 12, 1925.

22. *Derevenskaia gazeta*, no. 46, December 12, 1925; ibid., no. 19, March 11, 1928; ibid., no. 23, March 25, 1928.

23. *Derevenskaia gazeta*, no. 27, April 10, 1926.

24. For a brief discussion of Soviet medical views on masturbation see Eric Naiman, *Sex in Public: The Incarnation of Early Soviet Ideology* (Princeton, 1997), pp. 120–23. Compare prerevolutionary opinions in Engelstein, *Keys to Happiness*, pp. 226–28, 234–37, 244–48.

25. RIAMZ, III/828, No. 315, p. 38.

26. *Derevenskaia gazeta*, no. 25, April 3, 1926.

27. Ibid., no. 75, October 8, 1927.

28. Ibid., no. 45, December 9, 1925; ibid., no. 24, April 2, 1927; ibid., no. 87, November 24, 1927.

SUGGESTED READINGS

At present there are no studies dealing specifically with issues of sex and sexuality among peasants during the Soviet period. On the prerevolutionary countryside see Barbara Alpern Engel, "Peasant Morality and Pre-Marital Relations in Late 19th Century Russia," *Journal of Social History* 23 (1990): 695–714; Christine D. Worobec, *Peasant Russia: Family and Community in the Post-Emancipation Period* (Princeton, 1991); and Stephen P. Frank, " 'Simple Folk, Savage Customs?' Youth, Sociability, and the Dynamics of Culture in Rural Russia, 1856–1914," *Journal of Social History* 25 (1992): 711–36. Laura Engelstein, *The Keys to Happiness: Sex and the Search for Modernity in Fin-de-Siècle Russia* (Ithaca, 1992), treats the legal and medical discourses on sex before 1917. On the Soviet period, Peter Kenez, *The Birth of the Propaganda State: Soviet Methods of Mass Mobilization, 1917–1929* (Cambridge, 1985), and V. A. Kozlov, *Kulturnaia revoliutsiia i krestianstvo, 1921–1927. (Po materialam Evropeiskoi chasti RSFSR) [Cultural revolution and the peasantry, 1921–1927. Based on materials from the European part of the RSFSR]* (Moscow, 1983), provide good introductions to mass educational campaigns, although neither addresses sex education. Mark G. Field, *Soviet Socialized Medicine: An Introduction* (New York, 1967), contains a brief survey of the development of Soviet health policies.

Among many naive studies of Soviet health care by Western physicians see Edward Podolsky, *Red Miracle: The Story of Soviet Medicine* (New York, 1947). To date the only study to examine sex education in depth is Frances L. Bernstein, *The Dictatorship of Sex: Enlightenment, Health, and Deviance in Revolutionary Russia, 1918–1931* (forthcoming), which treats in much greater detail several of the issues raised in the present chapter. Others that deal with various aspects of Bolshevik and medical attitudes toward sex include Susan Gross Solomon and John F. Hutchinson, eds., *Health and Society in Revolutionary Russia* (Bloomington, IN, 1990); Sheila Fitzpatrick, "Sex and Revolution," in idem, *The Cultural Front: Power and Culture in Revolutionary Russia* (Ithaca, 1992), 65–90; Susan Gross Solomon, "Innocence and Sexuality in Soviet Medical Discourse," in *Women in Russia and Ukraine*, edited by Rosalind Marsh (Cambridge, MA, 1996), 121–30; and Eric Naiman, *Sex in Public: The Incarnation of Early Soviet Ideology* (Princeton, 1997).

PART III

THE GREAT TURN

One can scarcely exaggerate the impact of the Great Turn of 1928–29 on Soviet history. Following the political victory of Stalin, a program of rapid industrialization, the forced collectivization of agriculture, and the Cultural Revolution all moved forward simultaneously, and Soviet power abruptly ended the experimental period that was NEP. This Great Turn encompassed, paradoxically, radical measures to achieve socialism rapidly as well as the restoration of traditional standards of social stability, and in its most extreme form it signaled nothing short of the beginning of class warfare. During the succession struggle of 1924–1928, Stalin had consistently expressed general support for a more rapid, centrally planned transformation to socialism, but he allowed temporary allies such as Nikolai Bukharin to take the lead in public statements. Now confident of his authority, Stalin's pronouncements became more confrontational after 1928, and he consistently blamed class enemies for the nation's problems.

Even Stalin's most incendiary rhetoric, however, could not prepare the country for what took place. In industry, the implementation of the First Five-Year Plan set quotas that would have taxed a thriving industrial power and were impossible in a country as economically depressed as Soviet Russia. Large-scale projects and heightened work tempos nevertheless came to predominate in heavy industry and construction, while mobilization campaigns replaced planning (in any rational, economic sense of the term). And although some managers, economists, and local officials argued for a more realistic approach, Stalin blamed engineers and technical experts with unacceptable class backgrounds for shortfalls in industry and other failures, and he orchestrated show trials of these "wreckers" and "saboteurs." Simultaneously, party propaganda slogans belabored the theme of fulfilling the Five-Year Plan in four years.

The forced collectivization of agriculture and liquidation of the kulaks as a class were, if such were possible, even more draconian. Beginning in early 1928, Stalin vehemently upbraided local officials for leniency toward the most prosperous stratum of the peasantry, known as kulaks, whom he held responsible for the state's food shortages and grain procurement problems. Stalin's militant approach laid the foundation for a general collectivization of agriculture that began in October 1929. Originally presented as a gradual transformation of the countryside, the campaign quickly assumed the proportions of a civil war between state and

109

village. Relying extensively on coercion, Soviet power had moved more than 58 percent of peasant households onto collective farms by March 1930 and deported troublesome elements—the term "kulak" became elastic amid the lawlessness that prevailed—to distant regions. By 1936 nearly 90 percent of the peasants were collectivized, and in the process Soviet militants made a concerted effort to eradicate the traditional rural lifestyle. Not surprisingly, the displacement caused by this abrupt uprooting of so large a proportion of the population and the concomitant disruption of the agricultural cycle brought on a major famine and losses of livestock that would continue to be felt decades later.

Stalin also exploited the mood of radicalism and revolutionary impatience that had arisen during the revolution's first decade, especially but by no means exclusively among the young. At the end of the 1920s the state moved resolutely against the entrepreneurs known as NEPmen, whose position had been insecure even at the height of NEP. The state increased their business taxes exponentially, and often retroactively, as a prelude to depriving entrepreneurs of apartments, personal possessions, and ration cards for food. More broadly, during 1928–1932 a cultural revolution against gradualism took place in virtually every Soviet institution and sphere of life. Radicals scrapped the experimental social programs that characterized NEP, drove political moderates and others who remained from the tsarist period out of Soviet institutions, and intensified revolutionary vigilance. As this mood of socialist extremism ran its course, an emerging xenophobia and proletarian prudishness reverberated from law, film, and architecture to jazz, literature, history, and education.

By 1928–29 the party itself underwent a significant transformation. Membership expanded exponentially—the 25,000 members of February 1917 mushroomed to more than 1 million by the late 1920s—and the social and educational profile of the party changed significantly. The intellectuals who had dominated the prerevolutionary leadership exercised less sway over the young, urban, poorly educated males who predominated among the newer cadres. Moreover, the experiences of the early years of Soviet power caused the Communist Party to place the ability to complete assignments, even if ruthlessly, above the ideological sophistication that had been critical to prerevolutionary reputations. Stalin understood well this new mood among the party rank and file and the public. His ability to mix political and economic iconoclasm with social conservatism enabled him to appeal to cynics, opportunists, those desiring simply to build careers in the new order, and idealists alike. His consistently correct appraisals of popular attitudes resonated with proponents of a renewed socialist radicalism as well as citizens who primarily desired the return of security and normalcy. By the mid-1930s, NEP social engineering was largely a memory, and Soviet society returned to traditional Russian roots as a result of the so-called Great Retreat. In addition, even outside the circle of Stalinist henchmen and their dupes, the policies of the Great Turn held out the multiple prospects of settling real and imagined scores, satisfying a yearning for stability and tradition, and making the revolution fulfill the expectations of 1917.

Not all of the dimensions of the Great Turn were fully evident at the time. The scale of human and material waste was, of course, unprecedented in Russia, and it has few rivals anywhere in human history. Moreover, the Great Turn marked—if not the death of Marxist ideology in Soviet Russia—the demise of ideology as an active force that directly configured party policy and actions. Thus, although the tenets of Marxism acted effectively to limit leadership decisions prior to 1928 and prevented any unbridled recourse to expediency, it would be difficult to find ideological justification for the Great Turn. Individual guardians of ideological purity continued to appear among the leadership until the demise of the Soviet Union (the career of Mikhail Suslov under Nikita Khrushchev and Leonid Brezhnev stands out in this regard), but after the Great Turn, Marxism was reduced more to the dominant idiom of political discourse than a revolutionary force in the national mission. Finally, the Great Turn set new socialist initiatives into motion but squelched a number of others already extant. In this connection, the principle of reforging (*perekovka*), which was as old as the revolution itself, was central. We have already seen that from the outset the Bolsheviks believed they could recast citizens into proletarians, and the rise of Stalin did not influence the party to abandon this aspiration. On the contrary, even penal labor could, in the Stalinist schema, theoretically act as a positive force of social engineering.* But the abruptness with which the revolution changed direction at the end of the 1920s caused projects such as those to reform prostitutes to lose momentum (Chapter 8), provided evidence that earlier efforts to curb alcohol abuse among workers had come to little (Chapter 9), and brought to light contradictions and weaknesses within the Soviet regime (Chapter 10). In a large sense at odds with its own announced objectives, the effects of the Great Turn are being felt in Russia to the present day.

---

*On this point see Cynthia A. Ruder, *Making History for Stalin: The Story of the Belomor Canal* (Gainesville, FL, 1999).

CHAPTER 8

Prostitutes and Proletarians

The Soviet Labor Clinic as Revolutionary Laboratory

FRANCES L. BERNSTEIN

There could be no more symbolic victory of socialism over capitalism in the Soviet Union than the elimination of prostitution. Marxists regularly attributed the existence of prostitution to socioeconomic exploitation. German Social-Democrat August Bebel contended in the nineteenth century that "marriage represents one side of sex life in bourgeois society and prostitution the other"; Lenin wrote in 1913 that "as long as wage slavery exists, prostitution must inevitably continue." But the egalitarianism of socialism was to end exploitation and its social ramifications. Soviet society intended not only to create new economic opportunities for future generations of women but also to reclaim existing prostitutes as productive citizens.

The tsarist regime had been particularly vulnerable to criticism for its handling of the issue. The state criminalized procuring as early as the seventeenth century, but it elected to address prostitution itself through administrative regulation by the Ministry of Interior and the police. Prostitution received no official welcome in Russia, to be sure, but except for one relatively brief period (1845–1866) statutes against it were absent from the legal codes. The goal was to limit the spread of sexually transmitted diseases, and to this end Catherine the Great introduced the medical inspection of prostitutes during the second half of the eighteenth century. Her son, Tsar Paul I, forced some women to wear yellow dresses as a sign of their profession and banished others to forced labor in Siberia. Attention to the issue then became more systematic in 1843 when Nicholas I implemented detailed regulations modeled on the French State Regulation of Vice, which entailed the registration of prostitutes, mandatory periodic medical examinations, and licensing of brothels. Registered prostitutes in Russia were to undergo a weekly bath, change linen after each session of intercourse, not work during menstruation, and even be limited in the amount and type of makeup they wore. In practice, however, the police sometimes conducted a hundred of the required genital examinations per hour without requiring the women to disrobe fully, and the unregistered streetwalkers who plied the trade outside the brothels did not appear at all. Not surprisingly, by the 1890s venereal disease was spreading at alarming rates among the urban population, and syphilis reached epidemic levels in the countryside.

By the beginning of the twentieth century, the tsarist approach had achieved scant success. First, in addition to failing to control the spread of disease, regulation actually made it more difficult for prostitutes to leave the profession. During the Great Reforms, Alexander II had added a significant new rule. Every woman arrested for plying the trade—including desperate female workers who practiced so-called casual prostitution only periodically when they could not otherwise make ends meet—surrendered her passport and was issued a document called a "yellow ticket." This rule had serious ramifications. Every Russian citizen was required to carry an internal passport (which had to be shown to the police on demand) that listed one's social class and permanent residence. In addition to limiting personal mobility, the passport was required when applying for work or renting a room. The embarrassing yellow ticket consequently cut off its bearer from legitimate pursuits and mainstream society, even if she had desired to change her life. Second, with the marked increase in peasant migration to the cities during the second half of the nineteenth century, the corps of urban prostitutes expanded significantly and reached levels comparable to those of London, Paris, Berlin, and Vienna. Contrary to commonly repeated tales, new recruits usually were not inexperienced peasants who fell into the clutches of bordello operators immediately upon arrival, but typically had worked as domestics or in manufacturing for several years before taking up prostitution. By the turn of the century, independent philanthropic groups attempted to offset the state's ineffectual efforts to combat prostitution, usually by setting up shelters and attempting to smooth the reentry of former prostitutes into the work force.

To achieve revolutionary goals, Bolshevik approaches after 1917 not only had to wean women from the life of prostitution but also provide them the wherewithal to become economically independent and socially productive. Dismissing philanthropic efforts as bourgeois and self-serving, the state began in 1924 to establish labor clinics that would address socioeconomic considerations and, in the process, remove women infected with sexually transmitted diseases from circulation. In this essay, which concentrates on the objectives, biases, and perspectives of clinic organizers, Frances Bernstein examines both the success stories that dominated official publications on the subject and evidence of shortfalls. An innovation of the 1920s, the clinics were gradually closed during the 1930s when the social experimentation that had been associated with NEP fell out of favor.

Frances L. Bernstein, assistant professor of history at Drew University, is the author of The Dictatorship of Sex: Enlightenment, Health, and Deviance in Revolutionary Russia, 1918–1931 *(forthcoming). She received her Ph.D. from Columbia University.*

By the calm moonlight
In the month of May
The brothel where I lay
Was raided and I was taken that night.
The cold prison once more,
Witnesses, questions galore;
Mean questions, and brutal they are
When a prostitute stands at the bar.
Five years in a prison cell
From my young life men stole;
They took a heavy toll,
Those years of unforgotten hell.
But now it is past like a dream.
I am that country's daughter now,

Where the people's will is supreme
And their power with the years will grow,
The country that is true freedom's home,
Where to bourgeois tyranny none need bow,
That country's daughter where this fifteenth year
The workers' songs of triumph you hear.
No other land, we say,
Like this is to be found,
The past is swept away,
Of it we hear no sound.
I am the workers' child by right,
Daughter of peasants and of the Soviet State;
Workers of the world, unite,
The Red Flag shows the way to victory straight.[1]

$\mathcal{R}$eaders of a 1929 issue of the popular health newspaper *Toward a Healthy Life-style* would have come across a photograph that was fairly typical for the time—a young woman seated at a table in a textile workshop, intensely absorbed in her task. Behind her stands a female supervisor, smiling approvingly as she inspects the piece of finished cloth that the young woman holds in her hands. But this is neither an ordinary workshop scene nor an ordinary worker, a fact made evident by the title given to the photograph and the article that accompanies it: "We will remake her."[2] The woman in question, it turns out, is a former prostitute, saved from the street and given the chance to start over by a new institution devoted to her physical, material, and ideological redemption.

The period following the Revolution of 1917 was one of great experimentation, as supporters of the new state sought to redress the inequities of the past and shape the socialist future through a wide array of utopian programs, reforms, and practices. This essay examines one such visionary project, the labor clinic (*trudovoi profilaktorii*), one of the many efforts to create "the new Soviet person"—a central goal of the revolutionary agenda—and at the same time solve the vexing social problem of prostitution. First established in 1924, these voluntary institutions combined the treatment of prostitutes for venereal disease with political, cultural, and vocational reeducation. Once the women were deemed successfully "cured," they were rewarded with factory jobs (highly coveted in this age of mass unemployment) and lauded as heroes of the new order, "active collaborators in socialist construction."[3] Over the next several years, labor clinics were opened across the Soviet Union, reaching a total of forty-four at their peak, with a capacity to accommodate as many as 1,000 workers at a time.

The labor clinic can be seen as a kind of "revolutionary laboratory," a place where ideas about the possibility of remaking life in accordance with an ideological vision of the perfect society could be put into practice. The success of this program, whose test subjects were among the most unfortunate and backward segments of the population (prostitutes suffering from gonorrhea or syphilis), would prove that the great socialist endeavor was valid not only in theory but also in practice. The routine followed inside the clinic walls demonstrates precisely how members of the medical profession went about remaking life to meet their ideological and practical objectives. Drawn almost entirely on accounts in medical and popular health publications, this article should be read less as a record of the actual lived experiences of clinic residents than as a study of the objectives, biases, and perspective of the clinic organizers who conducted this revolutionary experiment.

The first labor clinic was opened in June 1924 by Venereal Dispensary No. 2, in the Baumanskii district of Moscow. Agitation efforts among prostitutes had led women to turn to clinics for examinations and treatment in ever growing numbers. Yet as doctors quickly recognized, neither treatment alone nor the health education that accompanied it was enough to "solve" this social ill: without an alternative source of income, these women would be forced to continue prostituting themselves, and the benefits of treatment would quickly be nullified. It was imperative that they be provided with financial assistance, at the very least, while their disease was still in the infectious stage. The fate of those women who completed their course of treatment was an additional problem. In this era of vast unemployment, when the supply of qualified workers greatly exceeded demand, factories were unwilling to hire such unskilled laborers.

Doctors attempted to address these concerns by developing a special living and curative facility where infected prostitutes would receive medical care, food and shelter, remunerated work to cover their expenses during their stay, and job training to provide for them after they left. The clinic would be organized strictly according to the principle of self-financing, with the profits from the sale of finished goods applied toward the maintenance of the institution and the salaries of the workers—all under the watchful eyes of medical and other supervisory personnel, to ensure that the women correctly followed their treatment regime and behaved properly in other respects as well. Finally, the workers would be required to participate in a program of political and cultural enlightenment that was considered to be the key to the success of this enterprise and ultimately to the women's rehabilitation. Venereologists subscribed to the prevailing socioeconomic interpretation of prostitution, which held hunger and need, rather than hereditary pathology or behavioral defect, responsible for driving women to the streets. Yet somewhat paradoxically, they also maintained that only proper education would guarantee the women's definitive break with their past. The regimen of the labor clinic would create conscious proletarians, fully reborn and ready to join the laboring family that was building socialism.

By early 1925 a group of 110 women was employed at the first workshop at Baumanskii. Initially, they sewed and repaired sacks, tasks demanding neither special skills nor a substantial financial outlay. Yet because of the health concerns associated with this type of work (the sacks produced a huge amount of dust) and continued financial losses, a second workshop eventually opened for the production of linen. Here, supervised by a paid instructor, women sewed sheets, hospital gowns, and underwear on the thirty machines donated to the clinic. This sewing workshop had the advantage of providing workers with the kind of industrial qualifications that would help them find employment after their departure and had the added benefit of being more profitable, since it could now fill much larger industrial orders. Soon the workshop was not only paying for itself but even turning a slight profit.

Ironically, this early financial success threatened the institution's very existence. Because the workshop had no legal status, various economic organs attempted to take control of it as soon as it became profitable; only the intervention of the Moscow City Council prevented its appropriation. The initial recruitment method endangered the institution in another respect as well. When it first opened, women received referrals either from venereal dispensaries or from the Zhenotdel, the women's section of the party. Since most of the women recommended by the Zhenotdel were unemployed but healthy, the workshop was in danger of losing its mandate as a treatment facility for infected prostitutes (or women on the verge of prostitution). By restricting the right of referral to the city's venereal dispensaries and officially registering the workshop as a health facility, the labor clinic, as it was now called, would preserve its original mission: to treat and provide for those women suffering from venereal disease who were in the greatest danger of spreading it further among the population.

The irony of rejecting impoverished yet healthy women desperate for employment—including even disease-free prostitutes—was not lost on either the clinic's organizers or those women eager to be admitted. More than one woman complained about the absurdity of having to become infected before being selected for entrance. Yet as the labor clinics became publicized, the numbers of women eager to enroll quickly exceeded the institutions' capacity to accommodate them; not long after the Leningrad facility opened in 1928, for instance, there was a list of 700 applicants for its 100 available spaces. Labor clinic selection committees (composed of representatives from Party organizations such as the Zhenotdel and the Communist Youth League as well as various health and volunteer associations) therefore were forced to employ a variety of methods and devices to determine the suitability of the applications. After initial difficulties in distinguishing "real" prostitutes from the many other women eager for admission (and for the concomitant guarantee of permanent employment in industry), the Baumanskii labor clinic hit upon a simple solution. As the committee discovered, only "pretenders" readily identified themselves as prostitutes; "true" prostitutes admitted to their profession only with great reluctance. Although other clinics employed different criteria, in general all the clinics preferred to admit women not older than twenty-five to thirty (because the physicians thought that they posed a small threat as disease carriers) as well as those for whom prostitution was not a long-standing occupation. In keeping with the preferential treatment afforded the proletariat in other facets of life during the 1920s, clinics opted when possible to admit women with either peasant or working-class credentials.

Although the selection board continued to accept the occasional healthy woman whose plight was particularly dire, the vast majority of those enrolled after the first few years were prostitutes infected with at least one, and sometimes as many as three, venereal diseases. Recruitment took place at the various venereal disease-treatment facilities, including city prisons. A significant role in the recruitment process as well as in the life of the clinic itself was played by the members of two volunteer organizations: the Council for the Fight against Prostitution (SBP) and the Committee to Make Labor and Everyday Life Healthy (KOTIB). Such volunteerism was strongly encouraged, since it helped to make the struggle for the women's transformation one in which the entire country—through these representatives of the worker community—could participate. In close cooperation with the venereal dispensaries (for whom they also conducted educational outreach work), group members scoured train stations, flophouses, restaurants, and cafés as well as the boulevards during working hours, trying to convince prostitutes to come in for an examination, break with the street, and give the labor clinics a chance.

Perhaps even more than accounts written by medical personnel, testaments by these volunteers display a heightened awareness of the difficulty and importance of their efforts and the obstacles that they were forced to endure as well as the sense of idealism mixed with condescension toward the prostitutes whom they encountered. Hence the description of the committee's accomplishments, provided by Comrade Filippova, a member of the SBP affiliated with one of Moscow's venereal dispensaries: "Work in the struggle against prostitution is difficult. We are not always met with sympathy and the desire to leave the street and quit this wasteful life. We often are forced to listen to insults from unfortunate drunken prostitutes. Regardless of these difficulties we have achieved a great deal. In eight months we have brought around 100 people for treatment and directed them to the labor clinic." Attempting to draw the women they encountered into conversation, the committee soon learned the reason for such distinct reactions to their offers of aid. Prostitutes, it seems, could be divided into those resorting to the street out of need and those selling themselves to acquire pretty and expensive clothing: "The first group are women who are looking for a helping hand, who without a doubt can be led to the path of labor and a normal healthy working life. The second group are prostitutes with whom we can do nothing: they don't want to listen to us and rarely even listen to the advice to go get treatment."[4]

Filippova's distinction between women on the one hand and prostitutes on the other is highly instructive. Throughout the years of the labor clinics' existence, efforts were made to explain the inexplicable: in effect, to reconcile reality with the ideological convictions that governed their approach. Why, for instance, would a woman turn down the opportunity to be rehabilitated? Differentiating between those unfortunate motives that nonetheless made sense in the current economic climate and those that were antithetical to the new political reality offered an acceptable explanation.

The women who did want this opportunity and were accepted into the labor clinic could expect a strict regimen that would teach the skills and, equally important, the behavior required of "true proletarians." The imposition of a set of rules of internal order was seen as necessary to prevent the breaches in discipline observed when the facilities first opened: at the Dnepropetrovsk clinic, for instance, women shirked work and even engaged in such "criminal acts" as theft and fighting. It was also hoped that by adopting a schedule and regimen as close as possible to that followed in actual factories (with the same breaks, work-day structure, etc.), the eventual transition to industrial work would be made easier. Thus, at the Leningrad labor clinic, women woke at 7 A.M., made their beds and tidied their sleep areas, and had breakfast at 7:30. Work began at 8 and continued until 5 P.M., with an hour's break for lunch. Dinner was served from 5:30 to 6:30, followed by the evening program of study, volunteer work, and entertainment as well as the women's treatment sessions. At 9 they drank their evening tea, and retired for bed at 11.

To counteract the pull of the streets, the women's comings and goings were also strictly controlled and monitored: during the first two months of their stay they could leave the clinic grounds only in exceptional cases, thereafter only with the director's permission, although most facilities allowed women to go out at night as long as they returned by

10 P.M. By 1934, when many of the clinics had closed and only those deemed "recalcitrant" remained, this regimen was revised: educational work and treatment sessions were moved to the morning, with the workday beginning at 2 in the afternoon and ending at 10, followed by bed. The clinic directors decided that women would no longer be permitted to leave the clinic in the evenings: for former professional prostitutes, the attraction of the street was apparently too great after dark.

Yet even before this reorganization, every effort was made to occupy as much of the residents' time as possible. While clinic organizers subscribed to the prevailing socioeconomic explanation of prostitution, they nonetheless sought to keep the women's contact with their former lives to a minimum, shielding them from negative influences and any danger of a relapse. Alcohol was forbidden, and venturing out of the clinic walls alone and unchaperoned strongly discouraged. Free time and days off were filled with supervised group expeditions to the countryside and excursions to the theater and cinema (provided that these productions had been screened for suitability: those with scintillating or sexual content were to be strictly avoided). At least one Moscow clinic sought to end the institution of Sunday visiting hours after observing among the women's visitors a number of "dubious" acquaintances from their former lives, not the least of which were their pimps.

Within the clinic walls themselves, the women were also under close and continued surveillance. In addition to the medical and workshop staff on hand, a paid "observer" watched over the residents from the end of the workday until bedtime, and the front door was guarded at all times by a female police officer. Women were also expected to keep a close eye on one another so that "the confidence shown in them is not too grossly abused."[5] Clinic residents also served as room captains of the dormitory and on the so-called control-conflict council, the body that regulated the facility's day-to-day functioning and reviewed breaches of its regulations. Cleanliness and decorum were to be observed at all times: women shared the responsibility for tidying the workshops, cafeteria, dormitory and study spaces, and foul language was strictly forbidden. Punishments also followed a set order. Women returning to the clinic intoxicated, engaging in hooliganism or theft, maintaining ties with criminals, or intentionally missing treatment sessions first received a warning. A second infraction resulted in a one- to six-day work suspension, and a third in expulsion.

The inculcation of labor discipline was viewed by clinic organizers as a fundamental component of successful transformation. It was not enough to simply provide these women with tasks to occupy themselves while being treated. As articles describing the clinic emphasized, this facility had nothing in common with the philanthropic endeavors to "save fallen women" so common to the bourgeois West. Writers offered as a comparison a description of the work given to the "unfortunates" who had landed in the workhouses for prostitutes run by the Salvation Army in England. These women, according to the authors, spent their days moving sacks of flour from one side of the room to the other, only to move them back on the following day. They concluded, "Not without reason does the English prostitute say, 'better death on the street, than work in the workhouse.' "[6] The absence of philanthropy was a basic tenet of the clinic: for the materials produced by their own labor, workers received a salary (anywhere upwards of 30 to 35 rubles per month) out of which they paid for their room and board.

The women's first step toward achieving labor discipline was the very basic yet crucial task of learning how to work and, it followed, recognizing what constituted the kind of socially useful work valued by clinic organizers. Only then could they be expected to master the qualifications and skills required for industrial labor. Yet this was no easy task, owing, in the opinion of two doctors affiliated with the Leningrad clinic, to the psychological condition of women torn from the streets: specifically, to their "hysteria" and "neurasthenia." They cited the director of the clinic's workshop to confirm this assessment: "You can't imagine how difficult it was to teach them to sit still for a period of time in one spot. [A woman] sits, suddenly cries out, jumps up from her seat, and races off somewhere unknown."[7] Another doctor credited the mechanization of the workshops through the introduction of sewing, cutting, and knitting machines with further helping in this regard: he explained that the noise prevented women from engaging in conversation which, given their "hysteria," often turned into fights and scandals.

Just as important as learning how to work was learning how to be a worker. Becoming a conscious proletarian, a fully worthy member of the laboring family required extensive political, cultural, and social preparation; hence the mandatory participation in the various educational programs and activities. The significance attributed to the power of enlightenment was enormous. Clinic organizers maintained that the knowledge, outlook, and ideological orientation acquired within the clinic walls would go a long way toward preventing a relapse, should misfortune again befall these women in the future. The proper ideological foundation would prevent conflicts and alienation from developing between the former clinic residents and their new comrades in the factories. It would also keep these same transferees from turning to "underground" prostitution as an additional source of income or as a way of acquiring expensive or hard-to-get goods.

Educational work fell into two separate categories. The first centered on more academic and formal instruction. Classes in literacy were held in every labor clinic, since the ability to read and write was considered to be a necessary prerequisite for raising the women's cultural and production level. Thus at one Moscow clinic, for instance, women spent eighteen hours per week studying Russian, arithmetic, geography, politics (known as political literacy), and physics. In the second "mass section," women participated in one of the many groups devoted to nurturing their "artistic and emotional side"; among the various clubs from which the residents could choose were drama, physical culture, string and wind orchestras, literature, art, choir, and chess. Groups or courses of a more political and social bent were also on offer, including the Red Cross, first aid, the League of the Godless, chemical defense, unionism, political ABCs, and the Defense, Aviation, and Chemical Construction Assistance Society. Women could choose to work on the clinic wall newspaper, a ubiquitous fixture of these facilities with titles such as "The Path of the Female Delegate" or "On New Rails." The more "advanced" residents had the option of taking adult education, pattern cutting, dressmaking, or hygiene classes offered at other locations in the city.

In accounts of the clinics' progress, directors shared their experiences and offered advice on how to facilitate the enlightenment process. The educational supervisor of one Moscow clinic stressed the need for artifice to induce the women to learn: they "shrink from brainwork . . . the mere words 'address,' 'lecture,' and 'liquidation of illiteracy' call forth such intense feelings of repugnance that it is impossible to lure them into the Red corner"[8] (the corner of a room devoted to political themes, which took the place of the icon corner). He recommended that the topic at hand be introduced through roundabout means, by using Pushkin's story, "The Young Peasant Lady," for instance. On the next occasion, he promised, they were sure to listen with interest "even to an extract from one of Stalin's speeches."

Regardless of the specific clubs and activities selected, every effort was made to relate these interests to the broader values and goals of the regime, thereby advancing the women's political education. Thus, for instance, the literature circle and literacy classes would read antireligious works or stories from the Russian Civil War. Sociopolitical concepts and messages, and the promotion of a rationalist and scientific viewpoint, were further emphasized through evening question-and-answer sessions, lecture series, and films that treated political, juridical, historical, natural-scientific, antireligious, production, or revolutionary topics. In the winter of 1931 one Moscow clinic offered the following lectures: "On Prehistoric Times," "On the Descent of Man," "What Is a Petty

Bourgeois?" Talks were supplemented by visits to the Darwin Museum, the Planetarium, the Museum of the Revolution, the Polytechnical Museum, and the Lenin Museum. Sanitary-hygiene lectures focused special attention on the causes of social diseases or highlighted the differences in the battle waged against prostitution and venereal disease in the West and prerevolutionary Russia as compared to the Soviet Union.

Politics permeated the life of the facility in other ways also. The mandatory Red corner held slogans and posters relating to whatever revolutionary holiday was being celebrated or campaign being waged. To further draw women into politics, ceremonial evenings were held on such holidays as May Day, International Women's Day, Paris Commune Day, or the anniversary of the revolution, with speeches by local party and state representatives followed by performances of the clinic's drama circle, physical culture club, or orchestra. Workers participated in the socialist competitions staged between different labor clinics, raising money in one instance for a Red Cross health education "agitation-plane," or they contributed some of their own wages to the Industrialization Loan by buying shares in a national project. Occasionally, women were drawn into political activity beyond the clinic walls as well, becoming delegates to the Zhenotdel, trade unions, or to local worker councils. On at least one occasion, residents of the Leningrad clinic marched in their own column at a May Day parade; on their banner, in bright gold letters, were the words: "We are against alcohol and debauchery. We are for cultural revolution."[9]

The facility with which many of the women appeared to achieve political consciousness or be successfully born anew is apparent from the countless testimonies produced in their literacy and cultural work—sources that clinics were only too eager to share in the popular and medical press. In poems (such as the one at the beginning of this article), drama sketches, newspaper addresses, and conference presentations, women offered their narratives of salvation, expressing gratitude for their deliverance to the clinics and, more generally, to the revolutionary regime itself. Certainly, the question of whether such a transformation was genuine is one that cannot be answered, given the one-sided nature of the sources and the immeasurability of such a concept. What can be gauged, however, is the degree to which clinic residents fulfilled the goals established for them, in the sense of employing the right vocabulary, displaying the appropriate world view, and conceiving of their story in terms that corresponded to those offered by clinic organizers. The ultimate measure of success was their transition to factory labor, followed by glowing reports of their performance record, their designation as shock workers, and their continued participation in the political life of the country.

For those still employed within the facility, these testimonials served a similar purpose, measuring and exhibiting the residents' (and the clinics') great achievement.

"Two Years," an article from *Toward a Healthy Life-style* by Comrade Zorina of the First Moscow Venereal Dispensary clinic, is fairly typical in this regard. Zorina described a May Day two years earlier, when she complained bitterly to another prostitute acquaintance that it couldn't really be a holiday as there was no alcohol to be had. Going out into the street, she witnessed a scene that changed her life forever: "When I saw tens of thousands of working men and women walking to Red Square in close ranks with their banners to the sounds of music, tears came to my eyes. Could it really be that all my life I would be rejected and never be in the ranks of the laboring proletariat? Was I really fated to perish in flophouses, surrounded by drunkenness, thievery, and debauchery? Looking at the columns of workers going by, I firmly resolved to stand on the honest working path."

Remembering what she had heard about the labor clinic from other women at her rooming house, she appealed to the facility directors and was accepted. At first, the task of sewing sacks was difficult for her:

> I'd sit there for a day, another, a third, and could barely use a needle. But hunger is no laughing matter. If you want to eat, you'll work. And step by step I began to sew the bags better and better. At first I barely sewed 10 a day, and then I did more and more. I stopped thinking about drinking, started thinking about how to make money and buy all that I needed, since I didn't have anything. And so the days and nights passed, one after another. Two years flew by quickly and I no longer recognize myself. I am better. I have long since left a lot of bad things behind me. I've gotten used to labor. I lead an honest working life. And I hope that in the future it will be even better and better.[10]

Marusia Kuznetsova's story, "How I Lived Before and How I Live Now," follows a similar pattern. First, she presented a picture of her former existence: hungry and cold, constantly harassed, sleeping on the streets. She feared that she was done for, with no one to turn to, no way to find work, and no means to escape her wretched life. The final blow came when she contracted a venereal disease, which landed her in the Korolenko Hospital. While there, Marusia learned about the labor clinic; she applied and was accepted. As with Comrade Zorina, the adjustment to productive work did not come easily. Initially, Kuznetsova found it difficult to break with her past, which pulled her back to the street and her former occupation. "But then I started going to movies and lectures, and, as I observed my friends, I began to struggle, began to do away with the evil inside me. Gradually, step by step I gave it all up and became a different person, and I am no longer drawn to the street. I participate in a drama circle, I study, am a member of the International Organization in Support of Fighters for Revolution, and I will never go back to the pit of shame. I will stand firmly on the path they put me on: the honest working path."[11]

Each of these narratives followed the same model, beginning with a depiction of the prostitutes' desperate life before entering the clinic, the obstacles that they were forced to overcome on their journey toward enlightenment, and their eventual transformation into conscious and capable workers. The script varied little from story to story, often repeating the same words and expressions: the women escaped lives of "vice," "shame," and "debauchery" and eventually attained the "honest working path," where they "hardly recognized [themselves]." Not surprisingly, all the published accounts by residents were unmitigated success stories; less than stellar models of rehabilitation were afforded no such access, as there was little gained from granting them the opportunity to speak. In the vast body of literature devoted to the clinics, therefore, only one or two works register the voices of the experiment's "failures."

Dr. Lev Fridland's account of his experience as a medical expert in venereal disease cases provides one of these rare examples. He described his encounter at the Leningrad courthouse with a prostitute who had left one of the Moscow clinics, blaming her departure on the inability to break with her previous occupation. "After nights with men, having to return to the clinic was too much for my conscience. They treat you humanely, they all want you to increase your pride in yourself, [acknowledge] that you are a real human being, if only you work. . . . I couldn't look the doctors in the eye. I suffered not from this damned life but because of that untruth. Then I decided I clearly can't be reformed."[12]

The two prostitutes whom Dr. Fridland quoted in a second incident offered a far less charitable assessment of the clinic's worth. Called before a judge for fighting, resisting arrest, and attacking a police officer, these two women were given the chance to enter the labor clinic rather than be sentenced so that they might "correct [themselves] and return to a productive life." The first prostitute responded: "Let others break their backs. I was there, I know. I won't give up my free life for a piece of bread and a cot." After a reproach from the judge, she continued: "All the same I'm free, I live as I want. What do I need with your sewing machine? Look: silk stockings. Who takes such luxuries to a convent? Thank you very much!" The second added, "I endured that drudgery for three months, busying myself with the sacks. I sewed them. To hell with it. A sweeter life awaits us somewhere else."[13]

A more realistic and balanced assessment of the clinics emerges from the sources written by (and principally for) members of the medical community. In fact, according to these accounts, a substantial proportion of women left the facilities throughout the life of these institutions, either of their own volition or as a result of discipline infractions; this number reached on average almost 50 percent of those enrolled each year. Others failed to make the transition to factory work: turning again to prostitution, some eventually returned to the clinics, while others simply disappeared. A small number managed to hold onto their factory jobs while continuing to engage in their former occupation. How were such statistics justified?

Assessing the behavior of the prostitutes who chose jail over the opportunity to remake themselves, Dr. Fridland offered the prevailing explanation for these failures: certain categories of women, he claimed, were hopeless. Originally turning to prostitution out of need, these women had become professionals for whom the occupation was now an end in itself.[14] Earlier in this essay, mention was made of the distinctions drawn between different prostitutes during the recruitment process: the separation of women into the worthy and unworthy, those with understandable (though regrettable) reasons for turning to the streets as opposed to inexcusable and reprehensible motives. As the mass industrialization of the country progressed and the problem of unemployment receded, sources reflected an increasing level of impatience with those who could not, or would not, be reformed.

Some observers fell back upon a psychological explanation for this failure: they reasoned that with the economic causes of prostitution eradicated, only psychologically imbalanced women would resort to such a base profession. Others pointed to the strong ties that supposedly persisted between the women and the criminal world. That women might have had a legitimate reason for wishing to remain in these clinics as long as possible, or even for preferring prostitution over the industrial work that was often grueling, dangerous, and monotonous, was never entertained. By the end of the decade, a number of medical writers were calling for more radical measures, such as forced correctional colonies, to deal with the prostitutes who could not be transformed using the clinics' methods. Expressions such as "socially dangerous element" began to be used to describe those women who were "not capable of reeducation and don't want to work."[15] Dr. Fridland envisioned a five-year plan for prostitution: he argued that the country had the right to be free from such "social anomalies" and proposed the use of correctional facilities to accomplish this goal. "The path to the laboring life will already lie there," he concluded.[16]

In the early 1930s the clinics gradually began to shut down, due in part to the transfer of many of the workers to permanent jobs in the ever expanding industrial sector. The closings were not always the result of such positive developments, however. By the middle of the decade their tax-exempt status had been revoked, making many of the workshops no longer financially viable. Others, like the Gorky labor clinic, were evicted from their buildings: in mid-1934 the facility was ordered to vacate the premises, which would now be used as a school. Appeals by the Commissariat of Public Health to the Council of People's Commissars on behalf of the clinics were ineffectual, despite an observed rise in prostitution that was presumably a result of the era's upheavals. Clearly, medical personnel were not the only ones becoming impatient with the approach toward prostitution employed by the clinics. Even though a few facilities continued to function after the middle of the decade, and at least one survived until 1940, the time for such experiments had passed. Prostitutes were now subjected to forced treatment and, along with other "dangerous elements," consigned to the rapidly growing prison system. Indeed, the fate of the labor clinics reflects a much broader shift away from the voluntary methods and approaches pursued in the 1920s for addressing the country's problems to the coercive measures such as industrialization and collectivization adopted in the 1930s. Gone was the faith in the possibility of transforming individual "human material" through education and consciousness-raising; in its place the authorities implemented a set of punitive policies aimed at forcing transformation on the entire population, willing and unwilling subjects alike.

NOTES

1. Cited in Fanina Halle, *Women in Soviet Russia* (New York, 1933), 240.

2. "My ee peredelaem," *Za zdorovyi byt* 7 (1929): 3.

3. Professor V. M. Bronner, one of the originators of the facilities, described them in this way in *La Lutte contre la prostitution en URSS* (Moscow, 1935), 42.

4. Chlen Raisoveta Filippova, "O rabote komissii po borbe s prostitutsiei," *Za zdorovyi byt* 1 (1928): 3.

5. Halle, *Women in Soviet Russia*, 237.

6. Drs. B. Rein and L. Zheleznov, *S ulitsy na proizvodstvo* (Moscow, 1929), 39.

7. Ibid., 40.

8. Halle, *Women in Soviet Russia*, 238.

9. Rein and Zheleznov, *S ulitsy na proizvodstvo*, 45.

10. Zorina, "Dva goda," *Za zdorovyi byt* 2 (1928): 4.

11. Marusia Kuznetsova, "Kak ia zhila ranshe i kak ia zhivu teper," *Za zdorovyi byt* 2 (1928): 1.

12. L. Fridland, *S raznyh storon: prostitutsiia v SSSR* (Berlin, 1931), 53.

13. Ibid., 60–61.

14. Ibid., 61.

15. V. Altgauzen and G. Murnek, "K voprosu ob efektivnosti raboty pokazatel-nogo trudovogo profilaktoriia NKZ za 2 1/2 goda," *Venerologiia i dermatologiia* 6–7 (1931): 20.

16. Fridland, *S raznyh storon*, 62.

SUGGESTED READINGS

As an introduction to the wide range of experimental projects associated with the revolutionary era see the collection of primary sources edited by William G. Rosenberg, *Bolshevik Visions: First Phase of the Cultural Revolution in Soviet Russia* (Ann Arbor, 1984). Richard Stites considers a number of these visionary programs in *Revolutionary Dreams: Utopian Vision and Experimental Life in the Russian Revolution* (Oxford, 1989); on similar experiments in the realms of art and culture see John E. Bowlt and Olga Matich, eds., *Laboratory of Dreams: The Russian Avant-Garde and Cultural Experiment* (Stanford, 1996).

Stephen Kotkin explores the process of creating new Soviet people in his study of the building of *Magnitagorsk, Magnetic Mountain: Stalinism as a Civilization* (Berkeley, 1995). On the history of prostitution in the prerevolutionary period see Laurie Bernstein, *Sonia's Daughters: Prostitutes and Their Regulation in Imperial Russia* (Berkeley, 1995). Olga Matich examines the prostitute's function in Russian literary classics in "A Typology of Fallen Women in Nineteenth Century Russian Literature," *American Contributions to the Ninth International Congress of Slavists*, vol. 2, *Literature, Politics, History*, ed. Paul Debreczeny (Columbus, 1983). There are no full-length analyses of prostitution after 1917 in English. See Chapter 11 in Richard Stites's general study, *The Women's Liberation Movement in Russia: Feminism, Nihilism, and Bolshevism, 1860–1930* (Princeton, 1978); and the following two articles: Elizabeth Waters, "Victim or Villain? Views on Prostitution in Post-Revolutionary Russia," in *Women in the Soviet Union and Eastern Europe: Papers from the IV World Congress of Soviet and East European Studies*, ed. L. Edmondson (Cambridge, MA), and Elizabeth Wood, "Prostitution Unbound: Representations of Sexual and Political Anxieties in Post-revolutionary Russia," in *Sexuality and the Body in Russian Culture*, ed. Jane T. Costlow, Stephanie Sandler, and Judith Vowles (Stanford, 1993).

CHAPTER 9

Liquid Assets

Vodka and Drinking in Early Soviet Factories

KATE TRANSCHEL

There may be no image more strongly associated with Russia than vodka. Other European countries outstripped Imperial Russia in the per capita consumption of intoxicants at the beginning of the twentieth century, and for much of its history vodka was reserved in the hierarchy of Russian beverages for celebrations and other specified functions, but the vodka-drinking Russian has been a dominant and sustaining cultural stereotype. Whether fully fair and accurate or not, the perception was strongly enough grounded in observed experience that the Russian national leadership periodically gave the issue of alcohol abuse serious attention. The tsarist government launched an antialcohol campaign as early as the sixteenth century. In the 1890s the Orthodox church, the state, and medical professionals all sponsored their own temperance organizations. And one of the first reforms implemented by Mikhail S. Gorbachëv when he became Soviet leader in 1985 took aim at drunkenness. It should therefore not cause surprise that as the Bolsheviks set out to create a socialist society in the 1920s and 1930s, the issues of improving labor productivity, inculcating "proletarian" values, improving public health, and raising political consciousness were only a few that led directly to confronting the use of alcohol.

Vodka was deeply embedded in diverse social traditions long before 1917. In addition to its obvious effectiveness as a way to become drunk for those so inclined, vodka was also inextricably entwined with church holidays and various rites of passage. Peasants used it as their preferred mode of celebration, to legitimize grief, and to seal new friendships and fortify existing ones. In the nonmonetary economy of the village, peasants provided vodka both to recruit the help of neighbors when needed and to remunerate them for services performed. When submitting to community self-justice, the perpetrator would buy vodka for fellow villagers as the final act of the punishment, thereby symbolically acknowledging the authority of the community. Vodka would also be employed as a bribe, and it was the element that bonded male culture. Drinking vodka to excess was, in short, both a rite and a right.

These traditions collided with the Bolshevik attempt to reconfigure the Soviet labor force, redefine rhythms of work and labor discipline, and inculcate new class identifications. At the root of this process of changing peasants into proletarians (and tsarist workers into Soviet ones) was a transition from the task-oriented rhythms of agricultural work to the time-oriented discipline of the factory. In this transformation, laborers must give up their extensive reliance on self-supervision and the perception of work and breaks as parts of an unbroken whole. Instead, they must accept the ownership of their time by an employer who demands efficiency, punctuality, and constancy; employs direct supervision; and demands a strict accounting. In other words, agrarian time is "passed" while industrial time is capital that is "spent," and the transition from one mode to the other involves not only learning new habits but also accepting different values.

As Kate Transchel shows in this article, such considerations were not abstractions in the Soviet factories of the 1920s and 1930s, and confronting the issue of drinking was unavoidable if the social revolution were to succeed. Experienced workers as well as those who entered industry after the revolution drank heavily before, during, and after work, but eliminating such behavior involved more than changing attitudes toward recreational drinking, however deeply rooted. New arrivals at the plants drank for fun, but they also needed to exchange drink for training, and everyone knew the effectiveness of bribing foremen and managers with vodka. In addition, patterns of drinking reflected and indeed reinforced divisions within the working class itself. Echoing the partisan vocabulary used by the state, experienced workers considered the former peasants new to industry to be "backward," and they observed separate drinking rites. Conversely, the recent arrivals legitimized their own values as they re-created a village subculture in the cities, and "peasant" drinking houses arose in every industrial center. And to complicate matters further, any attempt to inculcate greater responsibility in the use of alcohol ran afoul of existing constructions of gender among all workers. The ability to drink was basic to masculine self-images, and state antialcohol campaigns were perceived as encroaching on a basic male prerogative. In sum, alcohol mediated the differences between experienced workers and new ones; but it also reinforced preexisting ideas, and the identifications associated with drinking after 1917 could be divisive as well as solidifying. As Transchel argues, for the various strata of the working class—all aware of the position of the state on drinking—their unbroken allegiance to alcohol can be read as a conscious rejection of Soviet values.

Kate Transchel, who received her Ph.D. from the University of North Carolina at Chapel Hill, is assistant professor of history at California State University at Chico. She has published in Soviet and Post-Soviet Review *and is coeditor of* Daily Life under Stalin *(2000).*

*D*rinking, more than most leisure activities, derives meaning from its social context and setting. The essentially social nature of imbibing is indicated by the fact that solitary drinking is commonly considered to be problematic. Be it the televised camaraderie on *Cheers* or the lone drunk with a bottle, drinking is a defining activity for the individual and society. Nowhere is this more true than in Russia, where alcohol has held a central place in the social, cultural, economic, and political life of the country from the very first written accounts in the twelfth century to the reforms of Mikhail S. Gorbachëv in 1985. Since its introduction into Muscovy, vodka has evolved into a product of everyday consumption for ordinary Russians, as a regular accompaniment to food, and even as part of the most mundane social occasions, including business transactions of every sort. Having powerful associations with health, happiness, and even national character, vodka in Russia has become a symbol of mythic proportions. Moreover, because of alcohol's vital role in the daily lives of Russians, nowhere has the problem of alcoholism been more politicized. The tenacity of traditional drinking cultures, firmly embedded in Russian popular culture, has thwarted social reformers' best efforts for two centuries. Beginning in the nineteenth century, Russian, then Soviet, reformers have tried with little success to control the drinking behavior and, by extension, the social identities and cultural values of the lower classes.

Lack of successful reformism was particularly the case throughout the 1920s and 1930s when Soviet authorities harbored ambitious goals of creating a new socialist working class. Emphasizing sobriety and discipline as proper behaviors for Soviet workers, they hoped to transform former peasants into efficient workers who shared their world view and their commitment to building socialism. Yet the social and cultural landscape limited the possibilities for change and made the creation of a "new world with new people" nearly impossible. After seven years of war, revolution, and civil war, the Russian economy and society were in a state of near collapse. Millions of peasants flocked to the cities seeking jobs and ways out of rural destitution, and millions of workers fled to the countryside in search of food.

With the beginning of industrial recovery in 1923, moreover, waves of new workers from the villages joined the industrial labor force, radically altering the social composition of the working class and "ruralizing" the cities. Peasant migrants and established workers were thrown together in urban factories creating what Soviet leaders called "socialist" society. In truth, the industrial work force in the 1920s formed what Moshe Lewin has termed a "quicksand society" characterized by flux, uncertainty, and mobility. The 1920s and early 1930s were a period of dreadful poverty and social misery—an urban world of crime and unemployment, of dirty workers' dormitories, roving homeless waifs (*besprizorniki*), open prostitution, and drunkenness. Leading Bolsheviks insisted that in order to make a transition into a socialist future, these legacies of the past had to be overcome and a new socialist culture and morality had to be created. The workers, however, had other ideas.

Despite the revolution and Bolshevik expectations, alcohol continued to lubricate many shop floor customs and dominated life after work as well. As one commentator wrote, "Drunkenness permeates the everyday life of the people; it remains the traditional and unchanging companion of people's lives. From birth, all events in a person's life, including his death, are accompanied by vodka and drunkenness. They drink out of misery and happiness, they drink because there is nothing to do, or because they are tired from doing too much. . . . All holidays and celebrations are met with drunkenness."[1]

The behavior of the new working class, especially those fresh from the village, did not respond to Bolshevik desiderata: they came late to work, if at all; broke their machines; ignored the authority of bosses; and, above all, drank themselves into oblivion. These new peasant-workers did not fit Bolshevik visions of a socialist society. They were uncontrollable, unpredictable, and shared few of the values of the urban working class. The time-discipline and labor-discipline that industrial labor demanded were alien and oppressive concepts that many migrants found difficult to assimilate. On the farm, regular breaks to rest, smoke a cigarette, or talk were accepted. In the factories, such behavior incurred the wrath of foremen and other workers. These newcomers frequently missed work and regularly resorted to drinking, often even before and during the work day.

Not only new workers drank. Frequenting the neighborhood tavern remained a regular social ritual. A typical Saturday saw workers go home to clean up and then make the rounds of the beer halls, starting with third-rate bars and moving up. When the usual places had closed, the diehards would continue drinking in all-night basement tearooms. On paydays, the beer halls and taverns were full of workers, where often they would drink up their entire paychecks. Complaints about drunkenness appeared frequently in the press beginning in 1923. In the following year the *Rabochaia gazeta* (Workers' newspaper) portrayed a typical tavern scene on payday: "Accordions screech and corks pop. The entire shop is drunk. In one corner stumbles the boiler room staff, in the other the furnace workers. There is nothing but noise and fights. And in the street there are two lines. One—male—waits for free tables, the other—female—waits for their drunken husbands to come out."[2]

More important perhaps for the new regime, whose political authority was still tenuous, the worker-elite—those skilled workers who entered the factories before 1917—also did not respond to party imperatives to create a sober culture. They continued to come to work drunk, and they drank during working hours from bottles smuggled in and hidden in machinery, garbage cans, and rafters. For example, in 1927 at the Krasnoe Sormovo factory in Moscow, one-third of the workers were reported for either drinking on the job or coming to work drunk; of these, over one-half were highly skilled workers. Home brew was sold and even made in the factories, as evidenced by the large still found in the Sokolniki machine works in 1923.

Until the mid-1920s workers' drinking culture generally expressed a type of labor solidarity, and the tavern became the center of social activity. There the worker was able to enjoy himself and satisfy his need for companionship. For him, the tavern was a social center, club, and friend, and it provided him with a temporary escape from his dreary life. When asked in a questionnaire to discuss the causes of drinking, one worker replied: "There are 40,000 people living in my settlement and we have only two libraries, which are usually closed. We have no workers' club or theater. In short, there is nowhere for us to study or spend our leisure time."[3] Another respondent noted the lack of teahouses, even in Moscow, so workers went to the taverns: "When we get there, we don't really plan to get drunk. We just want to talk and rest. But if we sit there, we must drink or get out." Still another complained that an alternative to the tavern would be going to the theater, but workers "can't go because we don't have the right clothes." They also emphasized poor living conditions as the main reason for spending time in the taverns. As one respondent stated, "Imagine an apartment in which fifteen to twenty people live in a comparatively small space. It is stuffy and damp, water seeps from the walls, bedbugs swarm like ants—whether you want to or not, you run to the tavern."[4]

Practices centered around the intake of alcohol at the workplace also fortified social relations among some workers and excluded others. "Blue Monday" became widespread among male workers in shops, commercial firms, and factory enterprises. Arriving at their jobs hung over from weekend drinking, they used Monday as an occasion for more drinking. As one observer wrote, "Blue Monday is a regular ritual. Even the owner himself is prone to alcoholic binges."[5] Moreover, each new man underwent an initiation rite, which typically centered around buying and drinking vodka. In some factories, a new worker was not addressed by name but called "Mama's boy" until he provided drinks for the whole shop. The appointment of a shop foreman was accompanied by a ritual in which the workers gave homage and the foreman reciprocated by buying drinks for them all. Treating with vodka strengthened shop solidarities, reinforced hierarchies among workers, and symbolized a rite of passage into the world of "real" workers.

Worker solidarity expressed through drinking shifted in the late 1920s, when drinking practices at the workplace became more exclusionary and hierarchical. The reasons can be traced to the changing composition of the work force as the regime instituted a policy of rapid industrialization. The first year of the official policy of rapid industrialization, 1928, also marked the beginning of what has been termed the Stalin Revolution—a period of societal transformation even more profound than the political revolutions of 1917. One of its features, the collectivization of agriculture, fundamentally realigned the contours of agrarian life and methods of cultivation, shattering old rural structures and causing millions of peasants to flock into the towns. In industry, the First Five-Year Plan destroyed the NEP economy, replacing it with central planning designed to ensure large-scale industrial development and rapid economic growth that required unprecedented numbers of workers from an already depleted skilled labor market. Another feature of the Stalin Revolution, or Cultural Revolution, sought to destroy the remaining vestiges of "bourgeois" power and influence, launching political attacks against specialists and stripping them of their authority. Thousands of workers were admitted to educational institutions, creating a technical intelligentsia of working-class origins, and thousands more were promoted from the shop floor to positions of administration and management.

Alongside this process, rapid industrial expansion created an enormous need for skilled technicians, managers, and low-level supervisory personnel, which resulted in a great degree of social mobility. Many older experienced workers advanced directly from the shop floor to administrative posts, while many of the younger ones were recruited into higher education. In addition, experienced workers who remained on the shop floor were often appointed to the fast-growing number of posts for foremen. The newcomers who filled positions vacated by these promotions consisted primarily of males in their late teens or early twenties, unskilled and poorly paid, who tended to drift from factory to factory in search of higher wages. Having no long-term experience or employment at any one industrial enterprise, they could not have developed a sense of being part of an older work culture and community. They, therefore, most likely perceived themselves (and were perceived) as outsiders, on the margins of the working class.

The cultural dimensions of these developments had a great impact on the character and identity of the working class. Peasants who moved to the city did not remain rural prototypes, nor did they assimilate established shop-floor culture. The urban environment to which older workers were accustomed and that new ones encountered was constantly changing, in part because of the massive influx of peasants who reflected aspects of both city and village culture.

The Bolsheviks attached the labels "backward" to workers of peasant origin and "petty bourgeois" to their social and political outlook. Older workers judged them uncultured, ridiculing them in derogatory terms as yokels, "sandaled hicks," or "dark people." During the first years of rapid industrialization as factories filled with more and more immigrants from the countryside, they received considerable attention within the party and the press. By and large, the images of factory peasants were negative; they were backward and largely illiterate; they did not read newspapers, were not interested in political matters, did not master the skills of industrial work, had no qualifications, and did nothing to acquire them. Often accused of drunkenness, laziness, or cunningly avoiding work, "raw workers" were portrayed as wreckers, hooligans, slackers, and drunkards who were dangerously vulnerable to "socially alien" enemies of socialist construction.

New workers continually drew attacks from older ones and from management, and their political credentials with the party were very poor. In the factories, new workers were, in many respects, the antithesis of urban workers. They continued to draw upon peasant culture as they organized their lives in the cities. Having grown up in the village where they worked in accordance with the seasons and the weather, migrants were not familiar with the demands and order that defined industrial routines. They had been their own bosses in the village where work was task-oriented, the results tangible. In the factory they became just one of thousands of cogs in an incomprehensible machine, their work time-oriented and seemingly meaningless. Their lack of experience and the difficulty in operating unfamiliar machinery often resulted in equipment breakdowns, thus adding to their confusion and intensifying their alienation.

Not only were these newcomers excluded from the drunken camaraderie that was typical of the Russian working class, but their drinking behavior also drew criticism from older workers. Besieged by the tide of peasant migrants, threatened by increased mechanization, their labor devalued by assembly-line production that increased the demand for semi-skilled labor, these older skilled workers attacked drinking in part as a device to assert their superiority and maintain their status in the factory. While individual vanguard workers may have wished to uplift and enlighten their new comrades, this goal did not lessen overall expressions of condemnation and hostility that old workers as a group displayed toward migrants. A telling example comes from the Komintern factory in Kharkov, where the head of the machine shop (who also chaired the factory party cell) was brought to task for habitually punishing new workers for their indiscipline by hitting them, and they often struck back. When confronted at a committee meeting in 1928, he bellowed, "The real working class is quantitatively small and it is impossible to turn these peasant hicks into proletarians! To think so is utopian!"[6]

Alongside exhortations for newcomers to the factories to put down the bottle, old workers often demanded payment in vodka from new ones before they would train them. As one new man complained, "If you want to begin something, if you want to learn or understand . . . vodka is necessary. . . . If you don't play along, you can study for two hundred years, but nothing will ever get started."[7] Individual apprenticeship was everywhere linked to this type of payment—trainees had to "pay what they must and keep quiet."[8] For example, recruits at one textile mill were invited to buy vodka for the foreman in order to secure a decent loom. Trainees were also advised to contribute to the trainer's liquor cabinet unless they wanted to be reported to the factory committee for being unofficially recruited and trained. At a trade union meeting at the Krasnoe Sormovo factory in Moscow, it was revealed that the shop supervisor demanded a bottle of vodka from new workers before he would allow them to begin work. New men complained that they could not afford to buy vodka until they earned a paycheck. Their complaints, however, were dismissed since the supervisor shared his bribe with the administration. When a highly skilled worker at the Lenin factory in Saratov was promoted to overseeing the training of unskilled recruits, he used his position to stay drunk at work and extract vodka from his charges, whereas previously he had been a model worker. So widespread was this practice that in 1928 *Golos tekstilei* (Textile workers' voice) published cartoons showing new recruits approaching a mill loaded down with vodka and food while members of the factory committee looked on through their fingers. Not surprisingly, trade union reports in 1930 criticized apprenticeships for not providing the individual instruction that they were supposed to give.

Not all old workers extracted vodka for training, of course, nor did all of them drink on the job, but there is much evidence to suggest that skilled workers and foremen (promoted from the ranks of vanguard workers) who did drink could more or less do so with impunity on the shop floor. Until the mid-1930s, however, skilled workers were rarely punished or else received light reprimands. For example, in 1933, the head electrician at the Mikhalovskyi combine went to work drunk and promptly fell asleep. He therefore did not notice that one of the cooling pumps was malfunctioning, and it burned up. Despite the fact that the factory was without water and could not operate for two days, he was not reprimanded. At one regional factory committee meeting in Moscow, a member of the committee cited five highly skilled workers who were repeatedly written up for being drunk at work, but the factory could not fire them because their skills were needed. Noting that by contrast unskilled workers or workers with ties to the countryside were regularly fired for coming to work drunk, he argued that production in the factories would stop altogether if skilled men were fired for the same reason. In 1928 at several regional party committee meetings in Kharkov, the focus was the "systematic drunkenness" of older party members heading factory party cells. These vanguard workers were drunks who had established systems of patronage. They were not disciplined—not only because their skills were valuable, but also because they were allied with the administration in what the party termed "protectionist policies." This complaint was echoed repeatedly in trade union meetings and noted in factory reports by the Workers' and Peasants' Inspectorate (RKI). In Kharkov the problem was so prevalent that the RKI presented a three-page list to the Central Committee of the Ukrainian Communist Party of factory supervisors who were regularly drunk on the job.

The skilled workers' right to accept vodka from newcomers and to drink without much fear of retribution intensified new workers' resentment. An incident at the rolling mill workshop at the Enakievo metallurgical plant in Ukraine is particularly illustrative. Reacting to old skilled workers' refusals to work in protest of an increase in output quotas, the party secretary of the factory, N. A. Voznesenskii (who would become chairman of Gosplan in 1937), summoned all employees to a meeting in the factory club. At this meeting he emphasized the importance of the increase for building socialism and attacked skilled workers for frequent drinking and absences. His speech evoked a cry from the audience: "That's right! How much can we put up with [from them]? Chuck them out!" He replied, "Today, when each and every skilled worker is so important to us, we allow him a lot. But this is temporary. . . . Tomorrow we won't pardon anybody for drinking and truancy."[9]

Struggling against the alien and hostile environment encountered on the shop floor, new workers, who generally displayed strong collectivist tendencies among themselves as an aspect of village culture, forged and strengthened solidarities in the factories. In addition to lodging complaints against old workers' drinking, many unskilled workers joined to defend their right to drink on the job. As the drunken Kolka Leshii informed his foreman, who had threatened him with dismissal, "No one has the right to remove me from work."[10] Expressing solidarity among their own ranks, new workers often rallied to protest the firing of one of their comrades for drunkenness. In one such case, a certain Votskyi was dismissed after receiving six pink slips for truancy and coming to work drunk. His fellow workers petitioned the trade union to reinstate him, arguing that the offenses did not merit dismissal, especially since the punishment was not applied to all workers uniformly. In another case, the actions of an unskilled metal worker who came to work drunk, refused to leave, and started a fistfight with the night watchman were defended by his comrades, who argued that he was not to blame since he was suffering a "nervous breakdown." Further, they claimed that the administration had violated labor codes in dismissing him. When workers at the Kriukovskii factory in Kharkov were reprimanded for drinking, they blamed the executive committee of the regional soviet for lapses in discipline, noting that the soviet had allowed a beer hall to operate next door to the factory. Implying that drinking was a natural part of working-class life, workers defended their right to stop in for a shot or two at the beginning and end of the day and pointed out that they were merely doing their part to increase state revenues.

The vast number of such protests lodged by new workers against reprisals for drinking demonstrates that they were regularly dismissed or reprimanded for drinking on the job whereas old workers were not. It is impossible to determine with accuracy if new workers were indeed more often drunk at work, if they were victims of harassment by foremen and administrators, if it was simply a matter of their sheer numbers in relation to old workers, or a combination of factors. What is evident, however, is that new workers perceived that they were being harassed and unfairly reprimanded for drinking, which reinforced their sense of alienation.

Adding to this sense of alienation were the places where different workers drank. The complex lines of fraternization within the walls of taverns are impossible to discern from the sources, but it is logical to assume that while taverns often brought together workers from diverse crafts, boundaries and exclusions existed along social and cultural lines there as they did in the factory. For example, in Leningrad, seasonal workers and migrants from the countryside headed for a tavern on Gorodskaia Street. "Without this 'teahouse' things would be bad for us," one new arrival concluded. "Let's say you have come from the countryside. Where can you find people from your village? Here. . . . If someone is without work, where can he go? Here. Here you can see everyone . . . and you can sniff out work."[11] In Moscow the Stenka Razin pub was known for its boisterous peasant clientele. And in Kharkov, city officials complained that new workers gathered at a tavern called Bam before and after work.

The press cited these bars because they had gained notoriety for their peasant clienteles, which gives us a clue into the segregated nature of sociability outside work. But since taverns were not always accessible, workers also drank in public parks, dining halls, cooperatives, private homes, the streets, and even workers' clubs. Although there is no comprehensive list of places that sold alcohol, there is abundant evidence that many workers drank in various public areas despite official regulations prohibiting the consumption of alcohol. Since the Soviet regime and factory administrations would not tolerate the casual informality—gambling, singing, talking, and especially drinking—that had characterized work in the prerevolutionary factory or in the village, workers found or created new areas for socializing in public areas and communal leisure-time facilities. For example, workers' clubs, intended by the regime to be centers of culture and enlightenment, were constantly besieged by drunks or were passed up by workers on their way to the beer hall. In one account, two metallists who had been excluded from the trade union arrived at a club, ate, drank vodka, and threatened to shoot anyone who disturbed them. Similarly, a trade union paper noted that drunken youths frequently visited the club and started fistfights when asked to leave.

Dining halls also were places where male workers engaged in rough and drunken sociability. In 1924, *Vestnik profsoiuzov* (Trade-union herald) complained that the majority of dining halls were gradually being converted into beer halls. In Kharkov, where the factory party cell had banned the sale of beer in the dining hall, workers nonetheless brought their own. A reader of the *Kharkovskyi proletarii* (Kharkov proletariat) grumbled in 1929 that "many have already written about, and even more have talked about, the fact that the workers' dining hall doesn't sell beer. Well, it doesn't matter. On paydays the dining hall is turned into a tavern anyway and it is impossible to eat there. It is always full of troublesome drunks. There is smoke, swearing, and fights because everyone brings vodka in with them."[12]

The same newspaper ran a cartoon under the caption, "The Dining Hall as It Really Is"—a scene of chaos with drunken workers retching on the floor, others passed out on tables, still others fighting. The waiter, holding up a bottle of vodka, asks a drunken patron with a huge red nose, "Lunch? To drink here or to take out?" While this example was an exaggeration, it highlights the conflictual world of the worker in the 1920s and 1930s. The implied condemnation of workers' drinking was a clear refutation of their values and culture, whether former peasant or old worker. That this challenge to their traditional way of life by representatives of the workers' state was met by resistance demonstrates how deeply they resented the intrusion. They perceived it as an affront to their rights as workers and to their dignity as individuals capable of exerting their own wills in structuring their leisure and social activities.

While perhaps not actually drinking at the same table or bench, or even at the same pub, club, or dining hall, the use of these places by both new and old workers demonstrates their passive and outright resistance to the regime's calls for workers to adopt a sober life-style. It also implies a form of common male worker solidarity against what were perceived as unjust demands made on them by the state: to spend their work time in the sober creation of socialist production and their leisure in sober, cultured entertainment. In this case, workers as a class asserted and expressed their collective culture despite the split into two strata. Heavy drinking, coarse swearing, and physical roughness were bonds that united these individuals as men as well as workers. The rejection of official values in favor of peasant or prerevolutionary worker culture amounted to an act of self-definition for the members of the industrial work force. When they went to the beer hall instead of the club, they were rejecting the official model of proper behavior. Such activity not only reflected their culture but also served to reaffirm and consolidate their sense of social identity.

NOTES

1. N. Tiapugin, *Narodnye zabluzhdeniia* (Moscow, 1926), 12.
2. *Rabochaia gazeta*, no. 280 (1924): 2.
3. V. Ia Kanel, *Alkogolizm i borba s nim* (Moscow, 1914), 383.
4. Ibid., 384.
5. A. Buzinov, *Za Nevskoi zastavoi: Zapiski rabochego* (Moscow, 1930), 23–24.
6. Tsk KPU, op. 20, f. 1, d. 28L8, l. 1.
7. *Komsomolskaia pravda*, February 27, 1927.
8. *Rabochii krai*, March 11, 1927.
9. V. V. Kolotov, *Nikolai Alekseevich Voznesenskii* (Moscow, 1974), 101–7.
10. *Krasnyi putilovets*, November 14, 1929.
11. *Stroitel* 6 (1925): 42–44.
12. *Kharkovskyi proletarii*, July 14, 1929.

SUGGESTED READINGS

Christian, David. *"Living Water": Vodka and Russian Society on the Eve of Emancipation*. New York, 1990.
Frank, Stephan P., and Mark D. Steinberg, eds. *Cultures in Flux: Lower-Class Values, Practices, and Resistance in Late Imperial Russia*. Princeton, 1994.
Herlihy, Patricia. "Joy of Rus: Rites and Rituals of Russian Drinking." *Russian Review* 50 (April 1991): 131–47.
Hoffman, David L. *Peasant Metropolis: Social Identities in Moscow, 1929–1941*. Ithaca, 1994.

Segal, Boris. *The Drunken Society: Alcohol Abuse and Alcoholism in the Soviet Union*. New York, 1990.

White, Stephen. *Russia Goes Dry: Alcohol, State, and Society*. Cambridge, MA, 1996.

CHAPTER 10

The Cantor and the Commissar

Religious Persecution and Revolutionary Legality during the Cultural Revolution

William B. Husband

The Bolsheviks' approach to law was utilitarian. As Marxists, they viewed it as a manifestation of the socioeconomic and political order it served. Law was therefore an instrument for shaping and defending the existing order by reflecting established customs and values, and by embodying the ideals that those in power wished to promote. Under tsarism, according to this view, bourgeois law served the beneficiaries of the old regime, while Soviet law was to advance the class interests of the proletariat. The future Communist society, the argument ran, would have no need for law; but during the transition from the present to the ideal future, law was necessary, even desirable.

Bolshevik legal opinion thus left itself open to challenges on more than one ground. Most obviously, by employing repression and systematic terror, the revolutionary regime forfeited any claim to law as a supreme social value. The prevailing Soviet concept of "revolutionary legality" was therefore not an expression of abstract legal principles but a political instrument—a mandate for the least arbitrary and socially disruptive displacement of the status quo by the revolution. As circumstances dictated, revolutionary legality could be an alternative to the use of force or its supplement. In practice, however, implementing any such stratagem would entail at least a partial reliance on abstract (read "bourgeois") concepts of fairness and justice, even as these Marxists denied their ideological validity. To complicate matters further, the fact that the Bolsheviks were attempting a Marxist revolution in what was still a predominantly agrarian country multiplied the possibilities for friction. The absence of many of the economic and social prerequisites for a Marxist society consequently increased the Bolsheviks' reliance on interventionist tactics, which in turn tested the tensions among law, political pragmatism, and preexisting views of morality in society literally case by case.

During antireligious campaigns the Bolsheviks consequently utilized law to further their objectives, but revolutionary legality also unexpectedly became the refuge of the repressed. As this article shows, Soviet power used law extensively to attack religion from its first days in office, and at the beginning of the Cultural Revolution it placed additional restrictions on religious activity. By issuing detailed guidelines for the elimination of churches, however, the state unintentionally placed an effective weapon in the hands of those who defended religion. Even during the repressive days of 1928–1932, believers were able to appeal successfully to state authorities on legal grounds for the redress of injustices. So entrenched was this practice, in fact, that Boris Lvovich Shulman, a prominent religious figure in Moscow, carried his grievances to the top of the Soviet political hierarchy. Although ultimately unsuccessful, the Shulman case demonstrated the central role of revolutionary legality in the battle between state and society over religion in the early Soviet period.

William B. Husband is the author of "Godless Communists": Atheism and Society in Soviet Russia, 1917–1932 *(2000) and* The Revolution in the Factory: The Birth of the Soviet Textile Industry, 1917–1921 *(1990). He received his Ph.D. from Princeton University and is associate professor of history at Oregon State University.*

𝓑olshevik antireligious repression and the Cultural Revolution of 1928–1932 did not extract the maximum price from Boris Lvovich Shulman. He neither lost his life nor received the prison sentence and term of exile that befell uncounted other believers and clergy. But Shulman, once a celebrated religious cantor in Moscow, endured cruelty in a different form: ongoing life in a society that deprived him of everything that had given meaning to his previous existence. And that makes his story significant.

Shulman's standing as a prominent religious personage and alien class element caused him hardship long before the beginning of the Cultural Revolution. Like others whose social origins and occupation under the old regime left them vulnerable during the volatile 1920s, he acquired the status of a *lishenets* (literally, "a deprived one"). As such, Shulman lost his legal rights, lacked suitable housing, and found himself in a food ration category too low to ensure adequate regular sustenance. No longer able to support himself as a cantor, he was pushed further toward the economic margin, and—not to be underestimated—the loss of his former profession and public reputation took away the religious and personal fulfillment they provided. And when ideologically motivated attacks against vestiges of tsarist society and revolutionary gradualism broadened everywhere in the USSR after 1928, they only exacerbated his problems.

Shulman reacted with survival strategies born of desperation. Possibly considering emigration or political asylum in the United Kingdom, he acquired six-month visas for himself and wife, Millie, from the British

Consulate in August 1930. The Soviet government refused to issue them passports, however, and during the next year Shulman's circumstances further deteriorated. Seeking to improve his material condition and shed the stigma of his social status, he tried to attain the labor classification of "singer-artist" by accepting work from a state-sponsored entertainment agency in the vaudeville-cum-variety-show format known as *estrada*. But even so humiliating a concession came to nothing. Reduced to performing in a modest venue for employees in the trade bureaucracy, Shulman received scathing reviews for the aria he sang on August 13, 1931. The toll that more than a decade of living in deprivation had taken on his talent, quite likely in combination with the social and possibly anti-Semitic biases of the reviewer, left him "an old man who had lost his voice [and who] sped up where it wasn't needed and was out of time, although the accompanist tried to [adjust the tempo]." When his employers at the State Association of Musical, Estrada, and Circus Enterprises (GOMETs) refused to improve his lot, and in fact reduced his monthly salary from 240 to 150 rubles, Shulman appealed to higher state authorities. And to bolster his case, he publicly renounced his religious faith in an open letter that appeared in the newspaper *Bezbozhnik* (Godless) on August 31.

Although they recognized the obvious potential to exploit politically Shulman's denunciation of faith, officials of the Central Executive Committee of the All-Russian Congress of Soviets (VTsIK) could not reverse the fortunes of the former cantor. Shulman directed his complaint to Central Executive Committee chairman Mikhail Ivanovich Kalinin, who enjoyed a reputation as a "little father" to whom the wronged could turn for the redress of grievances; Kalinin monitored the affair while turning over specific appeals to his secretary, S. Vorobev, and fellow VTsIK member Peter G. Smidovich. But such intercession, although it came from the highest state political institution, failed even to resolve Shulman's housing problems quickly. A letter of September 1 from Smidovich to the head of the Moscow Oblast Housing Trust manifested more a tone of entreaty than of command. Citing Shulman's letter to *Bezbozhnik* as a politically significant concession to Soviet power, Smidovich asked only that Shulman and his family be allowed to occupy the corridor of someone else's apartment, but the Trust did not accede. In November—in a communication that, in contrast to recent reviews, praised Shulman's recent singing performances as socially useful labor as well as his letter to *Bezbozhnik*—Smidovich asked the chairman of the Moscow Oblast Executive Committee of Soviets to intervene. At the same time, Vorobev demanded that GOMETs explain the reduction of Shulman's salary. Housing eventually materialized, but GOMETs defiantly defended their action by responding that they could not use Shulman in their "production work."

The Cultural Revolution drew to an end, but the cantor's situation failed to improve. The Soviet government introduced its own internal passport system in 1932, which required citizens to receive permission to reside in specific cities, but Shulman's application to live in Moscow was not approved. Lacking the proper documentation, without which he could not obtain bread or vegetable ration cards, he lost consciousness on a Moscow street from hunger and poor health in October 1932. By January 1933, Shulman was living openly in an apartment on Nikolskaia Street, but he wrote to Kalinin that he had now been waiting for more than a year for legal permission to reside in Moscow, that his ration cards for January had therefore been confiscated, and that none for February had been issued to him. Once again, Smidovich wrote a letter explaining the political significance of the case—this time to the chairman of the soviet of the October district of Moscow in which Shulman lived—but without evidence of a speedy, positive result. The conclusion of the Cultural Revolution left Shulman with neither dignity nor health.[1]

How realistic was Shulman's appeal to the Central Executive Committee? In reality, his case accented two important dimensions of Soviet antireligious policy during the Cultural Revolution. The first, the repression of prominent individuals because of their spiritual beliefs, requires little explanation. The eradication of religion had been a revolutionary goal from the outset, and the Cultural Revolution brought the most aggressive and militant promoters of atheism to the forefront. But the second, the appeal to Soviet law and the principle of revolutionary legality by victims such as Shulman, is more complex. From 1917 onward, even the leadership of the Communist Party failed to manifest a unified position on antireligious policy and the best tactics for promoting atheism, although until the Cultural Revolution those who counseled pragmatic gradualism had been able to restrain militants who simply wanted to displace religious institutions by force. Soviet law, by serving as both a guiding ideal for Soviet antireligious campaigns and a mode of recourse for those wrongly oppressed, therefore played an operative role in Bolshevik efforts against religion throughout the 1920s and even during the more militant days of the Cultural Revolution.

Laws alone, of course, do not make a dictatorship, but the evolution of legislation on religion during the early Soviet period allows us at least to identify major turning points in Bolshevik thinking. Upon coming to office in 1917, despite their tenuous hold on power, Party leaders issued a series of decrees that seriously contravened the interests of religious institutions. A general land decree published soon after the October Revolution included the nationalization of church property; the Declaration on the Rights of the Peoples of Russia of November 2, 1917, abolished all religious privileges in the country; and on December 11,

Sovnarkom (the Council of People's Commissars) transferred all education under church control to the jurisdiction of the People's Commissariat of Enlightenment. Two additional decrees in December took away the authority that the Russian Orthodox Church exercised over marriage and divorce. The first empowered local judges to grant divorces to all citizens, regardless of their religious affiliation, while a second declared that the state would recognize only civil marriages, which did not outlaw church ceremonies but stripped them of their legal standing. An additional pronouncement ordered religious institutions to surrender their registers of births, marriages, and deaths to civil authorities.

The Sovnarkom Decree on the Separation of Church from State and School from Church issued on January 20, 1918, accelerated this assault and defined the short-term framework for church-state conflict. On the one hand, this act moved resolutely to negate religious organizations. It ended the use of religious oaths and ceremonies in state institutions, ordered the removal of religious symbols from public buildings, and outlawed catechism instruction in the schools. The decree forbade religious groups to own property, and it stripped religious societies of their rights as a juridical person. On the other hand, by directing its offensive principally against public ceremonies, church organizations, and property, the separation of church and state consciously spared individual observance. Citizens were free to profess any faith or none at all, they could conduct privately the religious education now excluded from the schools, and religious groups were entitled to petition central and local officials for the free use of buildings and objects intended for religious worship. The separation decree did not, therefore, prohibit private worship or mandate the persecution of individual believers, and it established entitlements under Soviet law that religious believers would subsequently employ to their advantage. The Soviet Constitution adopted in July 1918 reaffirmed the separation of church and state, but it also guaranteed "the freedom for all citizens to conduct religious and antireligious propaganda."

The principle of revolutionary legality, rooted in these early decrees, dictated that churches be closed only with advance authorization from responsible state organs and with the support of the local population, and that former religious structures be converted to socially useful purposes such as schools or clubs for workers. This legality was obviously one of pragmatism rather than of principle or compassion, for it strove for the maximum number of church closures with the minimum alienation of the population and disruption of communities. Nevertheless, even a politically pragmatic commitment to the use of law placed a potentially efficacious weapon in the hands of religious believers, for whom the distinction between confiscations carried out in accordance with

Sovnarkom decrees and those conducted without authorization was meaningless sophistry.

In practice, the actions of antireligious militants as well as responses by religious leaders frequently paid little heed to legalisms, and away from the direct influence of central authorities the church-state conflict created its own dynamics. Local antireligious activists and Soviet officials regularly disregarded legal requirements and confiscated church property in ways that violated both the spirit and letter of Soviet law. From the opposite camp, Patriarch Tikhon threatened to excommunicate those who attempted to implement the separation decree, and in early 1918 he ordered the followers of Orthodoxy to resist the seizure of ecclesiastical property by Soviet power. Parish priests—horrified by attacks on religious objects, faced with the loss of income and standing in their communities, and unshakable in their equation of Orthodoxy with singular truth—incited resistance at the local level when they represented the separation as a complete ban on prayer and worship and attributed it to demonic forces. And among parishioners, responses to church closings and other assaults on the sacred ranged from resignation to obstructionism and passive resistance to armed insurrection and terrorism.

The cumulative alienation among the population that antireligious militancy created influenced the Bolshevik leadership to push the party rank and file more resolutely toward agitation and propaganda as tactics of choice. Following the first major circular on strategic antireligious work from the Party Central Committee in 1921, the early 1920s witnessed the creation of a plethora of new state and party institutions with responsibility for raising the social and political consciousness of the population through cultural enlightenment work. But when the Twelfth Party Congress met in April 1923, Central Committee member Grigorii Zinoviev soberly reported to the delegates: "We have gone too far, much too far. We need serious antireligious propaganda."[2] The congress therefore resolved to limit the use of "deliberately coarse methods" in the future; to create "antireligious mass propaganda in the form of lively and understandable lectures" and approaches "relevant to the social setting"; and to establish special courses to train agitators, develop new techniques, and publish a larger volume of popular and ideological antireligious literature.[3] In October 1924 and again in April 1926, the Party Central Committee issued major antireligious directives that instructed subordinate bodies to follow revolutionary legality and stressed the importance of propaganda over repressive, extralegal measures. In reality, the extreme antireligious militance of the first years of Soviet rule did recede by the mid-1920s, but agitation never fully displaced the use of force against religion, and gains by atheism fell far short of expectations. Instead of the anticipated demise of religion, the second half of the 1920s witnessed dramatic gains by foreign and domestic sectarians and a widespread perception among Bolsheviks that religious belief was actually rising.

In this environment the concept of revolutionary legality unintentionally created avenues through and around Soviet legislation, and religious believers used the letter of the law to subvert its intent. Since open resistance to the tsarist government had proven futile in the past, Russians had long ago established strategies to thwart unwanted initiatives from above or to put their own plans into motion. After 1917 religious believers drew heavily on past experience and guile as they cited law whenever possible in local confrontations and, if unsuccessful, appealed to central authorities to have lower decisions overturned. The frequency of their success lay at the root of Kalinin's sympathetic reputation, and antireligious agitators complained that "believers know the path to VTsIK and Mikhail Ivanovich [Kalinin] very well."[4] A positive outcome for those who launched appeals was by no means assured. To fight religious repression through the Soviet bureaucracy required persistence, political acumen, a willingness to take risks, the ability to speak to the Soviet regime in its own language, and often more than a little luck.

Workers and peasants certainly required no instruction in composing petitions. Even during the internecine Russian Civil War, they did not hesitate to produce scores of signatures demanding the release of arrested clergy; and when the law on the separation of church and state made possible the transfer of nationalized places of worship to registered communes of believers, congregations quickly recognized the potential thereby to gain control of their parishes. They submitted literally hundreds of such documents to local soviets, which sometimes gave church buildings and sacred objects back to the petitioners, and the VTsIK Commission on Religious Issues reopened a significant number of churches that had been nationalized without prior authorization.[5] The expansion of sectarianism (*sektantsvo*) during the 1920s spawned additional episodes of recourse to Soviet law. Religious organizations capitalized on the opportunity to form economic communes voluntarily, and by 1926 hundreds of religious communes were masquerading as economic cooperatives. Moreover, the exemptions from military service granted to some denominations attracted new converts to their ranks. Indeed, by 1929 there were religious activists who were so familiar with the operations of the state apparatus that their petitions—which sometimes contained sophisticated references to previous legal decisions in their favor—moved quickly through the bureaucracy.

The radicalization of all spheres of party work that began with the Cultural Revolution in 1928 altered the legal position of religion in the

Soviet Union once again. In response to the lack of progress on the antireligious front, on April 8, 1929, VTsIK and Sovnarkom jointly issued "On Religious Associations," which superseded the 1918 separation of church and state and redefined freedom of conscience. Although it retained central aspects of the 1918 decree, the new law introduced important limitations. Twenty or more adults could still form a religious association—that is, a parish—but only if registered and approved in advance by government authorities. They retained their previous right to the free use of buildings for worship but still could not exist as a juridical person. Most important, the "freedom of religious and antireligious propaganda" guaranteed by the Soviet Constitution became the "freedom of religious belief and of antireligious propaganda for all citizens." In effect, proselytizing and instruction outside the home became illegal except in officially sanctioned classes, and religious rights of assembly and property were now more circumscribed.

During the Cultural Revolution, religious persecution intensified. The number and tempo of church closings rose dramatically, often on local initiative and therefore without the requisite prior authorization. Even when such acts did observe Soviet law, the sheer volume of new work reduced state agencies to approving long lists with only cursory discussion. Local officials and courts deprived clergy of housing and arrested, imprisoned, or exiled them to distant regions on contrived charges. Militants burned icons and seized church bells, and they routinely took from believers even what was necessary for family maintenance. Complaints abounded when religious believers were rounded up without regard for age, gender, or health to perform menial and difficult labor. Officials also unleashed economic weapons. In 1930 a large number of local soviets levied taxes on religious organizations some thirty to seventy times higher than during the previous year; by 1931 there were attempts to charge usurious rent for the land beneath the buildings to which Soviet law granted religious organizations free use. Kalinin's secretary categorically denounced the prevailing character of such assaults: "There exists no sign of elementary revolutionary legality toward them as *lishensty*. There reigns in the local areas complete arbitrary rule and a lack of understanding of the policy of the party in this politically important process."[6]

Believers, however, did not simply bow to lawlessness but sought recourse by filing documents of legitimate grievance as well as misrepresentations. Typically they resorted to their right to register a parish as a way to prevent a given church from closure. If unsuccessful locally, they would send delegations to superordinate regional organs or even dispatch a single representative directly to the VTsIK Commission on Religious Issues. It was the success of such tactics that both bolstered Kalinin's public image and outraged those responsible for implementing Bolshevik antireligious campaigns, especially since not all representations made to central organs were truthful. The Commission on Religious Issues therefore often found itself confronted not only with opposing versions of the same events but also with falsified documents that turned out to contain the signatures of children less than ten years old and even babes in arms. Nevertheless, although inundated with appeals from believers, the leadership of VTsIK continued throughout the Cultural Revolution to intervene—with mixed success—where laws had been breached.

In the end, the Shulman case cannot be dismissed as an idiosyncratic episode involving an unrealistic crank; rather, it represented an avenue regularly pursued by victims of religious persecution. Although driven by deprivation and desperation, the cantor followed a legal strategy not only common during the period but also successful in enough cases that it became a key weapon for defending churches and believers. As we have seen, the concern among the Bolshevik leadership for the principle of revolutionary legality enabled the oppressed to cite their entitlements under Soviet law in order to win the registration of parishes, the reopening of churches, the release of arrested clergy, and the return of sacred objects. The religious did not prevail in all cases, as the resolution of the Shulman case—an unalloyed tragedy and injustice in human terms—makes clear. But although Shulman attained little of what he sought, the process was as historically significant as the outcome. The persistence with which he appealed to Soviet law and the magnitude of the concessions that he was willing to make indicated that it was an approach viable enough for him to put his energies and hopes into it.

In a larger sense, the very failure of Shulman to attain relief, despite such high-level support, also demonstrates the limitations of authoritarian control. Shulman's experience illustrates that central organs exercised considerably less than complete authority over subordinates even during the Cultural Revolution, one of the most repressive and violent chapters in Soviet history. Moreover, it shows that there often existed a marked difference between the approach to eradicating religion taken at the highest state and party levels and the prevailing attitudes in the local areas. Variations abounded, but in general central officials more seriously weighed the relative merits of closing churches against the further alienation of a population whose loyalty was by no means assured; uncontrolled and unfocused militancy that disregarded political pragmatism more often held sway below. And most important in the long term, the case of Shulman brings into focus the strong awareness among the Soviet leadership of the problem of political legitimacy that they faced in the USSR, an issue whose ramifications far outlasted the upheaval of 1928–1932.

NOTES

1. The correspondence related to the Shulman case is located in the State Archive of the Russian Federation (GARF), Moscow, f. 5263, op. 1, d. 14, ll. 1, 4–5, 7–15, 23.

2. *Dvenadtsatyi sezd RKP(b): Stenograficheskii otchet, 17–25 aprelia 1923 g.* (Moscow, 1968), 44.

3. *Kommunisticheskaia partiia Sovetskogo soiuza v rezoliutsiiakh i resheniiakh sezdov, konferentsii i plenumov TsK, chast I, 1918–1925* (Moscow, 1953), 743–45.

4. *Bezbozhnik* 23 (June 12, 1929): 4.

5. Central State Archive of the City of Moscow (TsGIAgM), f. 1215, op. 2, dd. 75–170; Central State Archive of Moscow Oblast (TsGAMO), f. 66, op. 18, dd. 320–44; GARF, f. 353, op. 4, d. 378, l. 102; GARF, f. 5263, op. 1, d. 9, ll. 3, 7–10.

6. GARF, f. 5263, op. 1., d. 7, l. 71.

SUGGESTED READINGS

Anderson, John. *Religion, State and Politics in the Soviet Union and Successor States*. Cambridge, 1994.

Davies, Sarah. *Popular Opinion in Stalin's Russia: Terror, Propaganda and Dissent, 1934–1941*. Cambridge, 1997.

Engelstein, Laura. *Castration and the Heavenly Kingdom*. Ithaca, NY, 1999.

Fitzpatrick, Sheila. *Stalin's Peasants: Resistance and Survival in the Russian Village after Collectivization*. New York, 1994.

_____, ed. *Cultural Revolution in Russia, 1928–1931*. Bloomington, IN, 1978.

Husband, William B. *"Godless Communists": Atheism and Society in Soviet Russia, 1917–1932*. DeKalb, IL, 2000.

_____. "Soviet Atheism and Russian Orthodox Strategies of Resistance, 1917–1932." *Journal of Modern History* 70 (March 1998): 74–107.

Oda, Hiroshi. "Revolutionary Legality in the USSR, 1928–1930." *Review of Socialist Law* 6 (1980): 141–51.

Peris, Daniel. *Storming the Heavens: The Soviet League of the Militant Godless*. Ithaca, 1998.

_____. " 'God Is Now on Our Side': The Religious Revival in Unoccupied Soviet Territory during World War II." *Kritika* 1 (Autumn 1999): 97–118.

Solomon, Peter H., Jr. *Soviet Criminal Justice under Stalin*. Cambridge, 1996.

Stites, Richard. *Revolutionary Dreams: Utopian Vision and Experimental Life in the Russian Revolution*. New York, 1989.

Viola, Lynne. *Peasant Rebels under Stalin: Collectivization and the Culture of Peasant Resistance*. New York, 1996.

Young, Glennys. *Power and the Sacred in Revolutionary Russia: Religious Activists in the Village*. University Park, PA, 1997.

PART IV

STALINISM AND BEYOND

The reign of every Soviet and Russian leader since 1953 has been directly influenced by the long-term consequences of Stalinism. Not only does the experience of repression during the 1930s touch Russian life in countless ways to this day, but also the various attempts to deal with the legacy of Joseph Stalin have kept another central truth in focus: that even dictatorships need to reach a variety of accommodations with the society they seek to control. In short, public opinion, resistance to and the circumvention of authority, and the rule of law are in no way absent from single-party authoritarian regimes, even though they manifest themselves in ways dramatically different under dictatorships than in participatory systems.* Police terror, in fact, reached a point of diminishing returns even during Stalin's lifetime; his successors have had to find ways to deal with its multiple long-term reverberations.

Advocacy of reform in Soviet and post-Soviet Russia has accordingly been an instrument both of those who sought to alter the status quo and of others who desired to maintain it. Nikita Khrushchev, Leonid Brezhnev, Iurii Andropov, Konstantin Chernenko, Mikhail Gorbachëv, and Boris Yeltsin each addressed reform in his own fashion as leader, but not with a principled reconfiguration of Russian political and social existence in mind. Rather, like Tsar Alexander II, their motivations have been above all to protect and enhance their own authority while improving Russia's ability to pursue its national interests effectively. And with the exception of the brief rule of Chernenko, every Soviet and post-Soviet leader has pursued reform seriously for at least a portion of his tenure. They have attempted to overcome not only the ruinously centralized political and economic systems that they inherited, but also Stalinism's principal social legacies: the inculcation of a widespread pattern of preemptive obedience that has stifled the expression of ideas and undermined public confidence; a system of rewards and

*For illustrations of this point in recent scholarship see Sarah Davies, *Popular Opinion in Stalin's Russia: Terror, Propaganda and Dissent, 1934–1941* (Cambridge, 1997); Sheila Fitzpatrick, *Stalin's Peasants: Resistance and Survival in the Russian Village after Collectivization* (New York, 1994); Alena V. Ledeneva, *Russia's Economy of Favors: Blat, Networking, and Informal Exchanges* (Cambridge, 1998); Peter H. Solomon, Jr., *Soviet Criminal Justice under Stalin* (Cambridge, 1996); and Douglas R. Weiner, *A Little Corner of Freedom: Russian Nature Protection from Stalin to Gorbachëv* (Berkeley, 1999).

sanctions that placed consensus above competence, acquiescence above initiative, and rationalization over responsibility; an ethos of misdirection in matters public and private; and the predominance of dogged self-preservation rather than enterprise among citizens.

Soviet politics configured these social realities in stages. Although he emerged as party leader in 1928, Stalin consolidated his full dictatorial powers only during the late 1930s and following World War II. At the end of the Seventeenth Party Congress in January 1934, Stalin lacked the full authority he desired, and the cult of his personality did not yet dominate in society. The bloody purges of the second half of the decade were a watershed. A series of show trials convicted long-standing revolutionary leaders—Stalin's former rivals Bukharin, Zinoviev, and Kamenev among them—of preposterous charges such as spying for foreign powers. Arrest and execution befell a significant segment of the party leadership and their families, the military high command, and the upper tiers of industrial management. Intellectuals, religious activists, people with unacceptable political and class backgrounds, dissidents, and nonconformists of various stripes suffered disproportionately. Moreover, with widespread mechanisms of denunciation in place, the purges ultimately took on an element of randomness before they ran their course. The reverberations in society by the end of the 1930s were understandably chilling, but by no means final. In view of the massive sacrifices made during the war, the population anticipated a loosening of controls after 1945. Instead, Stalin declared the real war against capitalism to be only beginning, and a determined watchfulness for ideological deviations stretched from the arts to the study of genetics during his final years. By the time of Stalin's death in 1953, the Soviet Union had become a global military power, but he left behind an equally important social legacy of demoralization and fear.

Stalin's immediate successor, Nikita S. Khrushchev, therefore did not overlook the task of providing greater personal security for the population as he launched ambitious reforms to raise its standard of living. His so-called secret speech of 1956 assailed the crimes of the Stalin era and called for greater truthfulness in discussing, for example, the history of the Communist Party. In addition to his well-known efforts to improve diplomatic relations with the West, he set into motion ambitious labor-intensive agricultural programs in the Soviet Far East, attempted to mitigate some of the more draconian constraints on the collective farms, looked to science and technology to overcome structural faults in the economy, and boldly predicted surpassing the United States by 1960 in the production of commodities such as meat and butter.

Although initially promising—he withstood a serious challenge to his authority in 1957— Khrushchev's new path ultimately produced frustration and dislocation. His calls for greater openness in society left boundaries of acceptable public discourse undefined, and scholars and artists learned the limits of what was permissible only when they overstepped them. A backlash against his policies of de-Stalinization arose in society as well as the party, and his personal tolerance of dissenting opinion and artistic expression proved to be considerably short of absolute. He also exhibited impatience in spheres of reform. What began as long-term projects were frequently compressed into a short period of time, with predictably disastrous results. To complicate matters, he alienated important interest groups by cutting military spending and reorganizing economic and political bureaucracies. The humiliation suffered by the USSR from the Cuban Missile Crisis of October 1962 evaporated whatever goodwill that he had left, and two years later his own clients in the party leadership, led by Leonid Brezhnev, drove him from office.

From hindsight, Brezhnev might seem to fit the mold of reformer badly. The characterization of his eighteen-year rule as the Era of Stagnation has become part of standard political lexicon well beyond the borders of Russia. A leader so tolerant of corruption that he could not silence, even in the secretive USSR, scandals involving members of his immediate family, Brezhnev fiercely guarded the privileges of party members and unwaveringly championed the "haves" over the "have nots." Economic growth fell to virtually zero at the end of his reign, and by the time of his death in November 1982 cynicism and opportunism predominated throughout society. But this was not how Brezhnev began. Following a massive expansion of the USSR's arsenal of strategic weapons, in 1970 he attempted a policy of the relaxation of international tensions (what the West labeled détente). The idea was to halt military confrontations with the West as a prelude to negotiating arms control treaties and trade agreements. Accomplishing this goal would slow economically ruinous military spending on both sides and allow the Soviet Union to acquire consumer goods without significantly restructuring its industrial sector. By the mid-1970s, Brezhnev had negotiated trade agreements with the United States, Britain, France, and Japan. But old tensions revived, the promising picture in trade never materialized, and by the late 1970s his strategy lay in ruins. Brezhnev was too entrenched politically to dislodge from his post but too discredited to launch new meaningful, productive programs. The Era of Stagnation was the result.

Mikhail Gorbachëv and Boris Yeltsin consequently inherited both the distant legacy of Stalin and the more recent one of Brezhnev. Following brief periods of rule by Andropov and Chernenko (both of whom were ill when they assumed office), Gorbachëv attempted the broad restructuring of the national economy—*perestroika*—in a general environment of greater openness known as *glasnost*. The first Soviet leader to have spent his full professional career in the post-Stalin period, Gorbachëv understood well the negative effects of bureaucratism and the loss of legitimacy that the government had suffered from its chronic avoidance of public truth. While he was attempting to place the subsidized economy on a rational basis of cost accounting, Gorbachëv therefore opened lines of communication and invited criticism of shortfalls. What he did not anticipate—in the face of the sacrifices and hardships that *perestroika* brought on—was how much the criticism would be directed at the leader himself. By the late 1980s, Boris Yeltsin, an ousted party secretary, resurrected his career in a populist mode and became the foremost critic of the slow progress of Gorbachëv's reforms. He rallied society and was elected president of the Russian Republic; and when the Soviet Union collapsed at the end of 1991, Yeltsin inherited Gorbachëv's problems. What began with celebrations and optimism, however, disintegrated rapidly. Runaway inflation in 1992–93 wiped out the savings of whole generations, while hustlers and gangsters appeared to be the main beneficiaries of the new order. Unable to produce solutions, Yeltsin reigned over a government both unstable and corrupt. Mafia members, hoodlums, and the unscrupulous prospered while the government fell months behind in the payment of wages and pensions to ordinary citizens. Attempts to privatize the economy led more to opportunism than opportunity; ministers were appointed and dismissed seemingly at the whim of the leader, and by the end of the 1990s a large segment of the population lived worse than under the Communist regime.

The history of very few nations, in short, can match the drama experienced in Russia since the 1930s. Among the varied elements are the nature of the police state terror itself (Chapter 11), the plight of ordinary citizens trying to cope with the mechanics of the Soviet system (Chapter 12), and the hope and frustration at the end of the Soviet era (Chapter 13). Russia will inevitably be a prisoner of its political past for a long time into the future.

Mr. Ezhov Goes to Moscow

The Rise of a Stalinist Police Chief*

J. Arch Getty

Inhuman behavior by humans is in no way a recent invention, but the forms that it has taken in the present age have given rise to new historical questions. Examples of the macabre inventiveness and skill of our ancient, medieval, and modern ancestors in inflicting misery on one another abound. The dubious contribution of the twentieth century has been to expand dramatically the scale of individual episodes of atrocity. Thus, as the application of lessons of organization, mobilization, and efficiency borrowed from industry and technology have significantly increased the scope of the violence during the last century, a questioning of the underlying causality has inevitably followed. Not surprisingly, some answers have relied heavily on demonizing the perpetrators of mass violence as well as those who failed to prevent it, either by narrowly blaming a single leader or broadly indicting a group as amorphous as an entire nation. Another approach, however, has eschewed demonization in favor of probing the mechanisms of atrocity itself. Rather than imbuing the planners and perpetrators of mass violence with nonhuman characteristics and dismissing them simplistically as the embodiment of evil, other students of the issue have produced a portrait of what Hannah Arendt labeled "the banality of evil." In this view, explanation rests not on the implementation of sinister motivations on a mass scale, but the degree to which actions previously unthinkable became ordinary to those who perpetrated them. And while the dramatization of evil in the first explanation allows us to distance ourselves from these atrocities, the linking of extraordinary cruelty with conventional behavior makes the second picture the more chilling.

The great purges of the 1930s in the Soviet Union must stand near the center of any such discussion of mass violence in the twentieth century. Efforts to interpret and understand this episode of Soviet and human history have generated heated disagreements, but all responsible views—

*Research for this article was carried out between 1997 and 1999 in Moscow at the State Archive of the Russian Federation (GARF) and at the Russian State Archive of Social-Political History (RGASPI). Most of this article is based on Nikolai Ivanovich Ezhov's personal archive at the RGASPI.

including the one presented in this volume—give significant moral and political responsibility to Joseph Stalin. But blaming Stalin provides only a partial explanation. In a nation that covered one-sixth of the world's land mass, what kind of apparatus carried out this mass terror? Who were its executioners? Where did they come from, and what professional or personal experiences prepared them for their work? If there is anything surprising about the voluminous literature on Stalin's purges, it is that it provides not only few answers to such questions, but also that it gives them little attention.

In his essay, Arch Getty therefore explores the "banality of evil" that characterized the career of Stalin's henchman Nikolai Ivanovich Ezhov, whose formative experiences have been little studied previously. A dedicated Communist and talented administrator, Ezhov sacrificed for the cause both before and after 1917. Hard-working and ambitious, he orchestrated his transfer to Moscow and at every upward stage in his career won the favor of his superiors, culminating with Stalin himself. And as the chief architect of the purges, Ezhov followed his career to its logical extreme as a victim of the apparatus of terror that he had once headed.

J. Arch Getty, professor of history at the University of California at Los Angeles, has written widely on Stalinism. His chief publications include Origins of the Great Purges *(1985) and, as coeditor,* Stalinist Terror: New Perspectives *(1993). He received his Ph.D. from Boston College.*

The second half of the 1930s saw a violent eruption of terror in the Soviet Union, the great purges of the 1930s. Having their roots in existing social conflicts, traditions of political violence, a war scare, and Stalin's "sickly suspicion" (as Nikita Khrushchev would later put it), the great purges were a combination of vigilante actions from below, mutual denunciations of one's rivals, and secret police arrests from above. Purges and counterpurges swept the country in what became a war of all against all. Between 1936 and 1939, more than 750,000 persons were summarily executed, most without any trial. At least 1.5 million others were arrested for various political crimes, and an equal number for other reasons. Many of them also died from brutal treatment or terrible conditions after arrest. At the end of the decade, some 1.5 million people were in the harsh regime camps of the dreaded Gulag system; altogether, more than 4 million people were in prison, camp, or distant exile in the Soviet Union.

As leader of the party and state, Stalin is responsible for the bloodshed; his policies instigated parts of the terror and permitted others. His presumed motives have been discussed at length in historical works and included settling old scores, eliminating political rivals, and preempting future challenges to his power. Indeed, recent research seems to support Isaac Deutscher's guess nearly fifty years ago that Stalin and his lieutenants, fearing a war with Germany and Japan, decided to eliminate in advance any possibility of an antiregime "fifth column" in time of war.

Still, many social and political constituencies approved of or tolerated terror; and, although Stalin's motives have been analyzed at length, it is surprising that we know very little about those who actually carried out the terror. He had no shortage of enthusiastic assistants and supporters in the gruesome process. The vast majority of the arrests and executions, along with administration of the labor camps, were in the hands of the secret police: the People's Commissariat of Internal Affairs, or NKVD. Yet we know next to nothing about the backgrounds of these executives of terror. Where did they come from? And what life or career patterns prepared them for this grisly work?

One man, Nikolai Ivanovich Ezhov, headed the NKVD throughout the period of the great purges. At the height of his power in 1938, he held more offices and titles than anyone before or after in the entire history of the Soviet Union. In addition to his post as People's Commissar of Internal Affairs, he was Commissar for Water Transport, a member of the party's ruling Politburo and Orgburo, and a secretary of the Central Committee. He was a member of the Executive Committee of the Communist International and a member of the Presidium of the Executive Committee of the Supreme Soviet. Moreover, he headed the party's disciplinary body, the Commission of Party Control, and exercised general supervision over the assignment of party personnel through his deputy, Georgii Malenkov. Factories, bridges, towns, and rural districts were named after him.

In less than one year, he disappeared completely. By March 1939 he had been arrested and stripped of all his offices; his name was never again mentioned publicly in the Soviet Union during Stalin's lifetime. It was as if he had never existed. Until the 1990s there were no articles or books about him in any language, and to this date there are no documented scholarly studies of his life and activities. Recently declassified archives in Russia allow us for the first time to answer some basic questions: Who was Nikolai Ivanovich Ezhov? Where did he come from? And what prepared him to become Stalin's executive of terror?

Ezhov was born in 1895 in St. Petersburg, the capital of the Russian Empire. At the age of fifteen he left school and became a factory worker. St. Petersburg was then in the throes of industrial revolution. From 1897 to 1914 the population of the city swelled from 1.2 to 2.2 million, and between 1890 and 1914 its working class grew from 73,000 to 242,000, mostly concentrated in gigantic new plants. The Putilov factory, where young Ezhov found a job as an apprentice metal fitter, employed more than 30,000 workers in numerous shops and shipyards.

It was here that Ezhov received his real education in a cauldron of class hatred and conflict. Conditions for St. Petersburg workers were severe. Working-class neighborhoods were usually fetid, muddy places of stench and disease without paved streets and often without running water. On average, 4.1 Putilov workers shared a single room, usually in a basement or garret, and paid the highest rents in the country. Death rates in workers' districts were very high: 23 to 26 per 1,000, and one in four babies born there died before their first birthday. Workers spent an average of 50 percent of their miserable wages on food and another 25 percent on substandard housing and clothing. Young Ezhov was not alone in his new job. At Putilov, two-thirds of the workers had started at age fifteen or sixteen. These teenagers entered a factory system that was hierarchical, tense, and dangerous. Putilov employees labored an average of ten hours per day in shops that were poorly ventilated and lit and lacked safety rules, clothing, or equipment. The Putilov plant averaged one industrial accident every other day, usually involving worker injuries.

Unlike American factories, where engineers and foreman often work and consult side by side with workers on the line, factories in Russia were strictly segregated according to power and privilege. An authoritarian chain of command was the rule, and arbitrariness and petty tyranny were the standard modes of operation. Until 1905 workers could be beaten by capricious petty despots in the factory hierarchy. In later years, a series of constant and arbitrary fines were imposed on workers for any infraction. It is not surprising that Russian factory workers had a deep distrust and hatred of management, and Ezhov must have absorbed the bitter confrontational attitudes of his fellows.

St. Petersburg workers had a tradition of resistance and revolution. In 1905 they had formed Russia's first soviet and had led the general strike that spread to the entire country. The Putilov plant was always a hotbed of labor radicalism, and the seventeen-year-old Ezhov participated in union committee work and strikes. He would later recall with pride the "tough time" that union activists gave factory management. By 1916, Putilov workers were frequently on strike and that year were locked out of the factory after demanding a 70 percent wage hike to keep up with inflation during the World War. In February 1917 a strike at Putilov would set in motion a chain of labor strikes and actions that would topple the monarchy. As the February Revolution picked up steam across the city and country, the fiery Putilov workers would murder the plant manager and his aide and throw their bodies into a nearby canal.

Ezhov, however, was no longer at Putilov when his workmates perpetrated that act of class violence. His extremely short height—full grown he would only be four feet, eleven inches tall—disqualified him from combat service, but in 1914 or 1915 he was drafted into the Russian army along with 8,000 other workers identified as labor militants and troublemakers. Enrolled in a "punitive battalion" and sent to the town of Vitebsk, he served there as a metal fitter in a military workshop.

Military discipline does not seem to have inhibited Ezhov's radical views or activities. Contemporaries remember that at the time of the fall of the monarchy in February 1917, Ezhov was already a political activist. Sometime in the first half of the year, he attached himself to the Marxist RSDRP, most likely as an unaffiliated "internationalist," but by summer he had officially joined Lenin's Bolsheviks. Ezhov joined Lenin's party at a time when it was not particularly fashionable to do so, and throughout his life he would carry the positive credential of party member before the Bolshevik Revolution of October 1917. In Vitebsk, Ezhov was an active organizer of radical forces. In the summer of 1917 he was one of the founders of the Vitebsk Red Guard, one of many armed workers' and soldiers' detachments formed around the country. Like his future boss Stalin, Ezhov worked as a committeeman behind the scenes and hated public speaking.

Through clever tactics and sometimes bluff, Ezhov and his Red Guards helped hold Vitebsk for the radicals, struggled with the town's moderates and liberals, and prevented the passage of rightist forces on their way to the capital. According to one story, he managed to intimidate a detachment of counterrevolutionary soldiers marching on the revolutionary capital by pure trickery. Having few Red Guards at hand, he distracted an enemy detachment by sending out a party of women to parley with them. He then ran a troop train in a circle, loading and unloading the same boxcar of Red Guards several times in front of the confused counterrevolutionaries who, faced with the alarming combination of radical women and "thousands" of Red Guards, turned back.

Although he was a Bolshevik worker activist in 1917, he had not yet decided to become a professional Bolshevik politician. After the October uprising that brought the Bolsheviks to power, Ezhov continued to work in various factories and railroad shops in Vitebsk and other towns. Probably because of his height, the Red Army draft passed him by until April 1919 when, in the heat of their civil war struggle with the Whites, he was called up for military service.

Sent to the Volga town of Saratov, Ezhov was assigned to work in a communications detachment; and in October 1919, at the age of twenty-four, he became commissar of the detachment's radio school when it was evacuated to Kazan. As a political commissar, much of his work involved personnel selection and assignment. He spent the Civil War in Kazan, working his way up to the position of political commissar of the Kazan Radio Base while also serving on the propaganda staff (*agitprop*) of the Bolshevik Tatar regional party committee (*obkom*).

Like many young Bolsheviks flung into the viciousness of the struggle, he saw on a daily basis the culture of violence and unyielding hatreds during the Civil War. Reds and Whites were fighting for their lives, and it was common for no prisoners to be taken, no quarter to be asked or given. Massacres and torture were commonplace in an environment of treason, betrayal, and general chaos. Already tempered by his early experiences at Putilov, Ezhov was further hardened by service in the class-against-class and brother-against-brother atmosphere of the Civil War. Death was everywhere, and veterans of this struggle, imbued with the sense that politics was a life-and-death battle, became accustomed to solving political conflicts violently; one was either friend or foe.

The Bolshevik party was growing dramatically. Veteran members no longer knew everyone in the party, and the automatic acceptance previously given to unknown comrades was being replaced by a certain care and even suspicion. The enemy could be anywhere, and all kinds of untested recruits were flooding into the party in order to be on the winning side. Those like Ezhov who specialized in choosing and assigning cadres became grimly aware of the difficulty—and desperate importance—of deciding friend from foe. Such people would become indispensable to the new regime.

Working in propaganda and personnel selection in Kazan were Ezhov's first experiences with bureaucratic administration and office routine. He seems to have taken to it instantly. His boss, A. T. Uglov, the famous early Soviet radio expert who had installed Lenin's telephone system, gave him glowing evaluations and increasingly greater responsibility. In turn, Ezhov was a good supervisor, and his subordinates would remember a chief who reflexively shared his food and clothing with comrades who had none. With the Bolshevik victory in 1921, Ezhov returned to civilian life and married Antonina Titova, a local Kazan girl whom he had met in *agitprop* work. Demobilized from the Red Army, Nikolai and Antonina headed for Moscow sometime in the autumn of 1921 to seek their fortunes.

Just a few months later, Ezhov was named Responsible Party Secretary for the Mari Autonomous Region, a large territory just across the Volga where the population was mostly of the non-Russian Mari nationality. A major career advancement for Ezhov, it made him a member of the full-time staff of paid party officials known as the *nomenklatura* and subordinated him directly to the party's Central Committee. In the early 1920s the party had a crying need for dependable administrators with trustworthy backgrounds. Ezhov, as a Putilov worker, Red Guard organizer, and Civil War political commissar, had good credentials, and his experience as an administrator marked him for higher things. In March 1921, Nikolai and Antonina arrived in Krasnokokshaisk (soon to be renamed Iokshar-Ola) in the woods and swamps of Mari territory. They found there a small party organization of 437 members, led by a regional board of only 21 people.

In Mari, Ezhov added another element to his professional dossier: experience in the turbulent world of Bolshevik provincial politics. Local politics was often factionalized around two or more key party leaders who contended for control, patronage, and Moscow's favor. In this case, the Mari regional party was divided into a faction that followed one I. P. Petrov and another that gravitated to Ezhov. In a typical pattern the two Russian factions denounced one another to Moscow. It is difficult to determine who belonged to which faction, and loyalties revolved around personalities more than principles as the groups maneuvered against one another, sometimes even exchanging positions on the issues.

Ezhov embroiled himself in these intrigues against his rival Petrov, and their struggle soon frustrated the Central Committee in Moscow. In a pattern frequently repeated elsewhere in the periphery, Moscow first tried to reconcile the factions by dispatching peacemaking emissaries from the capital to the province. This effort often failed; and in late 1922 or early 1923, Moscow solved the Mari mess by taking what was often the second step: the Central Committee recalled both Ezhov and Petrov to Moscow and, without taking either side, assigned them to other posts.

Despite the backbiting in Mari, Ezhov's efficient administrative work continued to make a good impression on his Moscow party superiors. Shortly after his recall to the capital, in March 1923 he was appointed Responsible Party Secretary in the Semipalatinsk city party organization in Kirgizia. Again, this was a significant career step. Not only did Ezhov receive a bonus of three months' salary, but his new post also was in a party organization of about 2,500 members, nearly ten times larger than that in Mari, and he was one of the three leading party secretaries of a large territory.

Once again, his efficiency impressed his superiors, and Ezhov rose rapidly. After only three months in Semipalatinsk, G. A. Korostelov, the First Secretary of the Kirgiz party organization, moved Ezhov to the Kirgiz capital of Orenburg and appointed him chief of the entire region's party personnel appointment department (*orginstrukt*). Several months later the new First Secretary of Kirgizia, V. I. Naneishvili, made Ezhov a full secretary of the newly formed Kirgiz territorial party organization. At the time, one of Naneishvili's deputies had suggested to the Central Committee in Moscow that Ezhov should be made First Secretary of all

Kirgizia, "since Ezhov is already doing his [Naneishvili's] job anyway." The territory had more than 28,000 party members: once again, Ezhov had been promoted to help lead a party organization ten times larger than that where he previously worked.

In just four years, he had risen from being a minor commissar in a radio school to running the party personnel machine in a large province (where he may have been the de facto leading party secretary). He now had considerable experience with the party's bureaucratic system, the all-important work of assigning party personnel, the nuances of party intrigue, and the delicate implementation of party nationality policy. In Moscow's eyes, he was a competent and valued cadre of provincial administration.

No Bolshevik, however, wanted to spend his entire career in the non-Russian periphery, far from Moscow. As it is today, Moscow was the center of the country. It had the best cultural life, housing and food supplies, and living and working conditions. Moreover, it was the focus of power. The highly centralized party and state apparatus was there, and it was in Moscow that one made and used the personal connections that could advance career and status. Those assigned to provincial posts, and even the temporary circuit-riding inspectors sent out from Moscow, tried to minimize their time in the periphery.

Ezhov wanted to be in Moscow and did all he could to get there. As early as the autumn of 1923, Nikolai and Antonina had decided that she should study at the Timiriazev Agricultural Academy, partly for her career and partly to scout out possibilities and make connections for them in the capital. Ezhov was frequently a delegate to national party conferences in Moscow and did the same on these trips. In 1924 he had written from Kirgizia to Central Committee Secretary V. M. Molotov. In the letter, Ezhov fondly recalled their meeting at a recent party conference and reminded Molotov about how they had discussed the possibility of Ezhov moving to Moscow. But after replanting that seed in Molotov's mind, Ezhov went on to note in true, modest Bolshevik style that "in these difficult times since the death of Lenin, personal wishes do not count, especially given the weak party situation in Kirgizia." He soberly concluded that his Bolshevik duty required him to stay in the periphery. Nobody in Moscow took the hint. Molotov referred Ezhov's letter to L. M. Kaganovich, another top Stalin lieutenant, who seems to have ignored the matter. Or maybe he didn't. The party had a crying shortage of talented administrators at all levels, particularly in the provinces, and it may well have been that the top party leaders in Moscow thought that Ezhov was most useful exactly where he was.

Realizing that he was probably not going to get the golden summons from the capital, Ezhov took matters into his own hands. In January 1926 he persuaded his comrades in Kazakhstan (into which parts of Kirgizia had been reorganized) to send him to Moscow to take a series of party courses at the Communist Academy. Such study was eventually expected of "practical workers" such as Ezhov who had little formal education or schooling in Marxist-Leninist theory. Even though he was dispatched by the Kazakh party organization, it seems that no one in Moscow expected him. When he arrived, the entry class was already full and he was not accepted into the Marxism courses until mid-March.

Ezhov was a student at the Communist Academy for a little over one year, during which time his organizational talents again surfaced. By September 1926 he was a student representative to the Academy's party cell, and there he filed a written complaint on the students' behalf with the Academy's administration about the miserly stipends that they received. Stipends were based partially on the size of one's family, and from these papers we discover that Ezhov claimed to be supporting a family of eight: his mother, his wife, and five nieces and nephews. This claim made Ezhov's family the largest of any of the 114 students and entitled him to a stipend of 225 rubles per month.

When a party worker completed the Marxist course of study, he was supposed to return to the party organization that had sent him. But Ezhov never went back. After a little more than a year of study in Moscow, in July 1927 he landed a new job that would keep him in the capital: an "instructor" hired by the Central Committee's personnel assignment department (Orgraspred). Instructors were important functionaries who supervised personnel in specified geographical areas. Ezhov's experience in the non-Russian provinces was a good credential for the post, and the appointment made him a full-time worker in the central party apparatus. His boss, Orgraspred chief I. M. Moskvin, was a taciturn and ascetic Old Bolshevik who neither drank nor smoked and who had a reputation as a hard boss, difficult to get along with and hard to please. But Moskvin was impressed with his hard-working thirty-two-year-old instructor. After only one month, Moskvin made Ezhov his personal assistant, and three months later elevated him to be Deputy Chief of Orgraspred of the Central Committee.

For three years, Ezhov worked as Moskvin's deputy in the busy offices of Orgraspred. Responsible for the assignment of all party personnel, this agency was crucial to a system where patronage was vitally important. Orgraspred recommended cadres and, through Moskvin, reported to the powerful Orgburo where the party's supreme leaders (including Stalin, Kaganovich, and Molotov) sat. Ezhov's work continued to impress, so much so that other party leaders tried to poach him from Moskvin's preserve. In 1928 a secretary of the Tatar Province Party Organization wrote to the Central Committee Secretariat proposing that

Ezhov be made a secretary in Tataria: "He is a strong guy . . . he will put the Tatars in order." But Moskvin kept his talented assistant who, as in the past, had come to do much of his chief's work.

Ezhov's written reports were crisp and to the point. His remarks at Orgraspred conferences reflected impatience with the long-winded oratory of others, and he often insisted that speakers be specific and propose concrete steps, rather than simply talking in theoretical or vague generalities. Ezhov made reports on a wide variety of topics at Orgraspred conferences and thereby picked up considerable technical knowledge about labor statistics, transportation, party composition, and especially provision of party cadres for rural work in agriculture.

This expertise stood Ezhov in good stead, for in 1929 he was named Deputy Commissar (minister) of the newly formed USSR People's Commissariat of Agriculture (Narkomzem), with special responsibility for the assignment of personnel in the new drive for collectivization of agriculture. This post was Ezhov's first nonparty state appointment, and it illustrates an important point about Stalinist institutional practice. One typical Bolshevik solution to policy implementation was simply to form a new organization staffed with entirely new personnel committed to the new policy. Stalin was fond of saying that personnel selection was the most important aspect of the regime's activity: "personnel determine everything," as he would put it in 1935. The Stalinist tendency was not so much to think of institutional execution of policy but rather about appropriate staffing, or cadres. Who would do it was more important than which institution would do it.

Every new policy, every new initiative, and even repetition of previous initiatives thus became a matter of personnel assignment. Everything became a mobilization of cadres, whether it was an effort to bring in the harvest or a plan to restructure educational institutions. Appropriate personnel had to be identified, taken from their jobs, concentrated, trained, and dispatched to the new effort. Bolsheviks did not so much administer as they "stormed fronts" with mobilizations, and the collectivization of agriculture was a classic Bolshevik campaign conducted by organizing wave after wave of pro-Stalin cadres and dispatching them to the countryside. Ezhov's new appointment put him at the center of the regime's most important policy initiative.

The year 1930 was big for Nikolai Ezhov in other ways. He and Antonina had grown apart since their marriage. He was a dedicated party bureaucrat, working night and day in the Central Committee apparatus. Having completed her studies at the Agricultural Academy, she had followed academic pursuits, becoming a research specialist and published author on agriculture. In 1930 they separated. Divorce was not necessary because their marriage had never been official. It was customary for

Bolsheviks, who had always scorned religious or administrative forms, to marry without ceremony or registration merely by living together. Nikolai and Antonina went their separate ways in 1930. (She would continue to write and teach until her death in 1988 at the age of ninety-one.) In that same year, Ezhov married Evgeniia S. Gladuna, again without registering their union.

This year was also the one when Ezhov was formally received in Stalin's office for the first time. The records we have of meetings of party bodies (Politburo, Orgburo, Secretariat, and various other commissions), along with Stalin's office calendar, do not indicate that the two had met face to face until that year. Of course, Stalin made it his business to know key leaders and workers at all levels of the party, and without a doubt he had heard of the talented and hard-working Ezhov. But until 1930 there had been no formal reason for them to have direct dealings. According to the chain of command (and his custom), Stalin dealt with cadres through Orgraspred chief Moskvin and with agriculture through Commissar of Narkomzem I. A. Iakovlev. Both were themselves rare visitors to Stalin's office; and Ezhov, as their deputy, had no reason to be there until November 1930. At that time, another reorganization again moved Ezhov up the party ladder. G. K. Ordzhonikidze, in taking over the Supreme Council of National Economy (Vesenkha), took Orgraspred chief Moskvin to run personnel in his new agency. Ezhov was summoned to Stalin's office for an interview on November 11 and named chief of Orgraspred that same day.

Ezhov was now close to the inner circles of the party's leadership. He received copies of all Politburo paperwork circulated to members of the Central Committee and had the right to attend Politburo meetings, although he would not do so until 1934. Socially, he rubbed shoulders with the country's political and intellectual elite. Nadezhda Mandelshtam, wife of the famous poet Osip Mandelshtam, remembers meeting him at the elite resort in Sukhumi in 1930. Unlike his new wife, who spent her vacation time rather boorishly reading and reciting aloud from Marx's *Das Kapital*, Ezhov himself made a positive impression as a modest and agreeable fellow, an opinion shared by others present.

For the next four years, Ezhov continued to do the work he did so well in the party's personnel department. He studied various spheres of administrative and economic activity to determine and recommend appropriate staffing. Because everything was somehow a mobilization of cadres, Ezhov found himself a key player in a wide range of activities. He worked on the Schools, Industry, and Agriculture Departments of the Central Committee and served on ad hoc Politburo commissions on the Communist International, foreign travel, and police and judicial affairs. In a preview of things to come, he was appointed to the 1933 special

committee to supervise one of the party's periodic membership screen-
ings, or purges. The records of the Politburo show that nearly every
time a working group of senior leaders was formed to draft a resolution
on an agenda item—ranging from chauffeurs to military affairs—Ezhov
was the member in charge of personnel.

All the while, he expanded his knowledge of party personnel: their
backgrounds, abilities, strengths, weaknesses, and personal connections
with one another. According to Ezhov's personal papers, this work made
him more and more indispensable to the top leadership. From at least
1932 the most powerful party leaders, including Kaganovich, Molotov,
and Stalin himself, rerouted memos and requests to Ezhov with mar-
ginal notes: "For Comrade Ezhov," "Comrade Ezhov: what is this about?"
or "Comrade Ezhov: what to do about this?" With his good memory
and with a huge amount of information at his fingertips, Ezhov was able
promptly to respond, often with a draft resolution for Politburo approval.

Knowledge was power. In the way that people with concrete information can influence decision making, his recommendations often became the policies of the supreme leaders. Nevertheless, even as head of
the most important Central Committee department he was formally not
part of the inner policymaking circle. Central Committee departments,
however influential, were in the end technical rather than political. They
served the top bodies—Politburo, Orgburo, Secretariat—where the real
decisions were made; and although a body like Orgraspred could press
its "recommendations," its authority had to be expressly delegated from
the top.

This role changed at the Seventeenth Party Congress in early 1934.
At that meeting, Ezhov was made a member of the Central Committee
of the party. In February, he also became a member of the Orgburo,
which had supreme authority over personnel in the party and state, and
Deputy Chairman of the Party Control Commission, the party's main
disciplinary body. On February 20, 1934, he attended his first Politburo
meeting. Ezhov had arrived at the pinnacle of power.

Ezhov's lofty new appointments and his specialty in party personnel
put him in a position to participate in the most important and secret
decisions of the top leadership. Thus, in the spring of 1934, he served on
an important commission charged with reforming the system of courts
and prosecutors. At Stalin's personal request, he also helped draft new
regulations for the NKVD's Special Board, which had the right to arrest
and sentence people to exile or prison. This job, in April 1934, represents Ezhov's first formal involvement in police affairs. It would not be
his last.

In December 1934, Politburo member Serge Kirov was assassinated
in Leningrad. A Politburo group led by Stalin rushed to the city to ini-

tiate an investigation of the killing, the origins of which remain mysterious to this day. Some people believe that Stalin had arranged the killing as an excuse to blame and move against dissidents; others think that the murder was the work of a lone assassin. In any case, it is clear that after the event Stalin used it as a pretext to investigate and persecute members of the former oppositions of the 1920s. Since the Leningrad officers of the NKVD had been responsible for Kirov's security, suspicion instantly fell on them as either incompetent or complicit in the murder. Stalin took the investigation out of the hands of the Leningrad NKVD and, indeed, away from central NKVD leader Genrykh Iagoda altogether. He summoned an independent team of NKVD investigators from outside Leningrad to look into the matter and placed a Moscow party man in charge of the investigation: N. I. Ezhov.

In the weeks following the crime, Ezhov supervised the arrests and interrogations of suspects. His pocket notebook contains a schedule of interrogations with the times and rooms where they were to take place, and he attended or observed many of them. He also "verified" (a Stalinist term for purged) the NKVD. Ezhov's team interrogated or investigated more than 2,000 NKVD workers in Leningrad and fired or transferred 300 of them to other work for negligence. In the first of many attempts to discredit the NKVD with Stalin, Ezhov reported to his boss that the men of the NKVD were incompetent, careless, and incapable of operating intelligence networks that could have prevented the assassination.

Ezhov applied his usual businesslike style to "cleansing" Leningrad. In February 1935 he reported to Stalin that he had rounded up about 1,000 former Leningrad oppositionists, most of whom were exiled from the city. In the course of his investigation, the meticulous Ezhov assembled elaborate personnel card files on the oppositionists, their biographies and their connections, which are preserved in his personal papers. He would later put them to sinister use. Stalin was so impressed with Ezhov's performance that he appointed the personnel specialist to three more high positions: chairman of the Commission on Foreign Travel, chief of the Party Control Commission, and Secretary of the Central Committee, taking Kirov's vacant seat.

In early 1936, Stalin decided to reopen the 1934 Kirov investigation. In the period following Kirov's murder, the investigation had concluded that the assassination was the work of lower-level followers of oppositionists Grigorii Zinoviev and Lev Kamenev. Now, in 1936, Stalin wanted the matter reopened to find out if others were involved, and he made Ezhov the direct party supervisor of the NKVD. Chief Iagoda was put in a difficult position. He still believed in the old rules: the NKVD should confine itself to arresting nonparty counterrevolutionaries and should stay out of party political squabbles. With Ezhov now looking over his shoulder, Iagoda had no choice but to begin arrests of party members who had been followers of Zinoviev, Kamenev, or Trotsky.

These arrests began in earnest in the first quarter of 1936. Zinoviev and Kamenev were reinterrogated. Constant questioning, deprivation of sleep, and threats against family members forced one prisoner after another to sign confessions and implicate others. This chain of confessions led to the first of the famous Moscow show trials in August 1936, when Zinoviev, Kamenev, and thirteen other defendants were sentenced to death. Following on the heels of the trial, a growing climate of suspicion gripped the nation as the press pushed themes about hidden "enemies of the people." "Vigilance" became the watchword, and the press reminded the party that "the best quality of a Bolshevik is his ability to unmask the enemy." The country was slipping into the throes of spy mania and hysteria about secret, dangerous "fifth columns" of conspirators out to undermine the nation.

The archival documents we have from 1936 show another side of Nikolai Ezhov: his ambition and ability to play on Stalin's well-known suspicions. At several times in 1935 he had dropped vague references in memoranda and at party meetings about the "deficiencies" of the NKVD. They had allowed an assassin to get close to Kirov. They had not followed up on investigations. They had not gotten to the bottom of the Kirov matter. They were not vigorous enough in purging the party.

After he became party supervisor of the NKVD in early 1936, his undermining of Iagoda moved into high gear. Ezhov complained about his footdragging and on several occasions went outside the chain of command to turn Iagoda's deputies directly against their boss. He protested furiously that Iagoda was not copying important documents for him about investigations. At one point, he went so far as to inform Stalin that Iagoda himself had been named as a member of an underground conspiracy, although he rather coyly professed not to believe it. But, in August 1936, Ezhov's gloves came off about the NKVD's inability to investigate conspiracies. Writing directly to Stalin about Iagoda and his lieutenants, Ezhov claimed that in the NKVD there were

> so many inadequacies that, in my opinion, it is impossible to tolerate them any more. I have avoided talking about this up to now because the main effort has been smashing the Trotskyists and Zinovievists. But now, everything points to the unavoidable conclusion that we have to fundamentally rebuild the work of the NKVD. . . . Among the leaders at the very top of the NKVD there has developed more and more a mood of self-satisfaction, passivity, and bragging . . . they dream only of awards and honors.

In September 1936, while Stalin was out of town on vacation, Ezhov drafted a resolution for the Politburo making clear his differences with Iagoda on the question of dissidents. Entitled "Our Stance toward Counterrevolutionary Trotskyist-Zinovievist Elements," Ezhov's draft noted that "until very recently, the CC of the VKP(b) considered the Trotskyist-Zinovievist scoundrels as the leading political and organizational detachment of the international bourgeoisie." (Iagoda's view.) Now, however, "the latest facts tell us that these gentlemen . . . must therefore now be considered as foreign agents, spies, subversives, and wreckers representing the fascist bourgeoisie of Europe. . . . In connection with this, it is necessary for us to make short shrift of these Trotskyist-Zinovievist scoundrels." Ezhov proposed summarily executing "about 1,000" oppositionists already incarcerated for various offenses. On September 29 the Politburo approved Ezhov's draft resolution but, it is interesting to note, without the final recommendation on executions. Nevertheless, that same week, Stalin and Andrei Zhdanov sent a telegram to the Politburo proposing the appointment of Ezhov as head of the NKVD, replacing Iagoda.

Because most Politburo members were also on vacation at the time, the appointment was not formally made until October 11 and was not a cause for consternation in the leadership. Politburo member L. M. Kaganovich wrote to his friend and colleague G. K. Ordzhonikidze that Iagoda "took his transfer quite painfully," but that he had "turned out to be too weak for such a role." Kaganovich noted that Ezhov's appointment was "favorably received" inside the NKVD and that "surely, things will go smoothly with Ezhov at the helm." Nikolai Bukharin, who had been virtual co-ruler with Stalin in the 1920s before going into opposition over collectivization, told his wife that Ezhov's appointment was a good idea; Ezhov was an honest man who would not try to frame anyone.

Seen in retrospect, Bukharin's and Kaganovich's words carry a heavy irony. One of Ezhov's first major efforts at the NKVD would be to fabricate a case against Bukharin. With Ezhov "at the helm," hundreds of thousands of innocent people would be arrested and shot and millions of others would disappear forever into the torments of Gulag concentration camps. Countless lives were shattered and families destroyed as Stalin and Ezhov together purged the entire country of real and imagined "enemies of the people."

Our story of Ezhov's rise must end here. The archives documenting his role at the NKVD and his relations with Stalin remain closed at the present time. We do know, however, that after more than two bloody years at the NKVD, Stalin decided to end the purge. Ezhov had become an embarrassment. On November 23, 1938, charging Ezhov with mismanagement and corruption, Stalin removed him from his position. Arrested in June 1939, Ezhov was interrogated by his successor, Lavrenty Beria, and secretly executed on February 4, 1940.

Ezhov is often seen merely as a tool: identified early on by Stalin as an obedient and unquestioning robot, nurtured and prepared for his role as master purger. One often reads that Ezhov was deliberately brought to Moscow and put to work finding out who was who in the party so he could later orchestrate a long-planned purge of the ranks. Ezhov's rapid rise is thus seen purely as the result of Stalin's patronage and preparations. Although there is no doubt that after 1936 Ezhov was Stalin's tool for terror, the documents we now have suggest that our usual picture of his rise is far too simple.

This time was one of meteoric careers and rapid advance for an entire cohort of "new Bolsheviks." The rapid promotions of those such as Zhdanov, Georgii Malenkov, and Nikita Khrushchev and millions of lesser figures followed trajectories as steep as Ezhov's. There was a desperate shortage of administrative talent in the early Soviet regime, and as its activities dramatically expanded after 1929 with the takeover of agriculture and industry, loyal and skilled administrators shot up the ladder. Unlike the Old Bolshevik professional revolutionaries, whose glorious revolutionary biographies made them disdain administration and paperwork, the new Bolsheviks thrived on it. They were willing to take on any assignment, however routine, and complete it thoroughly and on time. They were not just obedient; they were energetic "can-do" types who worked day and night to finish a job. Ivan Moskvin, Ezhov's boss at Orgraspred in the 1920s, recalled that "I know of no more ideal administrator than Nikolai Ezhov. . . . Entrust him with some task and you have no need to check up—you can rest assured that he will do as he is told. . . . Ezhov never gives up." Molotov remembered him as "a good party worker."

Although his talents were certainly recognized and rewarded by his superiors, we have no evidence that Ezhov was pulled up the ladder entirely as a result of mere obedience. Actually, we do not need to find a powerful sponsor or protector to explain his rise; he was not pulled up the ladder so much as he climbed it. His advancement was the result of his personal qualities and his Bolshevik résumé. As a former Putilov worker, Red Guard organizer, and Civil War commissar, he had the right social and political pedigree. His experience in regional party organizations and in the non-Russian nationality areas also stood him in good stead. As an expert on party personnel, he mastered what was to become the key area of political administration in the Bolshevik regime. He was also simply good at what he did. Ezhov's popularity, modesty, and efficiency moved him forward, as did his ambition and ability to advance his own career. We have seen how he got to Moscow on his own devices, in spite of senior party leaders rather than because of them. We saw how he made himself an agriculture expert when collectivization was in the wind. And we observed how he angled for the NKVD job by playing to Stalin's suspicions.

Ezhov was a skilled bureaucrat who would have risen quickly in the new Soviet regime, even had there been no Stalin. His type was what was needed at a time when revolutionaries became administrators, as an underground conspiracy became a ruling institution. Ezhov would have gone far and fast in any new revolutionary regime in a backward country, where political correctness and administrative skill were in high demand. He was a key figure in monstrous events. But the more we learn about him, the less he seems like a monster. No one who met him found him repellent, dangerous, or frightening. No one found him rude. He was not a loud bully like Kaganovich or a brutal lout like Khrushchev. No one commented on his shifty eyes or malevolent aura, as they sometimes did about Stalin. No one was afraid of the generally pleasant, hardworking administrator.

As with Hitler's Holocaust administrator, Adolf Eichmann, Ezhov was more banal than monstrous. He was executor more than executioner, and he no doubt asked himself few questions about the morality of what he was doing. As a good party worker, purging the country was for him a technical problem to be solved. Like so many others of his generation, he was convinced that there were enemies out there. What to do about them—ignore them, isolate them, arrest them, or kill them—were mere policy options, none of which carried more or less moral baggage than the others. In his mind he had no doubts about actions that would haunt others forever: the party is always right; Stalin knows what is best. Having put these issues in their place, Ezhov's job was to do his best to make the process run properly and efficiently. And Ezhov's careerist approach to his job is somehow what is most frightening about him.

SUGGESTED READINGS

There are no books about Nikolai Ezhov in English, although several works on Stalinist police and purges touch on his career. Two Russian-language books deal with his career, but without documentation or source citation. Until the recent opening of Soviet-era archives, it has not been possible to properly research his career, and most works rely heavily on rumor and hearsay. The present author is now writing a book-length study of Ezhov and his times.

Briukhanov, B. B., and E. N. Shoshkov. *Opravdaniiu ne podlezhit: Ezhov i ezhovshchina, 1936–1938gg.* St. Petersburg, 1998
Conquest, Robert. *The Great Terror: A Reassessment.* Oxford, 1990.
———. *Inside Stalin's Secret Police: NKVD Politics, 1936–39.* Stanford, 1985.
Getty, J. Arch, and Oleg V. Naumov. *The Road to Terror: Stalin and the Self-Destruction of the Bolsheviks, 1932–1939.* New Haven, CT, 1999.

Kovalev, Valentin. *Dva stalinskikh narkoma*. Moscow, 1995.
Starkov, Boris A. "Narkom Ezhov." In J. Arch Getty and Roberta T. Manning, eds., *Stalinist Terror: New Perspectives*. New York, 1993.

CHAPTER 12

"Free, and Worth Every Kopeck"

Soviet Medicine and Women in Postwar Russia

GRETA BUCHER

*Issues of direct concern to women followed a dynamic in the USSR differ-
ent from much of the rest of the industrialized world. In contrast to Western Europe and North America, the appearance of "the women's question"
in nineteenth-century Russia preceded the definitive onset of industrialization, and improving the lot of women became an announced goal of
virtually every Russian revolutionary group. These groups included the
Bolsheviks, but well before 1917 male party members reacted negatively
to any attempt to pursue women's issues separately from the liberation of
the proletariat as a whole. Upon coming to power, therefore, the party was
plagued by internal contradictions on what it called "the women's question." On the one hand, it steadily promoted a vision of liberation and
cultural enlightenment for women that entailed a far-reaching
reconfiguration of daily life: free child care and the expansion of family
support services, including medical care; the establishment of communal
dining facilities; greater access to literacy training, education, and, by extension, more meaningful labor; and a redefinition of roles within the
family. On the other hand, not only were Bolshevik actions frequently at
odds with these goals—the party disbanded its Women's Section in 1929—
but also many Soviet women carried the double burden of work outside the
home and domestic responsibilities that left them feeling more overwhelmed
than liberated. Everywhere the "new Soviet woman" faced higher expectations, yet the problems of the nation's economy were exacerbated by the
party's inconsistent commitment and, at times, seeming indifference to her
condition.*

*There was no shortage of salient issues. The emotional topic of abor-
tion, for example, was one of serious complexity. In response to the large
number of illegal and self-induced abortions and related medical compli-
cations, and as an attempt to counteract the influence of midwives and
other nonprofessional healers, in November 1920 the Soviet government
made abortion available on demand and without charge in state hospitals. Although controversial, the issue was not framed in terms of personal
choice and the right of control of the body, but rather pivoted on medical,*

175

economic, and political questions. Presented by the Commissariats of Health and Justice as a temporary expedient—the better-educated Soviet woman of the future would possess a higher consciousness and thereby recognize the social obligation of childbearing—the legalization decree condoned neither abortion nor the rights of the individual over the collective.

Dissenting medical professionals, however, argued that even abortions performed in hospitals could produce harmful side effects, and they held that even as a short-term concession to pragmatism the tolerance of abortion undermined the party's other goal of promoting a scientific-hygienic life-style. When the state began to launch large-scale, labor-intensive industrialization campaigns at the end of the 1920s, it perceived a labor shortage, and a concern with the national birth rate became paramount. This concern, coupled with the broad revival of prerevolutionary attitudes on social issues in the country, led to the recriminalization of abortion in the mid-1930s. Labor outside the home, to cite a second example, provided an additional perspective on the plight of the Soviet woman. Employment became an obligation for all Soviet citizens—the unemployed could be criminally prosecuted as "parasites"—and women in the USSR were fully integrated into the work force. Integration into the economy and a sense of personal liberation, however, were not the same thing. Females continued to carry the twin burdens of domestic and professional duties, and their lower pay and access only to less desirable work were continuing realities of life.

In this essay on Soviet medicine and women, Greta Bucher brings together the micro- and macro-complexities of this situation. Unrealistically high party goals, chronic shortages of resources, an entrenched bureaucratism that blurred lines of responsibility, the pressures on medical personnel to promote the birth rate in the national interest, and the low status of obstetrics and gynecology within Soviet medicine all worked against the women who entered Soviet clinics. And in the personal sphere, the lack of adequate sustenance, the absence of effective contraception, and the scarcity of proper housing were disincentives for Soviet women to carry their pregnancies to term. Based on an interview with "Tanya," who required that her identity be protected, Bucher's essay thus integrates the personal dimension of life in the period following World War II with a probing analysis of Soviet society in the late 1940s and 1950s.

Greta Bucher received her Ph.D. from Ohio State University. Her articles have appeared in Loyd E. Lee, ed., World War II in Europe, Africa, and the Americas with General Sources *(1997) and the* Journal of Women's History. *She is coeditor of* Daily Life under Stalin *(2000) and is assistant professor of history at the United States Military Academy at West Point.*

$\mathcal{M}$edical care in the Soviet Union was always a mixed blessing. On the one hand, it was free—everyone, even foreign visitors, had access to clinics, hospitals, and doctors as necessary. On the other hand, personnel short-ages, lack of medical supplies, faulty training, and poor facilities resulted in spotty care. In the realm of female medicine, the fact that the Soviet leadership desperately wanted women to have as many healthy children as possible to repopulate the labor force could logically have resulted in special attention to gynecology and obstetrics. Instead, policymakers were reluctant to divert resources from their pet projects of heavy industry and defense to health care institutions, even in pursuit of a higher birth-rate.

World War II exacerbated every aspect of their situation with its massive destruction of both people and property. The Soviet Union mobilized a staggering 34.5 million people for the war effort, sending 29.6 million of them to the front. The most current research indicates that military deaths reached 8.6 million, not counting prisoners of war and those missing in action. Civilian losses are much more difficult to calculate, but estimates range from 16.9 to 24 million deaths related to the war.[1] When added to the population losses caused by collectivization and the terror in the 1930s and the casualties from World War I and the Civil War, the leadership's concern for the future of the Soviet work force seems eminently reasonable.

Since their lives were already difficult, women were often reluctant to add to their burden by having children in the numbers desired by the state. They already struggled to work full-time and find adequate food and clothes for their families, in addition to cooking, cleaning, and look-ing after husbands, children, and elderly relatives. Postwar life in the Soviet Union was especially arduous. Bread rationing continued until 1948; the pace of work maintained a high tempo as the country struggled to rebuild after the extensive destruction caused by Germany; and con-sumer goods, housing, and support services remained a low priority throughout the 1940s and much of the 1950s as the state-directed economy continued to emphasize heavy industry and defense produc-tion at the expense of the needs of everyday life. Although the state wanted women to have large families, they were also needed in industry to re-build the economy.

The Soviet leadership had to find a way to allow women to raise children and work at the same time. To this end, the state promised work-ing women that it would provide day care centers, dining halls, laun-dries, and, very important, good medical care. At the same time, the state set high quotas on industry, driving the country to rebuild. Unfor-tunately, the Soviet Union did not have the resources for both ends of the reconstruction project—the state could not give women adequate support to help them raise children and work as long as it chose to pump almost all of its resources into industry. Heavy industry won this tug of war over resources, and nowhere was the state's inability to live up to its promises more apparent than in women's medical care. The experiences of Tanya, a construction engineer interviewed in 1993, illustrate the problems of survival in postwar Russia and the complex issues that undermined women's medical care and the state's motherhood campaign.[2]

Tanya's life was typical for a young woman during this period. As a fifteen year old in 1943, she left school to work in a factory. This job gave her a good ration card (workers got the highest rations) and helped her family survive the war years. After the war, she studied to become a construction engineer. Once again, she needed a job in order to eat, so she worked during the day and attended a professional institute at night.

In addition to a preoccupation with proper rations, other aspects of Tanya's living situation reflected the common postwar life-style. The housing shortage created by returning war veterans and peasants fleeing from the poverty-stricken countryside reached acute proportions. Most families lived in one-room communal apartments and shared the kitchen and bathroom with all the other families in the house. Tanya lived with her mother, father, and brother in one room of twelve square meters. Living in such close quarters—she had to share a bed with her mother—not only with immediate family members but also with the other residents of the house created tensions that were exacerbated by the frustrating search for the necessities of daily life.

The emphasis on heavy industry over consumer goods meant that household items were difficult to find, if they were produced at all. Few kitchens contained a refrigerator; no one had a washer or dryer, a vacuum cleaner, or an electric iron. Fresh food had to be bought, cooked, and consumed every day; clothes had to be washed by hand in the kitchen, hung to dry in the family's already overcrowded single room, and ironed with an old-fashioned flatiron; floors and carpets had to be swept with a broom, and rugs were taken outdoors and beaten with a stick. To make matters worse, even simple household necessities such as soap went through periodic shortages, and clothes and shoes had to be mended by hand to last a long time, since these items were low on the state's list of production priorities. Food shortages also occurred frequently, particularly in the first years after the war, which meant that shopping for the family dinner could take hours. Women went daily from store to store in search of bread, potatoes, and meat.

Eventually, Tanya concluded that she could no longer live with her family in these conditions, but in order to rent her own room she had to quit school to find a full-time job. When she told the head engineer at work of her decision to resign in search of better housing, he expressed surprise that she did not already have housing. He discovered that although her supervisor had been responsible for providing her with a dormitory room, the unscrupulous man had instead given it to his three daughters. The outcome was that Tanya then was assigned a room in a corridor-style dorm and decided to remain at school to finish her degree. She lived in one room on a hallway. Everyone on her corridor—eleven rooms housing about fifty people in all—shared a single bathroom. Unlike a communal apartment, this building had no kitchen, so people either had to eat out or cook over a hotplate. Tanya considered herself lucky to have a room all to herself; her good fortune was due to the fact that she was training to be a construction engineer, one of the most important fields during the postwar reconstruction period. To encourage such students to complete their studies, the state tried to furnish them with housing.

Tanya also had to deal with the shortage of consumer goods and the search for affordable food. She spent her days working, her nights at the engineering institute, and the times in between looking for food. With her very low salary, she could not afford to eat very often in the cafeteria at the institute. Her interview revealed that in the immediate postwar years, she started the day with no breakfast, lunched on 100 grams of sausage and a piece of bread, and often went to bed without dinner. When she was still living with her parents, she got home too late to eat since the rest of the family was already in bed; and when she moved out on her own, she often did not have time to stand in lines to shop for her dinner. Only after she finished school—when she earned more money and more food was available—did her diet improve.

How could women work, attend school, study, and take care of the shopping, housework, and cooking and have time to raise children—all in one room with no kitchen? Tanya's daily struggle for survival demonstrates the problems with the state's plans to rebuild and repopulate quickly. The leadership continued its campaign to promote motherhood. At every opportunity the state encouraged both married and single women to experience the joys of motherhood and attempted to coerce them into having children by withholding contraception and outlawing abortion, except for women with specifically defined medical or mental problems. They responded by using the age-old rhythm method and, when that failed, by resorting to underground or self-induced abortions.

Tanya's experience with health care illustrates these aspects of the Soviet medical system. In the early 1950s, Tanya became pregnant. She was working by this time and had more money, but not enough to hire a baby-sitter. She decided to induce an abortion, which she did by pushing a heavy wardrobe around her room until she was completely exhausted—

a method often employed by women during this time. Afterward, she had to get "cleaned out" at a women's clinic. Since there was no evidence of abortion, she was not accused of breaking the law, but a note was put in her file that she was prone to miscarriage.

In 1957, Tanya married and became pregnant again. This time she decided to keep the baby since she could manage her home, work, and a child better now than she could in 1953. Her file still contained the note about miscarriage, and the medical personnel at her clinic watched her closely. Eventually, they decided to send her to a hospital for closer observation—a common practice that would offer added medical care as well as twenty-four-hour supervision to make sure that she did not abort. When Tanya arrived at the hospital, the staff was busy and no one asked her why she was there; she was simply told to put on a gown and stand in line with several other pregnant women. She described what she called a typical visit to a gynecology ward:

> It was a type of mincing machine—women waited before the operation where they cleaned you out. They didn't let us in a room, you just sat in the hall until you went in the office where they cleaned you out. We all sat in a line on the floor, they didn't ask me if I was there to be cleaned out or if I was there to save my baby. I went into the office. Two women stood there, doctors, in bloody, dirty oilskin aprons. They wore rubber gloves and high boots. . . . Hastily, without anesthetic, without anything, they would clean each woman out. The woman lay there, contorted, and the doctor and nurses would talk among themselves of household matters. No one asked me if I wanted to keep my baby or not, they just told me to lie down. A doctor finally asked me if I wanted to keep the baby and I said yes. Then the doctor examined me and called a student over: "Look, here is a woman with a dead womb"; and all the students came to examine me to see what a dead womb felt like. The doctor asked me if I wanted to be cleaned out then or the next day. . . . I asked to wait until the next day. . . . They put me in a room in a bed. Those women who wanted to save their babies were in beds, but those who were waiting to be cleaned out after [illegal] abortions lay on the floor—women covered in gray, bloody, dirty gowns. These were not women, they were creatures, dreadful creatures. I thought, "Is it possible that later this creature will be someone who accepts love from a man?"
>
> In the middle of the night, a young girl began screaming and throwing herself against a wall. She was about sixteen. I said, "Hey, someone help her, call a nurse, hey, this girl is in trouble!" They all glared at me and said she was going into labor. They gave her a stimulant. She was four months pregnant and it was too late to clean her out. A doctor could have come to her. Someone could have helped her, could have held her hand, and said, "Be patient, little one." No one came to help her, she had to do it all alone; she gave birth alone under those conditions for the first time in her life. She gave birth to a boy and it was dead, of course. A woman with an extrauterine birth began to yell, she was on the floor and her uterus ripped. No one helped her. I thought it was terrible.

> In the morning an old doctor came to me and I began to sob. She
> asked me why, and I told her my baby was dead. She said, "Who told you
> so?" and I pointed out the doctor [who had diagnosed me]. The old doctor
> said that I was fine, everything was normal, and she had me moved into
> another room. I was there for a time and everything was normal there. . . .
> The vision of women in heaps under bloody gowns has stayed with me all
> my life, and after that I was afraid of marriage and birth and abortion.

Tanya had a healthy baby girl but decided not to have any more children.
Her experience seems particularly horrific.

Reports from the Ministry of Health bear out Tanya's memory. The
Ministry's mission was to provide high-quality health care to all women,
with a special emphasis on pregnant women and nursing mothers, through
a network of clinics attached to factories and hospitals and within all city
districts and villages. The clinics had two purposes: 1) to provide prena-
tal and postnatal health care and to ensure that women of childbearing
age were not exposed to hazardous conditions at work or at home; and 2)
to monitor all the women under their care for signs of pregnancy and to
register these pregnancies quickly so that a woman could not lose a baby
without the state knowing about it. Health care workers, then, also had
two functions: 1) to ensure the medical safety of their patients; and 2) to
spy on their patients and report any of them who were suspected of having an abortion to the police—hence the poor treatment of women
thought to have induced abortion.

Supply and personnel shortages plagued women's medicine. Tanya
attributes the callous treatment by the doctors and nurses to the fact that
gynecology was not a popular specialty. According to reports by the Ministry of Health, medical institutes often had to force some of their students into gynecology and obstetrics. While this fact was not published,
Tanya's observation indicates that it was widely understood that many of
the medical staffers in women's clinics did not want to be there.

Many doctors considered gynecology to be routine unglamorous
work, and employment in a women's clinic was certainly not the way to
get ahead in the medical profession. The doctors and nurses who did
nothing but "clean out" women after abortions and miscarriages had
thankless jobs on a gruesome assembly line. Tanya believes that the doctor who pronounced her womb dead had never seen a healthy fetus and
did not recognize the difference. While this may be true, it does not
explain the rest of the incompetence at the hospital—even the administrative staff failed to find out why she had been sent to them, and since
she was pregnant they simply assumed that she had either aborted or
miscarried. If Tanya had not asked to wait until the next day to be cleaned
out, the doctor would have performed an abortion without her even

knowing the truth, and—in a multifaceted irony—the state would have lost another of the future workers whom the system was designed to protect. Complaints about incompetence regularly appeared in medical journals and the Ministry of Health took steps to improve medical training, but with little apparent success.

Gynecologists were also caught in the middle of the war on abortion and the motherhood campaign. Knowing that their duties would be at least partly given over to "police work" gave many medical students additional disincentives to specialize in women's health. These doctors and nurses were the state's first line of defense in the war on abortion. As already noted, they were expected to monitor the women under their care for any signs of pregnancy and then closely watch them to prevent both abortion and miscarriage. This situation was difficult for many doctors and nurses, and some reacted by distancing themselves as much as possible from their patients. Women, for their part, harbored deep suspicions of these clinics, since they knew that although their primary function was to provide care for pregnant women and new mothers, their role as "spies" occupied an important place in the medical profession. Thus, a very problematic relationship emerged between women and their doctors.

Despite the state's emphasis on women's health issues, clinics and hospitals were plagued by a lack of resources as well as personnel. Both the Ministry of Health records and medical journals reflected concern with personnel and equipment shortages and called for improvement. Although the Ministry reportedly allocated 25 percent of the overall health care budget to women's health in 1947, facilities continued to be overcrowded, understaffed, and plagued by supply shortages.[3] Most of the budget had to be used to build new facilities rather than to staff and supply existing clinics, since bed shortages were a consistent problem, particularly in the years immediately following the war. The rebuilding campaign was a success, and facilities surpassed prewar levels by 1948, but the continued migration of population to the capital cities meant that bed shortages were ongoing. Women often had to wait weeks for an appointment at a clinic, and Tanya's experience in the hospital testifies to the overcrowded conditions—in line for hours outside the surgery. The shortage of beds was so acute that the hospital created a ruthless hierarchy. Women who were suspected of having induced abortion were left to spend the night on the floor, regardless of their medical condition.

Aside from the fact that many women did not trust doctors, there was the very real possibility of infection. As Tanya's story suggests, in a clinic or especially in a hospital, doctors and nurses wore the same gown and gloves for an entire shift and did not change between patients. This unsanitary practice was not due to ignorance but rather to shortages of gowns and gloves as well as soap, washing machines, and cleaning equipment. The Ministry of Health issued resolution after resolution calling for more attention to hygiene, but clinics could not comply without increased resources. Little wonder, then, that women viewed clinics and modern medicine with suspicion and often preferred home remedies and traditional practices to treat themselves and their children—practices such as pushing a heavy wardrobe to induce abortion. The time and effort required to get an appointment at these overcrowded facilities, the fear of infection, and the distrust of doctors and nurses as state spies encouraged women to avoid the medical system whenever possible.

The problems in medical care were not unique. Acute shortages plagued all consumer and service industries in postwar Russia; resources simply did not exist to meet the demands of the Soviet population—demands that had been fostered by state promises. While deficits and incompetence in the consumer sector of the economy created daily headaches for women and discouraged them from having the large families desired by the state, the problems that beset medical care in some cases actually prevented women who wanted children from having healthy babies. It would make sense, then, for the leadership to take a more active approach to solving health care problems.

In fact, the leadership did show some interest in trying to improve health care for women. The Fourth and Fifth Five-Year Plans (1946–1950, 1951–1955) both allocated significant resources to maternity clinics and hospital maternity wards; industries were ordered to build women's clinics for their workers. While part of the problem certainly stemmed from the diversion of most resources into production, its heart lay in the bureaucracy that stifled progress in all areas of Soviet life. Government bureaucrats and industrial managers spent their lives juggling state demands. Through resolutions, laws, directives, and the Five-Year Plans, officials at the top required lower-level ones and industrial managers to increase production, build housing, provide support services, and take care of the health of the average person. The state's goals for rapid recovery after the war demanded an enormous level of productivity in all areas but did not provide resources sufficient to meet these goals. In order to ensure that all areas were covered, the responsibility for providing for the people fell to a number of different institutions.

For the most part, the Ministry met its goals for construction and staffing of clinics; after all, this was its main function. But the other sources for women's health—industry and local government—had a myriad of other duties to perform with very limited resources. In response to an impossible task, both industry and local government officials shifted blame, each accusing the other of failure to keep its part of the bargain and thereby jeopardizing the entire project. No doubt, the high government officials who passed resolutions requiring industry and local governments to work together believed that a combined effort would relieve each party of some of the burden and would result in more efficient implementation of their plans. In reality, the ability for each party to blame the other for failures resulted in a bureaucratic shuffle, with each side pointing to the other in a circle of accusations that made it impossible for anything to get done or for anyone to assign responsibility.

In addition, bureaucrats, like everyone else, had to deal with the problems of existence in the postwar Soviet Union, and they often used their position and access to resources to help themselves rather than to rebuild the country. Tanya encountered a petty bureaucrat who abused his position when he diverted her housing assignment to his own daughters. Had she not tendered her resignation to the head engineer who then investigated her problem, she would never have known that she had been cheated out of the room to which she was entitled. The unscrupulous bureaucrat was a ubiquitous figure in Soviet industry and government at all levels. While it is impossible to calculate the damage that this kind of activity inflicted on the Soviet economy, the presence of widespread mismanagement of funds and resources crippled all efforts to improve the standard of living.

In the final analysis, the central leadership must bear the blame for these problems. The bureaucratic shuffle and the unscrupulous bureaucrat were products of a planning system that placed outrageous demands on industry and local government and exacted a heavy price from anyone who did not meet these expectations. Bureaucrats had to shift the blame for shortfalls to others in order to survive, and it became accepted practice for each department to blame another—as long as the buck never stopped being passed, no one could be singled out for blame. In addition, the extremely poor living conditions fostered corruption at all levels, with administrators and managers taking advantage of any opportunity to raise their own living standard. Daily life was so difficult that finding one room for three adult daughters to occupy was impossible without resorting to unscrupulous methods. Medical care, like other aspects of the Soviet economy, suffered from all of these problems.

In sum, women's health care fell far short of the state's demands. Despite its pivotal role in the postwar plans for repopulation, the state could not bring itself to allocate enough resources to medicine for it to meet announced goals, thereby encouraging the bureaucratic manipulation of resources and responsibilities. Perhaps more important, however, were the conflicting roles that clinics and medical workers had to play in the "struggle for reproduction." These conflicts often led to adversarial relationships between doctors and patients, encouraging women to avoid medical care, lie to their doctors, and rely on home remedies. When women finally sought professional care, they had to brave the dangers of infection as well as the callous attitude of over-worked and underappreciated medical workers, and suffer through painful procedures without anesthetics or proper medication.

The state thus undermined its own motherhood campaign. The re-fusal to divert sufficient resources from heavy industry not only lowered the standard of medical care but also made women's lives too difficult for most of them to contemplate raising large families. The search for food and clothing and the difficulty of cooking and housework in overcrowded rooms was literally a daily grind for most women over and above their full-time jobs. As a result, women continued to limit the size of their families, despite the state's continued efforts to encourage and coerce them into having children.

NOTES

1. Richard Overy, *Russia's War: A History of the Soviet War Effort, 1941–1945* (New York, 1997), 288.
2. Interview with the author, Moscow, March 16, 1993. To ensure privacy, "Tanya" is a fictitious name.
3. F. I. Zborovskaia, "Okhrana materinstva i mladshchenstva k 30-letiiu sovetskoi vlast'," *Meditsinskaia sestra* 11 (1947): 5–7.

SUGGESTED READINGS

Buckley, Mary. *Women and Ideology in the Soviet Union.* Ann Arbor, MI, 1989.
Clements, Barbara, Barbara Alpern Engel, and Christine D. Worobec, eds. *Russia's Women: Accommodation, Resistance, Transformation.* Berkeley, 1991.
Dunham, Vera. *In Stalin's Time: Middle-class Values in Soviet Fiction.* Durham, NC, 1990.
Goscilo, Helena, ed. *Balancing Acts: Contemporary Stories by Russian Women.* Bloomington, IN, 1989.
Lapidus, Gail Warshofsky. *Women in Soviet Society: Equality, Development, and Social Change.* Berkeley, 1978.
Zubkova, Elena. *Russia after the War: Hopes, Illusions, and Disappointments, 1945–1957.* Trans. and ed. Hugh Ragsdale. New York, 1998.

CHAPTER 13

New Lives in the New Russia

Democratic Contradictions after the
Fall of the Soviet Regime

WILLIAM G. ROSENBERG

Tensions between ideas of personal freedom and material abundance are not new in Russia. As the Grand Inquisitor and Christ confront one another over human nature in Dostoevsky's The Brothers Karamazov *(1880), the Inquisitor taunts:*

Turn [stones] into bread and mankind will run after Thee like a flock of sheep, grateful and obedient, though forever trembling, lest Thou withdraw Thy hand and deny them Thy bread. Thou didst reply that man lives not by bread alone. Dost Thou know that the ages will pass, and humanity will proclaim by the lips of their sages that there is no crime, and therefore no sin; there is only hunger? Feed men, and then ask of them virtue! In the end they will lay their freedom at our feet, and say to us, "Make us your slaves, but feed us."*

Whether such thinking played itself out in the Soviet Union is a matter of interpretation.† If the vision of the Grand Inquisitor still lies in Russia's future can only be conjecture. But as an issue that informs every realistic debate about Russia's present circumstances, some interplay between freedom and material satisfaction is inescapable.

In this work of creative nonfiction, William Rosenberg surveys the national and personal ramifications for two distinct generations of Russians of the collapse of the Soviet Union. In so doing, he brings his more than three decades' experience in the study of Russia to bear on events since 1991. The veteran of numerous trips to Russia with a broad circle of personal and professional friends and acquaintances (an important distinction in Russia), Rosenberg presents an analysis that encompasses national scandals and outrages as well as personal strategies of survival. Real estate scams, voucher systems, pyramid schemes, abandoned careers, and the loss

---

*Fëdor Dostoevsky, *The Brothers Karamazov*, trans. Constance Garnett (New York, 1955), pt. 2, book 5, chap. 5, 300. Quotation is condensed without ellipses.

†See, for example, Linda J. Cook, *The Soviet Social Contract and Why It Failed: Welfare Policy and Workers' Politics from Brezhnev to Yeltsin* (Cambridge, MA, 1994).

of cherished emotional space all make an appearance. Boris Yeltsin's October 1993 assault on the parliament, the rise of the right-wing extremist Vladimir Zhirinovsky, and the opening of McDonald's on Moscow's Pushkin Square all play a part, as do the discovery of personal talents previously unknown even to family members, resilience in the face of adversity, and opportunities and privileges unimaginable under the old regime. In the process, material values and democracy both take on meanings in Russia far removed from their standard Western usages, but as the author unravels the complexities of definition he lays open, for better and worse, much of the internal logic of post-Soviet life. Like its political and economic system, the citizens of post-Soviet Russia appear as a work in progress.

William G. Rosenberg is professor of history at the University of Michigan. His publications include Liberals in the Russian Revolution *(1974),* Strikes and Revolution in Russia, 1917 *(as coauthor, 1989), and* Critical Companion to the Russian Revolution, 1914–1921 *(1997). He received his Ph.D. from Harvard University.*

℄ate in December 1991 I went with my young friend Boris to Red Square to see the blue, white, and red Russian tricolor flying for the first time over the Kremlin. The late afternoon was typical for Moscow at that time of year. A soft, cold breeze blew sparkling snowflakes from an already darkened sky, their brilliance amplified by the bright lights on the Kremlin's red brick walls. To my mind, Red Square had never looked more beautiful. St. Basil's Cathedral glistened magically, the old GUM department store glowed in Christmas greenery, the murmur of strollers and shoppers drifted quietly upward as if to meet the falling snow. The new Russian flag waved easily, a stunning contrast to the familiar red stars that still adorned the Kremlin towers. The scene was extraordinary, awesome really, and fully appropriate, I thought, to the extraordinary event it symbolized. Who could have imagined that the Soviet Union, one of history's great powers, would quietly dissolve into the darkness like the disappearing snow?

My friend Boris felt the power of the moment too, but both of us were also worried. My apprehensions were the intellectualized concerns of a historian long engaged in the problems of revolutionary transitions, moments in history where hopes invariably seem greater than the possibilities of achievement. My friend's were far more personal. An advanced graduate student in English history at the University of Moscow, Boris had been struggling like his country for the past several years to define his own identity and future, just as Soviet Russia had. The period had been incredibly difficult, and overflowing in contradiction. As hopes for a new Russia rose with *glasnost* and *perestroika*, material conditions worsened in what seemed an exact inverse proportion: the louder and more strident the promises for a better future, the more problematic my friend's assumptions about his possible career as a teacher and scholar. As we stood in the beautiful December darkness, he confessed his realization that the Soviet regime had actually transformed the public service to which he had hoped to devote himself into very private privilege, that following through on his plans to become a teacher and scholar would now mean a fierce engagement with every falsehood that this tradition-ally respected profession had now to represent. He wasn't sure it was worth it.

Our conversation mirrored one that I had had several nights earlier with other, older friends, Irina and Aleksei, who lived without apology in an incredibly cozy one-room apartment on the sixth floor of an incredibly shabby walk-up. ("Why should I apologize?" Irina would ask; "Khrushchev built these slums; he and his party should be the ones to say they're sorry!") I had visited them for years, even when to meet with a Western visitor put them both at great risk. Irina had not simply been fired from her job as an editor for failing to "play his game," but refused the official discharge form that would have allowed her to get another job. She was now on a medical pension. Aleksei worked as a trainer in a sports complex. A few years back he had begun to fiddle around with a computer that the complex had acquired. He quickly realized its poten-tial to track team performances. Writing his own clever software pro-gram, he had begun successfully to distribute on his own computer-generated team records, which were soon in great demand. As Aleksei prospered, however, and even managed to purchase a somewhat battered used car, suspicions grew among his neighbors that his dealings were shady and that he, too, was joining the ranks of the "privileged."

At the moment, "privilege" had a very special connotation in Russia. Boris Yeltsin's initial rise to democratic prominence was based in no small degree on his skill at identifying traditional Soviet "privileges" as "cor-ruptions," a position that challenged the party's monopoly over its defi-nitions of the "public" good every bit as strongly as his assault on the party's monopoly of power. (Two years earlier at a time of great confu-sion over where *perestroika* was going, I went to a special showing of a film about Yeltsin sponsored in Leningrad by a district party committee. The film showed his modest Moscow apartment and especially his kitchen, where he sat for an interminable length of footage simply look-ing out the window. His dress was ordinary, and he left his apartment for work on the metro, demonstratively repudiating special services—an authentic "man of the people.") When Yeltsin was elected president of the Russian Republic in 1990 in Russia's first truly free elections, his new position pitted his own democratic authority against Mikhail Gorbachëv's authoritarian power as head of the Soviet Union, a political balance that obviously could not last. In his person as well as his political success, Russia's new leader symbolized the two sets of enabling beliefs that, we all hoped on that late December evening, were finally bringing democracy to Russia.

The first set was rooted in a classic Western liberal discourse that identified democracy with individualism and individual rights, realizable only within a clearly protected civil order. Its key arguments, as presented so eloquently in the last years of Soviet rule by Andrei Sakharov and others, lodged freedom in personal civil liberties, and individual rights in the natural ability of every human being to reason out his or her own interests. The second set was quite different. Here, democracy was identified not with civil liberties per se but with material abundance. Individual initiative, unfettered by the state, would at last bring the Soviet community into the mainstream of global marketization.

The appeal of democracy in both of these sets of meanings was obviously enormous. The democratic claim to human rights not only met the yearnings of repressed nationalities in the USSR but also identified the Soviet state itself as the embodiment of a dysfunctional *state* rationality: the logic of central command that suppressed the ability of individuals themselves to reason effectively, and hence more productively. That Gorbachëv and his supporters initially failed to realize the correlation between monopolies of power and reason provided the opportunity for liberal democrats to open through *glasnost* a broad and convincing rights discourse, one that played a vital role in accelerating full reform.

At the same moment, rapidly growing *defitsity* (shortages) in many essential commodities strengthened the presumed linkage between individual rights and material betterment. In 1988 and 1989 essential foodstuffs were rationed for the first time since World War II. The disappearance of sugar, matches, flour, medicine, and virtually all foodstuffs from state stores prompted sensational televised raids on railroad depots and other places where the goods were allegedly hidden. Many were convinced that the "mafia" was taking over, which fueled the pressure for democratic change; others saw the problem more in terms of Gorbachëv's own hesitancy to reform more radically, but they came to the same conclusion. During a six-week period in the spring of 1990, Moscow reportedly consumed an entire year's supply of natural gas since, without the matches that were needed to light antiquated stoves and water heaters, Muscovites (my friends among them) simply left their burners on. The Bolsheviks' old slogan *"Tak zhit dalshe, nelzia!"* (We cannot live this way any longer!) became ironically relevant.

The arguments linking individual freedom with material abundance were thus absolutely compelling. While the collapse of the Soviet Union was also profoundly influenced by national and ethnic claims for independence—claims that directly called into question the legitimacy (and ultimately the very possibility) of retaining a Soviet *union*—it was the premises of civil rights and reason, linked to the promise of material betterment, which collapsed the Communist order bloodlessly from within. In a euphoric moment when the world's largest McDonald's opened for business in Moscow on Pushkin Square, the private taste of individual freedom was finally gained both metaphysically and literally by public access to a globally marketed "democratic" meal. Two all-beef patties momentarily captured Russia's hopes for a democratic future.

My friends very much liked McDonald's (although for Boris its arrival meant heated arguments with his in-laws, who saw creeping Western "imperialism" along with the wrapper trash). What worried them was something very different. For all the conviction that there was no alternative to a "democratic" future, and for all the powerful appeal of democracy's linked promises of individual freedom and material betterment, Aleksei, Irina, and Boris and his wife Natasha each understood the incredibly difficult tasks of social and cultural reconstruction that democratization would necessarily entail.

There was the problem, first, of simple popular understanding of what democratic behaviors and concepts actually meant; and, even if understood, would Yeltsin's regime have the power to assure their realization? Second, there was the sheer magnitude of the task of Russia's economic reconstruction, and whether all the good intentions in the world could actually facilitate a successful transition from a centralized command economy to a functioning market system. Finally, there was the fear that all of these changes, however necessary, might still ultimately destroy for my friends something special and precious in their intellectual and cultural life: the intimacy of family and friendship, and the ability to feel secure in the dignity that a deep opposition to Soviet injustice had accorded each of them. Irina and Aleksei worried particularly. They and their friends spent hours together in their one-room flat, despite the six flights of stairs that were now, with no lightbulbs available, entirely in darkness. Irina's homemade vodka (*samogon* in Russian), carefully brewed with pure bootleg American alcohol, fueled special and sustaining relationships during many intense and stimulating evenings.

While we know in hindsight that each of these concerns was well founded, no one in 1991 could really imagine what Russia would come to experience before the end of the century. However natural the yearning for individual freedom seems to be, the institutionalization of democratic practice requires an understanding of tolerance, an appreciation and respect for difference, and a belief in the moral efficacy of superordinate law: a set of constitutional principles whose application in social practice enables the effective mediation of social conflict in ways generally perceived as just and fair. Although my friends (and certainly all of their generation) fully understood democratic practice in these terms, the concept of "democracy" itself was historically something new. (As late as the 1880s, in fact, it had not yet found entry into the four-volume *Definitive Dictionary of the Living Russian Language*.) Nor did "democracy" have any indigenous historical referents in Russia, despite the peasants' communitarian practices in the countryside and the efforts of some liberal historians to find protodemocratic forms in fourteenth-century Novgorod or the "constitutional" crises of 1730 or 1905. The very concept of *demokratiia* thus implicitly signified something foreign in Russian, as did the related neologisms *legitimost* (political legitimacy) and *narodnyi suverenitet* (popular sovereignty). Indeed, the common understanding of sovereignty was that connected with the absolute power (*verkhovnaia vlast*) of the sovereign emperor or tsar. As discourse theorists might have it, the "democratic narrative of modernity" in Russia was coded Western. "Democracy" thus encompassed the question of Russia's very identity as a nation.

This issue came to underlie virtually all Russian politics after 1991, despite Yeltsin's own reelection to a second term as president. By 1995, 66 percent of the Russian population thought that their country "was not headed in the right direction"; 55 percent were negative toward "democracy" itself. Law, justice, fairness, and human rights topped a list of cherished values where democracy ranked only seventeenth. Four years later the percentages had only marginally improved. Less than 11 percent "trusted" their president or his cabinet, and fewer than 10 percent saw anything worthy in their parliament or Duma. The two leading contenders as Yeltsin's successor—the mayor of Moscow, Yuri Luzhkov, and former army general Alexander Lebed—were widely respected for their tough and effective "old school" politics, not for any discernable democratic commitments.

The awful loss of life aside, Yeltsin's war against Chechnya and his bombardment of the recalcitrant parliament in 1993 were underestimated disasters on the democratic road. The harm was done not so much to the constitutional legitimacy of the actions or of Yeltsin's regime, but to the vital processes of constitution-making itself. One by one, Yeltsin replaced members of the Constitutional Court and the Procurator's Office who did not support his forceful actions. Russia's new constitution, completed soon after the White House bombardment and right before the December 1993 elections, was written largely at the government's direction and on principles intended to strengthen the president's personal powers. It was designed as well to defeat the claims of Russian Federation republics, like Chechnya, to independence, a stance notable not so much for its understandable concern about the Federation's own unity as a nation but because it subordinated principles of negotiation and mediation to those of brute force. Only the proto-fascist Vladimir Zhirinovsky fully supported the new document: he and the reactionary right clearly understood, as did others, that Yeltsin was personalizing a process whose ultimate legitimacy would depend either on broad support for the legal precepts espoused by the new constitution, which was doubtful, or on the success of his government in restoring social stability and bringing demonstrative economic improvements, which seemed even more so. Absent these occurrences, Zhirinovsky, too, could readily change the constitutional foundation of power if politically well positioned, since it was essentially the personal regime of Yeltsin himself, rather than the rule of law, that was holding Russia together.

At the same time, as we know, Russia's economic situation was becoming far worse than most people believed possible in 1991, the result of bad policy, corruption, and the sheer difficulty of reconstructing antiquated plants, inefficient practices, and technologically primitive methods of production. And as material conditions worsened, the rhetorical linking of "private" property rights to individual freedom bore less and less resemblance to actual practice. As Simon Clarke has argued forcefully, effective privatization as a legal transfer from state to private ownership has historically required the assets being privatized to be profitable for their new owners. Along with financial guarantees of various sorts, privatization has consequently involved steps to economize production, often forcing the dismissal of workers thought to be "surplus" or "inefficient." The prerogatives of ownership have also been legally defined and guaranteed. In developed market economies, these assurances of future profit potential necessarily precede the privatization of "socialized" industries, or the enterprises themselves will have to be shut down.

In Yeltsin's Russia, however, privatization involved nothing of the sort. Nor could it, if any modicum of social stability was to be preserved. Without a pool of private capital, state property could not be purchased outright; it had to be transferred in some other way, or left in the hands of local state authorities. There also had to be at least some assurances that the transfers would cause only minimal job or wage reductions.

The principal "solutions" to these problems were the distribution in 1992 of "privatization vouchers" as a means of creating a broad private ownership sphere in commerce and industry, and the simultaneous transfer of apartments and other residences to their inhabitants on the basis of arbitrary valuations (assessments) only theoretically linked to their market value. The former was necessary because the overwhelming majority of Russians had no resources whatsoever to "invest"; the vouchers for them became surrogate stock certificates. The transfer of apartments and residences at arbitrary values was necessary for similar reasons: while some buying and selling was under way, legal title (ownership) had to be established before any residential market system could assure permanent and uncontested transfers.

Privatization vouchers had a nominal value of 10,000 rubles (U.S.$10 at the then current rate of exchange), and could be traded privately or by auction as well as exchanged for specific shares of privatizing firms. Like apartments and residences, firms themselves were also assigned somewhat arbitrary valuations. Ownership was to be acquired formally by using the vouchers to pay off the state. Partly because it was intrinsically complicated, and partly because the value of the vouchers fell rapidly when many Russians rushed to turn them into cash, the system was easily manipulated. It proved relatively simple for knowledgeable people to accumulate large nominal values for the property they controlled, and for others to accumulate large numbers of vouchers. Both profited substantially: those who gathered up vouchers by selling them to the firms themselves (who transferred them back to the state to legalize ownership rights), and those whose property was given high valuations by selling it outright to foreign firms or joint ventures. Ordinary Russians, however, did not know whether to hold their vouchers or sell, to become nominal shareowners of antiquated (and perhaps wholly artificial) "corporations," or to stay completely out of treacherous "capitalist" waters. Few, of course, could manage to buy. (Once in January 1993, on a bitterly cold and gloomy day in St. Petersburg, I passed two very forlorn voucher peddlers standing next to each other on Nevskii Prospekt. One carried a sign that said "I Buy Vouchers"; the other, "I Sell Vouchers." I mentally urged them to exchange what they had, get out of the cold, and go home.)

When the vouchers were eventually all surrendered, the "private" sector had expanded exponentially—and legally—by consolidating further the property and wealth of those, in the main, who had already taken it under their control. The same thing happened with the "privatization" of residential property. Former *apparatchiki* in large, fancy apartments were suddenly the proud owners of very marketable real estate. Those like Irina and Aleksei, who hardly felt market demand for their shabby one-room flat, soon found themselves forced instead to pay for water, heat, and a whole list of nonexistent "services." (So-called janitorial and maintenance fees were particularly galling, since the stairways were still dark and the vestibules always cluttered with litter.)

However necessary these transfers may have been in view of Russia's economic and social circumstances, and however much they constituted an important aspect of widely desired political change, "privatization" thus consolidated the position and power of former Soviet managers and their newly entrepreneurial local political allies. In a phrase, as Clarke has argued, the reconstitution of the private in Russia became sanctioned primitive accumulation; in a word, it was theft. In many places (including the army), supplies and goods were simply sold off by those who controlled them for their own (very private) profit. Elsewhere, factories were forced to barter for supplies and resources as purchasers went elsewhere, capital disappeared, and an effective market essentially ceased to exist. By the end of the decade, Russia's gross national product had fallen more than 40 percent since the last years of Soviet rule, the greatest and most cataclysmic decline of any industrial country in the world since the Great Depression.

The impact of this catastrophe was felt everywhere in Russia. Alcohol consumption per capita became the highest in the world, twice the level of potential fatality defined by the World Health Organization. Life expectancy among men dropped to 57.5 years, an almost unbelievably low level and 14 years earlier than women, the largest gender gap ever recorded in any country. According to the Department of Medical Demographics at Moscow's Public Health Research Center, early male deaths from alcohol poisoning, accidents, and even tuberculosis meant that many Russian men did not live long enough to incur the chronic diseases that commonly kill men in the West. Massive underemployment, wage arrears, low skill levels, and accompanying despondency were the cause and consequence of economic failure for all but a thin stratum of adroit *biznezmeny* (businessmen), who managed to use the vast resources that they came to control to great personal advantage. In the midst of deep poverty, a tiny but very visible stratum of "New Russian" rich emerged, closely tied to the channels of finance and power and soon fabulously wealthy beyond all imagination. In contrast to the $12 per month national minimum wage that Yeltsin's government maintained in 1995 to avoid "inflationary pressures," New Russians were soon able to drop as much as $8,000 on a shopping trip, $500 or more at a light lunch at a new foreign-owned café. Impoverished pensioners selling their household goods were soon pushed off the streets as Estee Lauder, Yves Rocher, and other deluxe Western shops modernized downtown Moscow into a decent Western imitation. Soon, New Russians were living in "gilded Gulags" in an astounding exaggeration of the benefits of "private" property, surrounded by their personal guards and security systems.

As my friends had feared, all this change took its predictable toll on what had long been intimate and treasured personal relationships: the contradictions of democracy reached well beyond the political and economic into the depths of individual psychologies and cultures. Under the Soviets, the privative trait of Russian privacy, in Hannah Arendt's formulation, was the consciousness of being deprived in circumstances where individuality could only be freely and openly expressed within the solitary space of one's mind or one's family, and then, especially for women, never consistently. The warmth and friendly coloration of Soviet home space in all of its mythologized forms, with its powerful intimacies and friendships, its private tragedies and truths, and especially its definition within a collective context of individuality, was a powerful emotional defense against the colorless conformities of formal public existence. Individual "privacy" under the Soviets, in its most profound and influential meanings, was thus located in the closed-off realm of personal thoughts and feelings, a condition that helps explain the extraordinary roles of great poets, artists, and musicians in Soviet life. The artistry of a Mandelshtam, Pasternak, or Plisetskaia touched common "private" understandings.

If these understandings contrasted with the property-based meanings of "privacy" in the West, so did conceptions of the "individual" and especially "individualism," or the ideological privileging of the individual over the group. Here, too, there are no comparable words in Russian. "Individual" elides instead with "personality" (*lichnost*) or simply "person" (*chelovek*). Pursuit of "self-interest" translates into selfishness. Consequently, while the commodification of post-Soviet public life was eagerly anticipated as the road to wealth and well-being, the reconstitution of the "private" was at odds with deeply rooted cultural meanings. Even in the worst moments of scarcity and anxiety in the early 1990s, the intimacies of home life remained for many an important if romanticized defense against the growing turbulence of life outside—a link to what was, for many, the best of an unlamented past. Increasingly, however, as the shock therapists arrived on their globalizing waves, even these defenses were assaulted. In varying forms and degrees, intimate spaces were gradually commodified as well, along with the material and spiritual resources that sustained them.

Irina and Aleksei suffered greatly from this combination of developments. In Aleksei's view, his own and Russia's future both required the mastery of Western ways; Irina agreed, but only if it did not mean giving up what was "authentically" Russian. Seizing the opportunity that his skills, intelligence, and initiative provided, Aleksei quit his job at the sports complex and went to work for a newly arrived Western communications firm, but his immersion in what seemed the crassness of private business initially violated all of the qualities of privacy that they revered. Long hours, weekend work, and a constantly ringing telephone soon replaced evenings of thoughtful talk and companionship. The busy phone infuriated neighbors who shared the line. So did the comings and goings of Westerners like me. Irina and Aleksei installed a thick steel door on their one-room flat to keep out intruders. Aleksei also had a gun.

Work for the Western firm was demanding. The American boss knew little Russian and even less about Russian ways but expressed his own shortcomings in disdain for "native backwardness." To bring Western-style practices to Moscow, the firm required suits and ties, proper businesslike attire. To enhance sociability, it also began a late Friday afternoon cocktail hour. Like most of his Russian colleagues, Aleksei did not own a decent suit; and his required Friday afternoon relaxation over cocktails violated every sense of how and where one could relax and enjoy real friendship. Not surprisingly, for a long stretch of time he talked frequently about quitting.

Gradually, however, Aleksei's challenges became his work's rewards. Because he understood Russian practices so well, he was soon able to extend the firm's communication links into a number of major Russian institutions, thus proving himself invaluable. Outlasting his first boss and a string of successors, he gathered equally able people around him and was soon in charge of almost fifty Russian colleagues. Friday cocktail hours disappeared; the turn by corporations in the West to casual dress was seized as the new local norm. Time at home was compromised, but Irina compensated by becoming active in neighborhood service work. Taking meals to pensioners or visiting the sick was a way of extending individual success to a broader community. She and Aleksei both began to prosper.

Taking advantage of extremely cheap rates, Aleksei and Irina began to plan vacation weeks in Crete or Bulgaria and once, too, a skiing trip to Austria. They thought as well about getting a slightly larger apartment, especially one with a "real" kitchen, as Irina described it, rather than the alcove that Khrushchev had provided her. Since there were no mortgages to be had—an innovation that Russia's inflation and shaky banking system had not allowed even seven years after the end of the Soviet Union—they borrowed privately to augment the savings that Aleksei's dollar salary had allowed, and gave $30,000 to a realtor for a new apartment nearby. In three weeks, before the deal was closed, both the realtor and their money had disappeared.

In hearing this disaster over Irina's hearty *samogon*, I found myself far more upset than they were. Aleksei saw their experience as emblematic of Russia's predicament more generally. He thought that what had happened was because the country's entire financial system was corrupt, not because their realtor was dishonest. (In all likelihood, the realtor had reinvested their funds in one of the many pyramid banking schemes at the time, a risky but common hedge against Russia's high inflation. Another friend of mine in St. Petersburg had done the same with precious research funds, and with exactly the same result.) Aleksei was even somewhat amused, a sentiment not fully shared by Irina.

My other friend, Boris, meanwhile, had taken a different direction. Soon after our sojourn to Red Square in 1991, he decided to abandon his graduate studies and his plans to teach in favor of more promising opportunities in business. His in-laws, who were still providing him and Natasha with some support, were distressed. For a while he explored a number of possibilities in "banking" (he insisted himself on the quotation marks in our discussions) and even thought about trying to emigrate. Somewhat paradoxically, however, the end of the Soviet regime had eliminated the principal basis for seeking most forms of asylum, and neither Boris nor Natasha, who had recently spent several stress-filled summer months teaching Russian in the United States, felt ready to forego their close ties to their families.

They chose well. Instead of becoming a "banker," Boris took on work as a string reporter for a new and progressive Moscow newspaper. His byline was soon appearing regularly. Within the year, he was traveling with Yeltsin on his trips abroad. Shortly afterward, around his thirty-second birthday, he was made entirely responsible for the newspaper's Saturday edition. Meantime, after trying like Aleksei and Irina to find a new apartment, Natasha herself "went into real estate," as she liked to describe it. Capitalizing on the sale of their own newly privatized (and nicely valued) apartment, and also using borrowed funds, she took on the difficult and complicated business of finding new individual flats for poorer Muscovites still inhabiting *kommunalkas*, the communal living space that the Soviet regime had long ago created out of the old luxurious apartments confiscated from the "counterrevolutionary bourgeoisie." Taking entrepreneurial advantage of the inflationary spiral, Natasha managed, among other accomplishments, to gain title for herself and Boris to a spectacular seven-room flat within walking distance from McDonald's, undoubtedly once the home of a tsarist baron. After thousands of dollars of remodeling, the apartment was ready for rental at upwards of $3,000 per month—more than twenty times the average Russian's yearly income!

Elegance followed, but at some real cost to friendship as Boris and Natasha moved far beyond the social reach of their former student comrades. On the basis of what were proving to be his outstanding abilities—skills that his in-laws quietly admitted to me they found surprising—Boris continued his remarkable ascent in the genuinely sophisticated world of Russian commercial journalism. One day he took me to his office complex, which the newspaper's owners had set up in an old elementary school purchased from the city. Behind locked doors, he used the firm's private ATM to get some cash, took me through the completely computerized editorial and composing rooms, and then out to lunch, on the way filling up the Volvo station wagon that the paper was providing him with the firm's own debit card. Sometime later, when I was walking with his wife along Tverskaia Street, her beautiful new fur coat earned the same kind of stares that my own American attire had attracted ten years earlier. Within the year, and still well before his fortieth birthday, Boris had become the newspaper's editor-in-chief. His in-laws had sold their dacha outside Moscow—wonderfully intimate and cozy in my admittedly romantic perspective—for a regular summer rental on the French Riviera.

Aleksei and Irina, meanwhile, had also found a new flat, and this time successfully managed the transaction. Two blocks or so from the old one, it was also a walk-up but built sturdily in Stalin's time, and its three rooms now modestly but nicely redone. The kitchen was bright, the "dining room" table no longer had to be pulled out of the wall, and the "living room" couch no longer served as a bed. As I sat in their new place for the first time, and Irina, impatient with Aleksei for once again being delayed at his office, served me her *samogon*, it was clear that only the dysfunctional world around them had fundamentally changed.

SUGGESTED READINGS

Aslund, Anders. *How Russia Became a Market Economy*. Washington, DC, 1995.

Chenet, L., D. Leon, and M. McKee. "Death from Alcohol and Violence in Moscow: Socio-Economic Determinants." *European Journal of Population* (1998): 312–18.

Clarke, Simon. *The Restructuring of Employment and the Formation of a Labour Market in Russia*. Coventry, Eng., 1996.

Feshbach, Murray. *Ecological Disaster: Cleaning Up the Hidden Legacy of the Soviet Regime*. New York, 1995.

Goldman, Merle. *Lost Opportunities: Why Economic Reforms in Russia Have Not Worked*. New York, 1994.

Kagarlitsky, Boris. *Restoration in Russia: Why Capitalism Failed*. New York, 1995.

———. *Square Wheels: How Russian Democracy Got Derailed*. New York, 1994.

Lewin, Moshe. *Russia/USSR/Russia*. New York, 1994.

Lynch, Allen. *Does Russia Have a Democratic Future?* New York, 1997.

Remnick, David. *Resurrection: The Struggle for a New Russia*. New York, 1997.

Saikal, Amin, and William Maley. *Russia in Search of Its Future*. Cambridge, Eng., 1995.

Silverman, Bertram, and Murray Yanowitch. *New Rich, New Poor, New Russia: Winners and Losers on the Russian Road to Capitalism*. Armonk, NY, 1997.

Smith, Alan. *Challenges for Russian Economic Reform*. Washington, DC, 1995.

White, Stephen. *After Gorbachev*. Cambridge, Eng., 1993.

———, Alex Pravda, and Zvi Gitelman, eds. *Developments in Russian and Post-Soviet Politics*. Durham, NC, 1994.

Index

ISBN 0-8420-2856-0

90000 >

9 780842 028561